Crippled Grace

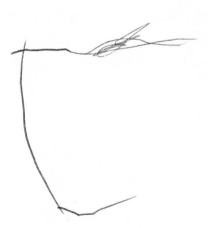

SRTD
STUDIES IN RELIGION, THEOLOGY, AND DISABILITY

SERIES EDITORS

Sarah J. Melcher
Xavier University, Cincinnati, Ohio

and

Amos Yong
Fuller Theological Seminary, Pasadena, California

Crippled Grace

Disability, Virtue Ethics, and the Good Life

Shane Clifton

BAYLOR UNIVERSITY PRESS

Cover design by Savanah N. Landerholm
Cover image: Rachel Gadsden, rachelgadsden.com, *Universal Journey*, 2016, mixed media on paper, 30x40 cm

The NIV translation has been used for biblical quotations throughout unless otherwise noted.

This book was first issued in paperback in 2019 under ISBN 978-1-4813-0747-5.

The Library of Congress has cataloged the hardback as follows:

Names: Clifton, Shane, author.
Title: Crippled grace : disability, virtue ethics, and the good life / Shane Clifton.
Description: Waco, Texas : Baylor University Press, [2018] | Series: Studies in religion, theology, and disability / series editors, Sarah J. Melcher and Amos Yong | Includes bibliographical references and index.
Identifiers: LCCN 2017034040 (print) | LCCN 2017048553 (ebook) | ISBN 9781481308144 (web PDF) | ISBN 9781481308137 (ebook: Mobi/Kindle) | ISBN 9781481307482 (ePub) | ISBN 9781481307468 (cloth : alk. paper) | ISBN 9781481307475 (pbk. : alk. paper)
Subjects: LCSH: People with disabilities--Religious aspects--Christianity. | Suffering--Religious aspects--Christianity. | Virtues. | Disabilities--Religious aspects--Christianity.
Classification: LCC BT732.7 (ebook) | LCC BT732.7 .C55 2018 (print) | DDC 261.8/324--dc23
LC record available at https://lccn.loc.gov/2017034040

Series Introduction

Studies in Religion, Theology, and Disability brings newly established and emerging scholars together to explore issues at the intersection of religion, theology, and disability. The series editors encourage theoretical engagement with secular disability studies while supporting the reexamination of established religious doctrine and practice. The series fosters research that takes account of the voices of people with disabilities and the voices of their family and friends.

The volumes in the series address issues and concerns of the global religious studies / theological studies academy. Authors come from a variety of religious traditions with diverse perspectives to reflect on the intersection of the study of religion/theology and the human experience of disability. This series is intentional about seeking out and publishing books that engage with disability in dialogue with Jewish, Christian, Buddhist, or other religious and philosophical perspectives.

Themes explored include religious life, ethics, doctrine, proclamation, liturgical practices, physical space, spirituality, and the interpretation of sacred texts through the lens of disability. Authors in the series are aware of conversation in the field of disability studies and bring that discussion to bear methodologically and theoretically in their analyses at the intersection of religion and disability.

Studies in Religion, Theology, and Disability reflects the following developments in the field: First, the emergence of disability studies as an interdisciplinary endeavor that has had an impact on theological studies, broadly defined. More and more scholars are deploying disability perspectives in their work, and this applies also to those working in the theological academy. Second, there is a growing need for critical reflection on disability in world religions. While books from a Christian standpoint have dominated the discussion at the interface of religion and disability so far, Jewish, Muslim, Buddhist, and Hindu scholars, among those from other religious traditions, have begun to resource their own religious traditions to rethink disability in the twenty-first century. Third, passage of the Americans with Disabilities Act in the United States has raised the consciousness of the general public about the importance of critical reflection on disability in religious communities. General and intelligent lay readers are looking for scholarly discussions of religion and disability as these bring together and address two of the most important existential aspects of human lives. Fourth, the work of activists in the disability rights movement has mandated fresh critical reflection by religious practitioners and theologians. Persons with disabilities remain the most disaffected group from religious organizations. Fifth, government representatives in several countries have prioritized the greater social inclusion of persons with disabilities. Disability policy often proceeds from core cultural and worldview assumptions that are religiously informed. Work at the interface of religion and disability thus could have much broader purchase in social, economic, political, and legal domains.

Under the general topic of thoughtful reflection on the religious understanding of disability, Studies in Religion, Theology, and Disability includes shorter crisply argued volumes that articulate a bold vision within a field; longer scholarly monographs, more fully developed and meticulously documented, with the same goal of engaging wider conversations; textbooks that provide a state of the discussion at this intersection and chart constructive ways forward; and select edited volumes that achieve one or more of the preceding goals.

Contents

Acknowledgments

I owe an incalculable debt to the many people who have helped me in the writing of this book. I am grateful to: Jay, Helena, and Sunshine McNeill, Mark Tonga, and Sara Chesterman, for their willingness to share their stories and wisdom openly; Neil Ormerod, Amos Yong, and Gwynnyth Llewellyn for their scholarly support; Lauren McGrow for her beautifully heretical insight; the faculty and staff of Alphacrucis College for their long support of my scholarship, and for granting the sabbatical that enabled me to bring the project near to completion; the Centre for Disability Research and Policy at the University of Sydney for accommodating me during my sabbatical, and for its ongoing encouragement; the Ian Potter Foundation for funding travel associated with the scholarship of the book; Baylor University Press for their commitment to excellence and for guiding me through the process of publication—especially Jordan Rowan Fannin for her careful and perceptive review and suggestions; Rachel Gadsden for allowing her stunning art to grace the cover; the many crips who have welcomed me as one of them and shown me how to live with this cantankerous body and inaccessible world; and above all, Elly, Jeremy, Jacob, Lachlan, and my wider family for the love that I hope imbues the argument that follows.

Introduction

A Disabled Account of Flourishing

Disability is not something we generally think about, but when we do, we imagine tragedy. We hear of a person rendered a quadriplegic, and we think to ourselves, "they'd be better off dead." So we say to our loved ones, "If that ever happens to me, turn off the machine." We are also told by charismatic preachers and motivational speakers that to concede to the constraints of disability is to fail in faith; to give in to doubt rather than choose to be positive and overcome adversity by the power of self-belief. But the prevailing view that disability, happiness, and faith are self-contradictory occurs because our vision of each is too narrow.

The danger of writing a book about happiness and faith with disability as the subject is that it is categorized as a minority study, and so, like people with disabilities, it is marginalized as specialty reading. Yet, disability should not be a fringe topic. On the contrary, to reflect on disability is to explore the fragility and potency, dependence and independence, constraints and possibilities, and hardships and joys that are a part of every human life. As Alasdair MacIntyre observes, we are born utterly dependent upon our parents, who do their best to raise us up to become "independent practical reasoners," people who are capable of taking responsibility for our own decisions and futures.[1] But even at the height of our independence, when we seem to have made something of ourselves, in reality, we are always dependent on our families, communities, nations, and in a globalized society, the entire world—to say nothing of our dependence upon the natural environment. And even though we

1

rarely admit it, our bodies are inherently fragile, always at risk of injury, illness, and permanent disability, and as we age, we inevitably deteriorate in body and mind. Old age generally involves disablement of one type or another. These realities of human existence are often obscured in our consumerist technological society, especially because we shunt the aged and the disabled into what are euphemistically labeled "homes," but are really ways in which we avoid facing up to our own dependency and the responsibilities that go with it.

This book is about disability, and it is certainly written with the benefit of people with disabilities front and center. But it also understands disability as symbolic of the human condition, and so utilizes the experience of disability as a lens through which we can seek to understand happiness, and what is meant when we use the term, and how we go about attaining it. I have been enriched through encounters with people with disabilities, as I have listened to their stories and tried to look at the world (or hear it, as the case may be) from their perspective. And it is my hope that my readers find the journey of this book similarly illuminating. My goal, then, is to reflect upon what disability might have to teach us about living well in the face of the challenges of life.

Even so, there is a danger in setting up people with a disability as being inspirational. Disability advocate Stella Young rails against what she has labeled "inspiration porn," which uses stories of people with a disability to inspire and motivate.[2] Inspiration porn usually draws on trite aphorisms, such as "your excuse is invalid" or "before you quit, try."[3] Young's rage is especially directed at the phrase "the only disability in life is a bad attitude," which blames victims for any limitations arising from their disability (unless they manage to overcome), and ignores the fact that we cannot wish away physical or psychological impairment or the constraints of our social environment. The problem with inspiration porn is that its purpose is to make nondisabled people feel better about their lot in life, and it functions by making them think "well, it could be worse . . . I could be that person."[4] In this way, labeling people with disabilities as inspirational, heroic, and superhuman exacerbates the disabled difference, and denies people the right to be fully human in their strengths, frailties, virtues, and vices. In objectifying disability to teach so-called normal people a lesson, inspiration porn is not actually about disability at all.

In drawing upon disability as the lens through which to explore happiness, my point is not to elevate disability, but, on the contrary, to recognize that it is central to the human experience.

MY JOURNEY AND ITS INFLUENCE ON THIS BOOK

Every book on disability must begin with an explanation of the author's right to speak about the topic, referencing either one's own disability or that of a close relative or friend. Disability is not the only discourse with such demands. Can a man write a book about feminism, or claim to be a feminist? And since the fundamental problem of disability is paternalism—that people with disabilities have always been spoken about and on behalf of—it makes sense that the emerging disability movement wants to speak for itself. Even so, it does seem a little passé —at least to me—to lay my credentials before you, as though the argument that follows only has merit because of my experience. But if that were the case, this would be a thin book indeed, because really I am an interloper.

Nevertheless, the logic and shape of this book draw on my own story. For more than twenty years I have studied and taught theology at Alphacrucis College in Sydney. My principal scholarly contribution has been in the field of Pentecostal theology, but my postgraduate study was with an evangelical college, and my Ph.D. at a Catholic university. So I am ecumenical in orientation, and liberal (by which I mean open-minded) in inclination. Like most theologians, I am schooled in the Christian classics, the big names of twentieth-century theology, and I am passionate about feminist and political theology. But until not too long ago I knew nothing—and had read nothing— about disability.

And then I had an accident while jumping a bicycle that left me a quadriplegic (C5 incomplete). I have written about my experiences of rehabilitation at Prince of Wales Hospital in Sydney, and of the struggles faced after returning home to my family to live with a permanent disability, in my memoir, *Husbands Should Not Break*.[5] So I won't repeat myself here. But if I may be indulged a citation from that book, the following anecdote of my first day home after a lengthy hospital stay sets the context for this present work:

Eventually I arrived home, and entered a house bedecked with balloons and streamers, to the cheers and tears of my wife and children. We were all excited but, although we didn't voice our concerns, we were also a little nervous—like newlyweds on a honeymoon, in love, but tentative. Not long after I arrived, Elly looked my way, smiled, and wrapped her arms around my shoulders. Looking on, the boys joined in spontaneously, a five-person hug that expressed our love and constrained our fear. There was one problem. I had forgotten to turn my chair's power off, and with Jacob accidentally leaning against my joystick, we were propelled like a rugby scrum into the kitchen table, which in turn smashed through our rear window, spraying shards of glass in every direction. It put an end to our cuddle, but did give us something to laugh about.

What we didn't realise at the time was that this event would turn out to be symbolic, representative of the fact that my homecoming would not be the end of our challenges, nor the panacea for the mounting unhappiness that I had attributed to being trapped for seven months at POW [Prince of Wales Hospital]. If you are in hospital for long enough, it starts to eat away at the soul. In my case, this focused my attention on discharge but, after a seven-month build up, my homecoming was never going to be able to carry the weight of the expectations I had heaped upon it. I suspect that, unconsciously, I had assumed getting home would bring back my former life. In fact, it was only at home that I really came to understand what the acquisition of an SCI [spinal cord injury] had cost me—had cost us as a family—and this realization was crushing.[6]

In the months and years that followed, I slipped into a deepening unhappiness. I say unhappy since I was not diagnosed with depression, at least in any formal sense, and my mood had an obvious cause that was not to be helped by chemical intervention (as valuable as such treatments are in other situations). Gradually, though, I emerged from the funk of despair and while I am still some way from what some might call happy, I am at least coming to terms with my lot, and can envisage a meaningful future. I have learned, at least, that I would not have been better off dead, and I am glad they did not turn off the machines.

In addition to the loving solicitation of my family and friends, I owe my emerging happiness to an unlikely source. In the week before my accident I was reading Alasdair MacIntyre's *Dependent Rational Animals* (a follow-up to his seminal *After Virtue*), which explores the potential contribution of virtue ethics for disability. MacIntyre notes that the ill and the disabled are almost never considered in the analyses of moral philosophy, and when they are, it is inevitably as subjects of charity, so that "we are invited, when we do think of disability, to think of the 'disabled' as 'them,' as other than 'us,' as a separate class, not as ourselves as we have been, sometimes are now and may well be in the future."[7] I was halfway through this book when I became a quadriplegic and "they" became "me" (providence, it seems, has a wry sense of humor).

After returning home, I remembered that unfinished book and discovered within its pages a spark of hope. The virtue tradition is not just about ethics. It is a tradition that explores the meaning of happiness and outlines the virtues needed to attain it. Prior to the injury, I had read the tradition as a scholar, but now it spoke to my experience. In the midst of the unhappiness that accompanied the losses resulting from my quadriplegia, the virtue tradition captured my imagination by reminding me about a way of conceiving of happiness that could transcend my disability: happiness as a life lived well in and through its difficulties.

At around the same time I also came across books written by scholars with a disability, including Paul Longmore's *Why I Burned My Book and Other Essays* and Tom Shakespeare's *Disability Rights and Wrongs*.[8] Here was a scholarship with a critical passion that mirrored feminism and that spoke directly to my situation. In this literature I began to understand myself, discovering what it means to live with a disability. I also glimpsed an opportunity to participate in a scholarly conversation, and once again this provided me with a reason to hope. Quadriplegia had robbed me of many things, but it had given me time to read (what better way to spend the hours once devoted to housework and sport?). More substantially, it introduced me to a community of people, and a literature that is fascinating, rich, challenging, and inspiring.

Thus, *Crippled Grace* brings into conversation the three fields of study that have shaped my journey: the virtue tradition, disability studies, and Christian theology. It is a work of theology because the virtue tradition, which has its origins in Greek philosophy, particularly in Aristotle, assumes teleology—i.e., that life has a meaning and purpose—and so has been appropriated and developed within

Christian tradition, especially in the writings of Thomas Aquinas and, thereafter, in both Catholic and Protestant moral theory. In building on the insight of Aquinas, the theological notion of grace underlies the project, even when not made explicit, because grace perfects and elevates nature, especially the habits of virtue that facilitate flourishing. That is to say, in discussing virtue and flourishing, grace is always in view. In the pages that follow, I also bring the critical and constructive resources of Christian theology to the analysis of disability and happiness. My intention is not to assume the superiority of theology over and against the field of disability studies but, rather, to bring the distinct insights of theological, ethical, and disability scholarship into critical and constructive dialogue. For this reason, this is not a book for Christians alone. Indeed, the virtue tradition has its philosophical origins in the writing of Aristotle, and has achieved something of a reemergence in the discussions of contemporary secular moral philosophy.[9] And it is my belief that the unique perspective that comes from Christian theology is capable of providing fresh insight, irrespective of whether a person is a believer, agnostic, or atheist. Conversely, the Christian church has much that it can learn from the experiences of people with a disability and the social and political analysis of disability scholarship.

DISABILITY AND ITS MEANINGS

Disability itself is a complex notion, and its meaning is disputed. Indeed, the line between a disabled and nondisabled person is fuzzy, not least because no one actually satisfies the mythical "normal," so that difference from the norm is always a matter of degree. In medical contexts there are various taxonomies that identify disability. The World Health Organization's International Classification of Functioning, Disability, and Health (ICF) identifies body functions and structure, domains of activity and participation, and environmental factors that constitute and classify disability.[10] Classifications such as those of the ICF are important, not only because they shape the medical and rehabilitative care received by an individual, but also because they direct a person's treatment under the law, determining welfare support, personal care allocations, technological assistance, and so forth, and more broadly, help to frame government legislation and policy.

Approaching disability by way of impairment and classification is not without controversy. During the latter half of the twentieth century, disability advocates and researchers began to differentiate between two models of disability, the medical and the social.[11] While the former focuses on the impairment of the individual, the latter insists that disability is a social creation; that society disables people by isolating and excluding them. This exclusion results from the inaccessibility of the built environment (such as the lack of ramps and elevators into buildings, inaccessible bathrooms, narrow and obstructed doorways and aisles) as well as the failure to implement social and technological supports (such as the failure to provide sign language interpreters to people who are deaf). Disability advocates thus argue that people with disabilities are not limited by their impairment, but by the interaction between the individual's functioning requirement and an environment designed without taking that requirement into account.[12]

From the perspective of the social model, discrimination and exclusion result from a lack of knowledge about the experience of disability, along with prejudiced attitudes that arise from "deep-seated, pervasive cultural devaluation and systematic institutionalised discrimination."[13] It is easily within our capacity to reshape our environment in ways that include people with disabilities, but this does not happen because ignorance and prejudice make us unaware of the importance of access and inclusion, and so we consider the social, economic, and political costs of change an unreasonable burden.[14] Since the social model of disability unmasks prejudice and its effects, it becomes the foundation for social change.

To make sense of the social model of disability, it helps to understand what it is we are talking about when we use the term "society," which is made up of social structures and the cultural values that frame personal meanings and virtues.[15] At the most basic level, societies exist to satisfy the vital necessities of life: health, food, shelter, sanitation, reproduction, and so on. That people with disabilities are too often poor, have inadequate housing, suffer from multiple health challenges with unequal access to medical support, and are too often denied reproductive rights is now widely documented.[16] Provision of these vital human needs is dependent on the social structures that are constituted by family networks, economic systems, political structures, and technological supports, and here again it is apparent that people with disabilities are too often socially marginalized. Too many have been taken out of family homes and housed in institutional settings. Their economic disadvantage arises from high rates of unemployment, inadequate social welfare, and higher costs of living—disability is expensive, and so are the technological supports that might ameliorate functional loss and social disadvantage. And above all, people with a disability are too often silenced and without political power. The status quo of social systems resides in cultural values: the meanings and values that direct our social living. These values are mediated to us by stories (especially religious narratives), discussed and criticized in philosophies and theologies, and expressed in art and the popular media. As critical disability scholarship reveals, ancient and modern religious texts, including the Bible, reflect and reinforce prejudice, as do important philosophies (especially the virtue tradition), novels, popular movies, television programs, and so on.[17] The overarching impact of cultural values on unjust social systems has led some commentators to move from the social model to a cultural model of disability. The latter is said to incorporate and extend the former, but one might equally argue that the social model can and should absorb the insight of the cultural model (I take this view, preferring the social model for its historical importance and wider frame of reference).[18] Finally, cultures are sustained and propagated by personal values. This is a vital reminder that, while derogatory and alienating attitudes and actions of individuals and groups are inevitably shaped by culture, persons are equally capable of effecting cultural and social change. And to that end the analysis of personal virtue that is central to the argument of this book has social significance, even when social justice is not the primary focus. The great advantage of the social model of disability is that it shifts the focus away from a person's deficits and on to the society that excludes that person, from cure to social transformation.[19] Rather than trying to normalize people with disabilities, it seeks to normalize the social and cultural environment.

In her powerful letter "To My Eighty-Year-Old Self" (published in the year before she died, aged thirty-two), Stella Young reveals the liberating power of transitioning from the medical to the social model. She writes:

Remember those days before you came out as a disabled woman? You used to spend a lot of energy on "passing." Pretending you were just like everyone else, that you didn't need any "special treatment," that your life experience didn't mean anything in particular. It certainly didn't make you different from other people. Difference, as you knew it then, was a terrible thing. I used to think of myself in terms of who I'd be if I didn't have this pesky old disability.

Then, at seventeen, something shifted. To borrow from Janis Ian, I learned the truth at seventeen.

That I was not wrong for the world I live in. The world I live in was not yet right for me . . .

I stopped unconsciously apologising for taking up space. I'm sure you can scarcely imagine that now; a world where all disabled people, women in particular, are made to feel like we're not really entitled to inhabit public spaces.

I started changing my language. To jog your memory, back when you're still thirty there are all kinds of fights about whether we are allowed to say "disabled people" at all. It's "people with disabilities" that's all the rage. Cause we're like, people first, you know? And if we don't say that we're people, folks might get confused. But I've never had to say that I'm a person who is a woman, or a person who is Australian, or a person who knits. Somehow, we're supposed to buy this notion that if we use the term disabled too much, it might strip us of our personhood. But that shame has become attached to the notion of disability, it's not your shame. It took a while to learn that, so I hope you've never forgotten.

I started calling myself a disabled woman, and a crip. A good thirteen years after seventeen-year-old me started saying crip, it still horrifies people. I do it because it's a word that makes me feel strong and powerful. It's a word other activists have used before me, and I use it to honour them.[20]

It is Young's spirit and pride that most powerfully reflect the impetus behind the social model of disability. She also highlights the importance of language. The way we talk about things that are important to us, the words and phrases we choose, reveals and sustains implicit values and attitudes. One of the contributions of the social model of disability has been to unmask the prejudices implicit in our linguistic choices. It is noteworthy that social advocacy has already had some impact on the language we use to speak about disability. It is no longer acceptable, for example, to use the term handicapped, which is oriented to a person's deficit. Likewise, pejorative labels such as crippled, dumb, deformed, imbecile, lunatic, simpleton, spastic, and so forth are now generally recognized as offensive.

However, the public is not yet conscious of the culturally ubiquitous use of disability metaphors with negative connotations. Few of us would "blink an eye" at the use of blindness as a metaphor for inattention, ignorance, or stupidity (the blind leading the blind), but blindness cannot be used as a signifier without implying something about blindness itself.[21] Equally problematic are everyday references to deafness (her pleas fell on deaf ears), paralysis (he is crippled with indecision), mental illness (he is crazy, a schizo), and the like. A person with a disability is surely right to insist, "I am not your metaphor."

To caution care with language may seem like nothing more than political correctness, and the widespread adoption of politically correct language has come under fire in recent years. But while political correctness can be taken too far, hindering our ability to listen to different perspectives, it can also be the case that the dismissal of political correctness arises from a refusal to accept that the language we choose to use can reflect an underlying prejudice. Indeed, changing the way we speak is one of the strategies used to get people to change how they think. Hans Reinders notes, though, that there is a history in the disabilities movement of replacing old bitter words with new sweeter ones: "idiots" became "morons," then "feeble-minded," then "mentally retarded," then "mentally disabled," and finally "persons with intellectual disabilities." That the language attending to disability has been in permanent flux suggests that the problem runs deeper—that the attitudes we have toward disability are so entrenched that choosing new terminology is not enough. As Reinders goes on to say, "persons with disabilities do not need different words; they need different people."[22]

One of the more common linguistic recommendations is to replace the phrase "disabled people" with "people with disabilities," because people are much more than their impairment—the person comes first. Thus far in the chapter I have taken this approach. It stands out (at least to me as a writer) because it is grammatically cumbersome. For this reason, and because I agree with Young that there is no need to be embarrassed about disability, I will use the two constructions interchangeably from here on.

Young also highlights that we can reclaim pejorative language, here mirroring the political actions of some feminists ("sluts") and gays and lesbians ("queers"). In her case, she adopts the label "crip" because she is proud to be a part of this marginalized community, and the shock value of using the term is politically significant. This is an issue I will address in more detail later, but for now it is enough to note that my goal in the writing that follows is not to be politically correct so as to avoid offense. Rather, my goal is to choose my language carefully, usually to reflect and reinforce inclusive values, but occasionally to shock. Because sometimes we need to be offended, and sometimes there is value in causing offense. The title of this book, *Crippled Grace*, plays with the shock of the label "cripple," and invites the ambiguous interpretation that coincides with its association with grace.

The contribution of the social model to understanding disability and to advocacy is substantive. Indeed, the social model understands disability as a political category, and for good reason. Recently, however, some scholars have been critical of the tendency of those using the social model to promote a dichotomy that sets the social and medical models against one another, treating the latter negatively.[23] This arises from the broader inclination to set the disciplines of philosophy and humanities (drawn on by proponents of the social model) against the empirical sciences (the primary resource of medical and rehabilitation professionals). The result is reductionist, conflating disability into the single category of social exclusion, and so ignoring the radically diverse experiences of disabled people. It is also to forget that disability is both a social and bodily reality, and while not everyone with a disability has a problem that needs a cure, for many others, disability entails loss, pain, and hardship that can benefit from scientific advances. Significantly, some disabled people long for a cure, or at least, for whatever medical and technological supports science can achieve to ameliorate their hardships and so advance their happiness. The force of this critique is that our analysis of and engagement with disability is richer if we take a multifactorial approach, seeking consensus between the disciplines and drawing on all the insights and resources available.[24]

The rich diversity inherent to the experience of disability is part of the joy of exploring the topic, but it also complicates such exploration. In the wide range of types of disabilities, each disability has its own constraints, challenges, and opportunities. The experience of disability is as unique as are individual persons, and is radically impacted by the different environments in which people live. Poverty has an especially negative effect, limiting access to medical, technological, and social supports, so that the experience of disability in wealthy nations is very different from that of people in the developing world. Disability is also differentiated by whether or not a person is born disabled or becomes disabled, and then by the stage in life in which disability occurs. The issues confronting people with an intellectual disability are very different from the issues of those with a physical disability. The social challenges of people with an invisible disability (such as a mental illness) are unlike the challenges of those who have an obvious impairment. Disability can be temporary or permanent, stable or degenerating, singular or comorbid, painful or painless. Disability is experienced differently by men and women and from one culture to another. As stated earlier, the line between the disabled and nondisabled is fuzzy, and as Alison Kafer observes, there are innumerable people "who might be recognized by others as part of the disabled we, but who do not recognize themselves as such."[25] Her point is not only that disability is central to the human condition, but that disability politics envisions a better future for us all.

All of this diversity raises the issue of whether it is possible to speak meaningfully about disability. Yet, that everyone's experience is unique does not mean that disabled people do not also share similar issues, challenges, and perspectives. These common experiences are readily apparent in the social model, since the disabled difference is what creates prejudice and exclusion, and necessitates political action. And while impairments may differ, the medical model also identifies functional limitations shared across different types of disability. Communication, for example, may be a challenge for a broad spectrum of disabilities: for the blind, deaf, some people with cerebral palsy, people with intellectual disabilities, people with autism, and some people with high-level quadriplegia, to name just a few. And collectively, the disabled community has always had difficulty having their voices heard. Similarly, while not every disability results in health concerns, many do, so that engagement with medical and rehabilitative professionals is common, as is the difficulty of dealing with pain, limitation, and loss. In the context of Christian faith, there are common questions about divine providence (why did God make me like this? and why am I not healed?) and shared experiences of being misunderstood and ignored by the church. And amidst all the diversity of disability there is the universal human experience of fragility, vulnerability, and weakness, alongside the universal longing for happiness, and the determination, strength, and virtue that are needed to flourish with nonstandard bodies.

Given this complexity, in the writing of this book I can address some of the shared experiences of living with a disability, but I cannot hope to provide a comprehensive account of its rich diversity. I shall thus draw on a variety of insights from disability scholars and disabled people as serves the argument in view, and leave it to the reader to decide whether the insight that emerges is of relevance to her unique situation. In my early planning for the book, I contemplated focusing on physical disabilities, worried that my particular experience with a physical disability would mean that I would be unable to do justice to the challenges of people with an intellectual disability. But I realized that making this division would be another instance where intellectually disabled people would be left out of the discussion. And in any event, the distinction between physical and intellectual disability is ambiguous, because many people have both types of disability (the brain is a physical organ after all), and because people are too often treated as though they are physically and intellectually incompetent, irrespective of their functional capacities.

Rather than pretend to be completely objective, it is important that I admit that my own experiences will inform my outlook. I am a white, well-educated, Christian, married man and father, residing in the wealthy city of Sydney, Australia, and so live with immense privilege, even as a quadriplegic—unlike far too many disabled people. And my experience of quadriplegia did not begin until a few weeks before my fortieth birthday. This background not only colors my perspective, but the fact that I came to disability late in life means that I am still learning about what it is to be disabled. Even so, as Bernard Lonergan observes, "genuine objectivity is the fruit of authentic subjectivity."[26] That is to say, while I bring my own experiences and biases to my study of disability, I am nevertheless capable of at least some self-transcendence as I learn from the experiences and scholarship of others. And while my intention is not to focus on myself, I will draw on my own experience where relevant, so as to make my subjectivity explicit. I also seek to prioritize the voices of others who have lived with disability for longer than I, and whose experiences are very different than my own.

THE SHAPE OF THINGS TO COME

My encounter with disability has been a challenging but rich journey of discovery, and the shape of this book intends to take the reader on a similar path. My first experience of spinal cord injury was as loss, as I spent the nighttime hours trapped in bed, staring at the ceiling, and wondering, "Why me, God?" Whether it is parents confronted with their child's disability at birth (chapter 1), or individuals, later in life, acquiring a disability, the experience is almost always earth-shattering, and the problem of pain—"Why would a good God allow this to happen?"—is more than abstract speculation; it is existential crisis (chapters 1 and 2). Gradually, as impairment gives way to the realization that one is disabled, the mourning of loss gives way to a new question, "How can I live and be happy with this disabled body in a society not well fitted to its peculiar qualities?" To answer that question, I turn to ancient sources, to the Bible, Aristotle, and Thomas Aquinas, and their deep meditations on happiness and the good life. These were texts that I had studied before my accident, but as I read them resting in my electric wheelchair, I had fresh insight into the ways they might help me and others emerge from the despondency of our loss. I also saw what I had previously failed to notice; that time and again these ancient and now authoritative scripts reinforced paternalistic and discriminatory beliefs and practices about disabled bodies. So, if they were going to be of use to me and to others, I would need to make explicit both their insight and their ideology (chapter 3).

Rehabilitating from a spinal cord injury is largely an inner journey, and inevitably self-focused. But it was in meeting peers who had lived with the injury over the medium- to long-term, and in hearing their stories, that I began to see that it might be possible, not only to achieve equilibrium, but to flourish (chapters 4 and 8). Those writing about virtue emphasized the importance of narrative for learning about the good life, and I also discovered that reflecting on the stories of peers gave fresh insight into the tradition's meanings and its shortcomings.

And then, not long after I had escaped from hospital, I came across a presentation by Martin Seligman, "The New Era of Positive

Psychology."[27] In a TED Talk, Seligman was presenting what he thought was a new approach to the psychology of happiness, but which sounded very much like the ancient virtue tradition to me. Digging deeper I found in the empirical studies of hedonic psychology another set of resources that seemed to affirm my intuition that a virtue-based account of happiness was relevant to living well with a disability (chapter 5).

In the months and years that followed my rehabilitation, I had the joy of meeting disabled people with extraordinary and unique bodies and minds. I began to wonder whether the virtue tradition had anything that might speak to their situations. My friend Jay and his daughter Sunshine were at the forefront of my mind. Sunshine was born with severe cerebral palsy, and is completely dependent on her parents for all the basic necessities of life (chapter 1). I realized that unless the logic of virtue could be applied to her situation—to the experience of profound disability—then it was not of much use. Thus, I wrestled with the seeming paradox of the importance of independent agency for the exercise of virtue, and the concomitant but seemingly irreconcilable fact of inter/dependency that is central to disability. What was needed was an account of individual moral agency that incorporates interdependency and friendship (chapter 6). Thinking about friendship led naturally to an exploration of sexual intimacy. In fact, the impact of spinal cord injury on sexual capacity meant that I had impelling motivation to examine the topic. In the process, I came to see that my sexual challenges were not unique, and that many disabled people struggled to flourish sexually in a society that too often assumes they are asexual.[28] These assumptions are exacerbated by Christian notions of faith and chastity, so I set out to discover more open and creative ways of conceiving of sexual virtue (chapter 7).

During these years of learning new things about disability and virtue, I was struggling with my crabby and leaky body. Dealing with the messiness of piss and poo is the everyday reality of many disabled people, for whom the question "Are the toilets accessible?" is always in mind, so much so that the politics of pissing has become something of a rallying call among disabled advocates.[29] Meditating on the practical resources needed to accept the messiness of life led not only to questions of policies and social practice but to a concomitant exploration of those virtues needed to live with fragile bodies in a fractious society—namely, humility, pride, anger, and forgiveness (chapter 9). Not the least of those resources is faith. And while faith can contribute to the flourishing of people with disabilities, the experience of disability, too, has something profound to say about how to exercise faith in a world sorely in need of the powers of hope and love (conclusion).

If the book is shaped by my narrative, I hope it is not dominated by it. As already noted, I have not pretended to hide my own experiences, but this book is not about me. My goal is that it stimulates reflection on your own journey, that of your disabled friends and family members, and on the virtues and values of the society in which you live. Notwithstanding the many and varied trajectories that follow, the aim of the book comes down to the following questions: "What does it mean for people with disabilities (and all of us fragile humans) to flourish, and what are the personal and social virtues needed to make that possible?"

1

The Experience of Disability
The Journey We Would Not Have Chosen

paralysis that affects all a person's limbs

This book had its impetus in my personal experience of quadriplegia, but my understanding of the struggles and joys of living with disability has been framed through interaction with others. Of special importance has been an ongoing conversation with Jay McNeill, a friend and father of twin girls, one with a severe disability. His reflections on his family's hardships and joys—set out in his blog and in personal correspondence—have been in the forefront of my mind as I developed my argument.[1] For that reason, I have decided to give my readers the opportunity to hear directly from him, as well as his wife Helena. As you will discover, they raise many of the issues that will occupy us for the remainder of the book, and their placement here is as a reminder that the inevitable abstractions of philosophy and theology are meaningful only when grounded in real-life experiences.

Jay will say that he is not a theologian, but although he has had no formal training, he has the spirit of a philosopher. He is willing to ask the hard questions of faith, and follow the answers wherever they take him. Jay is a musician, and where I can be dry and logical, he is colorful and open-ended, and I suspect the contrast will prove to be stimulating.

Jay

It was a disturbing way to start a family; a mad rush of speed through several red lights, two Aussie soon-to-be-parents in a foreign country, headed into the wilderness with no compass. Naivety was my friend until it abandoned me in a tidal wave

17

of reality. Our twin girls, Sunshine and Jazmine, were three months premature and born awfully sick. Sunshine was on a ventilator for four months and lived the first six months of her life in the Neonatal Intensive Care Unit (NICU). Even after bringing her home, we faced emergency dashes to the hospital on more occasions than I care to remember. Eleven years later, Sunshine is stable but has been profoundly affected and has severe cerebral palsy, along with all its complications. She needs assistance for most things and is not able to talk, eat, hold her head or walk. Jazmine was in the NICU for two months and has since joined the clan of the "average"; today you wouldn't even know she was a preterm.

The instant transition we found ourselves in came with a twist I wouldn't fully understand until later—we were worship pastors at a megachurch in Chicago USA. The assumption would be that my vocation would somehow be advantageous if I were to find myself in a crisis—instead, it made it more complicated. The very essence of our job was to bring focus and contemplation to a congregation, just at the time when our lives were turned upside down. Most days I wanted to quit, but my survival instinct would have me consider practical things as paramount. I needed a job, and I was in a foreign country with a specific visa for a specific role. Plus, my pride would have me be strong and push through like all good leaders should. Even today when I reflect on that period, I can feel the heaviness and contradiction lingering in the background of my mind.

After leading thousands of people in an intimate, upward focus in the worship of God on a Sunday, I would leave the church building and drive to the hospital, wondering if God even cared about what was going on in my world. I felt like a fraud. I remember one evening, in the very early days, I stood in front of the NICU pod where Sunshine was lying encased in a plastic shroud. She weighed a little over one kilogram, and her translucent skin emitted a sickly red color. She was arching her back in a pulse-like rhythm from severe pain, yet I couldn't hear her whimpers. She was suffering, alone, without the comfort of a human touch because she was too sick to hold. I have never experienced a more confronting picture of vulnerability. I pleaded with the nurse to do something; she tried to comfort me with a reminder that they were doing all they could. But doing all they could wasn't easing Sunshine's pain. While I looked at

Sunshine through the plastic shroud, I became deeply disturbed and fractured, and something inside me shifted. In my mind, injustice had a new poster child, a new thumbnail portrait that would permeate all of my future thinking. Sunshine was innocent and had done nothing wrong. In that moment, I wondered if the Christian view of God to which I had subscribed—God as an accessible healer and intimate friend—may have been bogus. *Fake*

No prayer or petition would change Sunshine's situation. My only option was to clench my teeth and fight through it. Sunshine would be among the many in this world who has had to suffer without the soothing balm of purpose. She would be in the elite group of people, like Holocaust survivors or displaced indigenous groups, that would not escape the brutality of our world. No future commentary would ever soften the pain or change the experience; nor would I likely heal from the emotional turmoil of watching the trauma unfold. I realized that, like many who have gone before me in this world, a full recovery from a brutal experience was a naive presumption. Nothing would ever remove what felt like scars of war, and to think otherwise would be to disrespect or diminish Sunshine's suffering.

Some time later, when Sunshine was around one year old, a case manager asked about our goals for her physiotherapy. I felt agitated because I thought the answer would be obvious to everyone. I wanted Sunshine to walk. In the early days, my heritage of Pentecostal faith, mixed in with the fact that I had no real understanding of the nature of cerebral palsy, made it far easier to believe something magical could happen. More than a decade later I have been sobered, and my ultimate dream is not a YouTube recording of Sunshine's first steps, but a simple conversation with her—just the two of us. Depending on the development of technology and Sunshine's unknown potential, it could actually happen—with or without faith.

My faith journey has become entwined with Sunshine's journey. They are linked, which demonstrates to me that my faith is, in fact, not broken but alive and responsive. At every stage of Sunshine's horrific health challenges (and there have been many over the years), I have been forced to reconcile my beliefs. Over and over again, I've had to allow my thinking to be tested, and each time I've had to surrender to something bigger than me. During the early years, I remember my faith slowly disintegrating, but I chose to ignore the transition long enough

compared his faith with his daughter

for the culture of Christianity to function autonomously, not connected to anything of substance. That was when I realized that faith can be faithless. Blind or habitual faith without substance still has a centering quality because it brings a focus and a sense of belonging, which is why the church could continue with or without God, and many wouldn't notice.

Sunshine's journey tipped my already fragile faith into a crisis, and I realized that I had a significant problem on my hands. The lens through which I judged the quality of my relationship with God had been polished by the fine granules of uncertainty and now I could see infinitely clearer. I would no longer be able to separate the stark contrast and contradiction of Sunshine's health from who I thought God was. The next chapter of my spiritual walk was possibly the most upsetting and disruptive experience I have had—the word that comes to mind is "loneliness." Once I started evaluating all the things I thought were true about my faith by the light of the brutal reality of my daily life with Sunshine, the intricate and self-serving theology that I had created turned out to be redundant. I realized that I had built my life on sand, and I no longer sensed God as a close friend—it was shattering. No words from seasoned ministers or close friends managed to change my mind at the time, because Sunshine presented as "exhibit A" of why God's healing, purposefulness, and accessibility weren't true. Few were prepared to present an alternate view with any sort of conviction, partly because the very problems presented challenged the faith of many who came in contact with our family. People knew that absorbing our reality was a precarious choice and could risk shaking their own foundations of faith.

I began to think about things that I never thought possible. There are serious ethical questions about disability and faith that rarely get questioned, which is a shame, because disability provokes the kinds of questions that I suspect are a gateway to a stronger faith. Disability in a child is a line in the sand for me. It says one of two things: either God has allowed innocence to be corrupted, or that God is not in complete control. But what if the idea that God is not in control of the finer details of this troubled world meant that our faith could have substance? What if uncertainty and mystery took a front seat in the car; and certainty was banished from the driver's seat? Would the possibility of a quality faith in God be worth the risk?

When Sunshine struggles to breathe during a typical winter cycle, there isn't a voice in me that says, "There is a reason for suffering, God must be teaching me something." I have come to the conclusion that there is no spiritual purpose for pain or suffering. In my mind a God who teaches someone else a lesson at the expense of an innocent child is not the kind of God who is working towards a perfect and flawless heaven—pain and suffering are a selective and mechanical concept that fits far better in a Darwinist theory. The miracle that I think doesn't get talked about enough is how, in many cases, God can turn that pain and suffering into something good. That is the miracle—it doesn't have the lustre of a lame person walking, but it surely serves a greater purpose, if an individual finds peace.

The trauma Sunshine experienced in the NICU left her with profound hearing loss. As a musician you would think that discovery would have been a huge disappointment. Surprisingly, I didn't react on hearing the news. Maybe it was because at that point we had had so much bad news that it all just blended into one big chorus. The option we chose was the modern miracle of cochlear implant technology. It would be one forward step in our journey that would be remembered as a breath of hope. The day we arrived to have her implant turned on was full of anticipation, as Sunshine had been living in silence for eighteen months. What would she do? Would she cry, laugh, or not respond at all? We were told to prepare for all of it. We didn't have a way to communicate with Sunshine what was about to happen, so she would just have to manage the surprise of an instant sensory experience. The audiologist counted down and flicked the switch. It was a genuine miracle; Sunshine heard our voices for the first time. Yes, there were a few tears, and in a long line of disappointments, those tears of joy were very welcome. I have often contemplated the practicality of that moment and how devoid of mystery it was—we took the act of a miracle into our own hands. It was a transaction. We handed over money (along with the right insurance), and we got the outcome we had planned for. It wasn't that different to how I used to see God—pray, commit, and give money in exchange for a relationship with a creator who offered spiritual insurance against life's challenges.

[Note: cochlear implants are controversial within the Deaf community.[2] However, since Sunshine is unable to use her hands or communicate in any way, the cochlear implant means that she is no longer completely isolated from the world around her.]

The most difficult thing for me to process was not the physical impairment Sunshine would live with, but the ethical dilemma disability presented when it came to the relationship between cognitive ability and the eternal consequence of establishing a core belief. So much of our Christian thinking revolves around a pivotal decision at a certain moment in time and then a series of moral choices after that. Initiating a Christian pilgrimage relies on understanding a set of complex ideas such as atonement. If you have ever sought the opinion of several people of equal intellect on any given subject on faith, you will soon realize that there are subtle nuances and differences that make a conclusive and holistic agreement unlikely. A deductive mind becomes important if an individual wishes to form a perspective that fits into an acceptable Christian framework. So what, then, if my daughter Sunshine is not able to comprehend the life of Jesus or even the concept of a God? If faith genuinely relies on some level of intellect or reasoning, then the most vulnerable in our community are at a disadvantage. It makes Jesus' call to have faith like a child a far more provocative idea. So how important is a conclusive view on Christianity then? The more people argue about an intricate theology that promises to unlock a new profound understanding, the more removed I feel from Christianity because it excludes my daughter. For my daughter, deductive thinking or perception is more an obstacle than a pathway to faith. The sense of injustice nestled in under my skin causes me to push back against the idea that intelligence plays a role in any way at all when it comes to faith. It seems unlikely that God would endorse inequality by elevating thinking as a primary way to His heart when there are so many variables to human beings. It is important to note that I am reflecting on the journey of faith from my own perspective, and not from Sunshine's point of view. At the moment, Sunshine can't speak for herself. And until she can, I won't dare to presume what it is she might think and say.

At the end of all the speculation and hypothesis, the truth is I would lay my life down for Sunshine. That is because I think her life is more valuable than mine. The world will continue to value productivity over love, because that is how efficient economies operate. Sunshine is not economically productive. In fact, she requires an enormous amount of resources to get through each day. But on my death bed, I won't be mindful of my financial footprint, I will be mindful of how much love I have given and received from others. In the case of Sunshine, there will not be one moment that I will regret where I have denied a preference of mine to fulfill a task that Sunshine needed from me. I know, without a doubt, that every diaper, every late night or broken sleep, every surgery, every opportunity turned down, every financial nicety denied, and every spiritual wrestle will be worth it.

I have paid a price to be Sunshine's father. It would be pretentious of me not to acknowledge that I do lament the challenges, but I have earned a privilege that you can't buy. Sunshine trusts me; she knows that I will be there and because of that she gives me a life-changing love in return that is far more sophisticated than words. Her love and presence keep pushing me to believe in God and have the courage to continue denying the magic, alluring promises that some parts of the modern Christian movement offer. I am a better man because of this journey, but I'll admit I live in more uncertainty than I am comfortable with. My lessening expectations of resolve and welcoming of uncertainty have become bitter medicines that I know I need.

At night, when I put Sunshine to bed, her precious face beams satisfaction, and I wonder if inside that broken body of hers is a more content human being than the average. Sunshine's life brings love from its lofty heights of the unobtainable to the tactile and useful interaction of an assuring smile. If disability can ground humanity and inform acts of compassion, then we should embrace and normalize its presence, rather than see disability as a problem to fix.

Disability is more painful than it ought to be because we have elevated perfection as a primary indicator to success. I struggled with Sunshine's disability for several reasons; the first and most powerful reason was that of the injustice of cerebral palsy. But the other powerful driver was unrealistic expectations, where I believed that life was not meant to be difficult—difficulty was just a phase that I would eventually overcome, by willpower and spiritual assistance.

Delayed gratification has helped me embrace discipline and achieve many goals in this life, but in the context of dealing with real challenges, it has been a blunt tool that, at times, has

Uncertainty = oxygen in faith

caused me to deny reality. The brain gets a chemical kickback from denial when there is an expectation of success at the end. The longer we delay our gratification, the more powerful is our elation when we reach our goal. That is why we exercise, study, save money or more provocatively, resonate with the idea of heaven. In the early days, I used delayed gratification as I processed Sunshine's illness, expecting it would all work out if I kept pushing through, and did not waver in my beliefs. But eleven years later my brain hasn't been rewarded with the chemical kickback it was expecting. Now I understand, and I have learned something far more important. My intimacy with God can only happen if my <u>faith embraces uncertainty.</u> Uncertainty is useful in the context of faith, and peace is an indicator that uncertainty is positioned correctly in the psyche. Uncertainty has become oxygen for my faith and makes sure that all my senses are working properly, and are not dulled from listening to philosophy or ideas that attempt to put a full stop at the end of every sentence.

I don't thank God for Sunshine's illness and the lessons that I have learned. It would be macabre to think that way. In fact, I am still angry about the injustice of it. I would not choose this pathway, because I am weak. It is only because it has been thrust on me that I have benefited. There is nothing noble in this story. I will always feel a pang in my heart when I think about Sunshine, because no self-respecting human would allow himself or herself to justify, in any way, the suffering of a child. But this crisis has elicited an honesty that I would not have reached on my own. So I have a predicament . . . would I trade my unique relationship with Sunshine and the lessons learned for a simpler life? If I allow this tension to remain unresolved, it will help me to live authentically and willingly embrace a more humble posture.

Life with Sunshine is good. Fortunately for us, she can respond in her unique way, and we have the benefit of sharing joyful moments. I know that for many families impacted by a profound disability, this isn't the case, and maybe those people are able to share wisdom that is beyond my reach. After eleven years of experiencing joy and pain, I can honestly say I am more resolved than I thought I would ever be. Yes, the scars are still red raw and visible to all, but they aren't bleeding or weeping anymore. As for my relationship with God, it is different, and there is no sugarcoating it; but the surprising outcome is that I have more respect for God. It is the contrast between a spoiled five-year-old child, demanding they have chocolate for lunch, and a seasoned athlete who listens to a coach's advice on diet.

I think we would all benefit from having a "Sunshine" in our life. I am not saying I would wish my journey on anybody, but I wonder if the world would be in less turmoil if we were all forced to lay down our selfishness to make someone else's life better. I know beyond a shadow of a doubt that without the crisis of Sunshine's journey crashing my party, the extra freedom and disposable time would have been directed to making me feel better about myself through experiences and buying lots of stuff. Instead, through no noble choice, disability has been wedged into my world and I am a far better human because of it.

Helena

Introductory note by Shane Clifton: because Sunshine is referenced repeatedly in this book, I asked her mother, Helena, to review what I had written to ensure my understanding of her impairment was accurate. Helena suggested various amendments to my text, which I implemented. But she also gave an overview of Sunshine's condition that I thought best shared in full. Helena did not write expecting publication, so the tone is casual, but hearing her voice will give a richer insight than any summation I might develop.

I appreciate you allowing for my feedback to make sure Sunny's disability is represented correctly in the context of your discussion. This is important not only to me as her mother, but also regarding how people with cerebral palsy (CP), who communicate with alternative means, are understood and viewed in general.

I like the clarification you are making between physical disabilities and intellectual disabilities, which are a completely different diagnosis. Unfortunately, I find that many people ignorantly presume a nonverbal person with severe CP automatically has an intellectual impairment as well. CP is a brain injury that affects the control of body muscles, but usually not someone's cognitive ability. That person is usually a fully thinking person trapped in a body that doesn't work properly! When the CP is so severe that it affects people's physical ability to produce speech, the challenge is to find an alternative means of them expressing their "voice" (cue entry into the world of alternative communication that ranges from simple to complex, from

Auslan [Australian Sign Language], eye blinking, pointing to pictures/phrases, switches operated by different body parts and technology of varying degrees. Thank God for it all!). So this is a communication issue within their disability, nothing to do with their cognitive or intellectual capability.

When there is an added impairment like deafness, as in Sunny's case, it adds another complexity to the communication issue, because we have to address not only how she expresses language, but how she receives it and then comprehends and understands it; only then might she be in a position to use it. Even with a cochlear implant, Sunny cannot access the clarity of everyday language like other hearing people, whether they have CP or not. So while someone else with CP can soak in information and comprehension just from observing and listening, Sunny needs the layer of receptive communication taught to her too.

This means Sunny's learning and education process takes even longer than someone with CP who can hear and/or speak, which is why her cognitive development is delayed and we must have a long-term view of her development in this area. There is no indication that her cognitive abilities are impaired, so we just have to be patient and do the journey of language input, and she will show us what she's capable of.

Sunny's form of communication (her "voice") is a PODD (pragmatic organized dynamic display) communication book, which is now also on her iPad. We introduced this to her at age four. The PODD is a device created by speech therapists. It is a series of symbols or pictures accompanied with a word or phrase, which can be put into sentences or just used as phrases to communicate facts, opinions, wants, needs, questions, etc. The PODD begins simple and then grows more complex as the individual develops capacity to use more language.

Sunny cannot use her hand or fingers to point to the symbols, nor does she have enough head control to give us consistent reliable "yes/no" head movements. So she uses two switches carefully positioned on her wheelchair tray to select what she wants to say or express, scrolling through the pages on her iPad via bluetooth (we are lucky she has good control of her hands). Here are some examples of messages she can sometimes navigate and select to "speak" using voice output on the iPad:

"I want—watch TV—DVD movie."

"Hurry up." (often used at school to the teachers while waiting!)

"I want—to go to the toilet." (successfully used at school this term, yay!)

"Let's go—to the movies."

"Hello."

"My name is Sunny."

"Let's go—home."

When asked a question using the iPad, she can respond, for example:

ME: Sunny, do you want to watch TV? Tell me "yes" or "no."

SUNNY: Chooses "yes" from the chat page.

Unfortunately, successful communication messages like these do not occur consistently. It is dependent on how fatigued she is, how her body is behaving, and how she is managing to focus above her everyday respiratory issues. But it gives you a glimpse of what she is capable of.

Obviously, these communications are simple compared to Jaz's complex language and comprehension skills. Sunny can only expressively use symbols that have meaning and comprehension attached to them, like TV or home or school or hello.

I have made a page in her communication book/iPad about God. It contains symbols such as pray, church, sing, Bible, love, people, Jesus. It was pretty tricky for me to decide what symbol to put with the word "God"!!! I decided on a big love heart. However, for "Jesus" I decided to do the classic bearded-guy figure, much like in the kids' Bible stories. I guess, down the track, she can learn Bible stories about Jesus, but how do you explain God?? It's hard enough to explain it to Jaz, even with the rich communication available to her.

The final point I need to make about Sunny's understanding is that it has a lot to do with experiential learning that comes through human relationship, being nurtured in your spirit, being loved. Sunny knows about love, not because of stories, but because she's experienced it.

She has been extravagantly loved and nurtured since day one. This is the message reflected to her from our faces, body language, and words. So this is the message she gives back to us and the world in general. I think this is the same principle for any child with or without a disability; if you pour love and affirmation into them, it feeds their spirit, and that is the language they learn.

I was tempted to round out this chapter by offering a commentary on Jay and Helena's accounts, but soon realized that it would be wrong to pretend to a theological expertise that gives me special insight into their experience. Their telling of their story reveals its own meaning, and our responsibility at this juncture is simply to listen to their questions and meditate on their insight.

I will return to their story at various places in the chapters that follow. For now, though, one of the fundamental issues Jay confronted was the problem of disability for his Christian faith. Sunshine's suffering and loss unmasked his faith as shallow, and caused him to question his understanding of the character and actions of God. In technical terms, he was exploring the problem of pain. Why has God allowed Sunshine to suffer? This is a question that I have struggled with in the context of my spinal cord injury, and it is thus the topic I take up next.

2

Disability, Theodicy, and the Problem of Pain
Why Me, God?

In the years since the accident that left me a quadriplegic, I have struggled with the problem of pain; how could a good, loving, and sovereign God have caused or allowed me to break my neck? While this book is primarily concerned with happiness, in my own case the challenge of happiness is that the hardships of my spinal cord injury (SCI) left me terribly unhappy. Disability and suffering do not always go together and, indeed, it is a fundamental premise of this book that disabled people can and do flourish. But often disability is accompanied by pain and loss, so that before we can attend to happiness, we need to try to make sense of suffering.[1]

To that end, I bring my experience of SCI into dialogue with the insights of philosophical theodicy and theology, to explore the activity of God at those times when God seems to be absent, or worse, malicious. Given the breadth of material, I cannot presume to do justice to the range of issues and potential solutions that have framed centuries of academic thought on the topic. Instead, I bring relevant threads and moments from twenty-first-century theodicies to bear on the question in front of us, weighing their potential contribution to the challenge of suffering and disability. I do not mount a comprehensive defense of theism but, rather, respond to my struggle to believe in the existence and love of God. I thus follow the modern impulse to set aside abstractions and reflect on particular experiences of suffering in the world, and only thereafter suggest generalizable conclusions.[2]

PAIN, SUFFERING, AND DISABILITY

The problem of pain is not about pain per se. Pain is a survival mechanism that functions to show us our limits; this is nowhere more obvious
than with a spinal cord injury, where the absence of the capacity to feel
certain pains is itself a danger. The issue, then, is not pain but suffering, which is prolonged hardship (physical, psychological, and social)
that serves no meaningful purpose.[3] Suffering undermines a person's
flourishing, and can be understood objectively and subjectively. Objectively, "the good" refers to the flourishing of the physical, psychological,
intellectual, moral, and relational capacities central to our nature as
human beings; suffering is what keeps a person from the "well-being
that, without the evil, he could and should have had."[4] Subjectively, a
person can also suffer the loss of desires of the heart that are particular
to the individual,[5] such as the loss of a love, personal goals, and identity.

Spinal cord injury is presumed to entail the loss of sensation and
movement, but it is also the distortion of neurological function. Normal
sensation is replaced by permanent neuropathic pain (that feels like
burning skin) and arthritic-type aches, and the ability to decide what
and when to move is traded for spasm and uncontrolled bladder and
bowel activity. It is a catastrophic injury that impacts every aspect of life;
the initial terror of finding oneself trapped in bed in ICU is followed by
months of hospitalization and years of rehabilitation, which eventually
give way to a stable disability that requires ongoing medical intervention
and care; this understandably creates difficulties for family relationships
(and sexuality), vocation, and recreation. This process involves a loss
of independence, and so impacts one's sense of self.[6] Thus spinal cord
injury undermines the various capacities that enable a person to flourish,
and it makes impossible the fulfillment of at least some of the heart's
desires. The point is not to elicit sympathy or to suggest that life with
the injury is meaningless. Indeed, the experience of disability can be
simultaneously more difficult and yet better than is generally imagined.
Many people, looking from the outside, assume that the paralyzed
person would choose euthanasia if it were legal (attitudes formed by fear
and prejudice, "masked by an avowed compassion, contempt cloaking
itself in paternalism").[7] But most people with the injury want to live
and flourish—even those with high-level quadriplegia.[8]

The brute fact is that life begins and ends in dependency—both youth and old age are a form of disability—and at every point in time we are vulnerable to affliction and death.[9] Our vulnerability has two fundamental aspects: first, our fragile bodies (including our brain), and second, our social embeddedness. Like any disability, spinal cord injury is a medical and social problem. We suffer our bodies, and we suffer our fitting into society with these bodies. And in the context of suffering the inevitable question arises, "Why me, God?"

In more recent explorations of theodicy, there has been a tendency to reject supposedly intractable, abstract, and theoretical analysis of the problem of pain, and to redirect attention to consolation and resistance,[10] highlighting, for example, Jesus' partaking in our experience of "godforsakenness" and the cross as a symbol of resistance to evil. One recent approach, written explicitly from the perspective of disability, argues that the problem with philosophical theodicy is that it asks questions about the character of God that are "simply inappropriate and perhaps even idolatrous." In relying on human reason rather than on the evidence of the love and power of God revealed in the incarnation and resurrection of Jesus, theodicy comes to be seen as a mark of faithlessness. Instead, figures like John Swinton have offered a pastoral theodicy of action and resistance.[11] But while practical responses to suffering are essential, so too is the logical coherence of faith. In my experience of crisis and ongoing disability, the consolations of faith have been intimately connected to my struggles to make sense of the power, character, and existence of God. While some have attempted helpfully to distinguish between the practical lament, "Why me, Lord?" which seeks a pastoral response, and the abstract and intellectual treatises of theodicy, the logic of this chapter is that the former is supported by the latter, and—conversely—that the best theodicies are compassionate and consoling responses to the hardships of life.[12]

SUFFERING AND SIN

Central to the problem of suffering are conceptions of the nature of divine causation. Christian theology has traditionally distinguished between primary and secondary causation; as creator, God is the source, ground, and primary cause of all that exists, including all secondary causes. Yet, because God imbues creation with its own power, secondary causes are real causes and can be understood in and of themselves.[13] This autonomous agency (not independence) does not detract from the divine power but, rather, reveals it, since the "perfection of the creature" (its creative causal power) reflects the divine power.[14] The logic of natural theology and the various proofs of the existence of God flow out of this conception of creation, but so does the problem of suffering.[15]

One of the responses to this problem is to distinguish between the will of God in creation and the rejection of that will in the human decision to transgress it (i.e., sin). Thus argues Augustine in his *Confessions*, where he teaches that evil is not caused by the divine will but, on the contrary, is the rejection of that will. In this way evil is understood as privation, as the negation of God.[16] On this account, while God is the primary cause of all good secondary causes, God is not the cause of sin, which God explicitly condemns. It is often further argued that all suffering (moral and natural) is a consequence of sin.[17] Evangelicals who reject the theory of evolution and interpret the Genesis accounts literally assert that life in the Garden of Eden was free of suffering and death, and that suffering and death are a consequence of the fall and the divine curse. In this view, original sin affects even the natural world.[18] An alternate proposal suggests that God took a population of prehuman ancestors and gave them the gift of free will along with preternatural powers to live in harmony with others and protect themselves from wild beasts, disease, and random destructive and natural events.[19] The subsequent choice to abuse the gift of free will (original sin, or the fall) caused Adam and Eve and their descendants to be separated from God, lose their "paranormal abilities,"[20] and so be subject to suffering.[21]

In taking this approach, scholars/theologians and philosophers set faith against the now overwhelming evidence for the theory of evolution, and invent an explanation for suffering that is implausible. But the bigger problem in the context of disability (and any illness) is that identifying suffering with sin needs to be handled with care. It is true that some suffering, even some permanent disability, is caused by a person's own sin. Often enough, a person's suffering is a consequence of someone else's sin—a drunk driver makes a quadriplegic of an innocent woman walking along the sidewalk. In this case, sin is the cause of the disability, but the injured person is still entitled to lament its unfairness: "Why, God, didn't you keep me safe?" One common response (often found in the Evangelical tradition) is to highlight the seriousness of universal human sinfulness, arguing, for example, that "plague, congenital birth defects, and many other afflictions," while not a product of specific sin, are nevertheless a consequence of divine wrath against the sin in which we are all complicit.[22] The problem here is not only the implications of this view for the character of God, but that identifying disability with sin is inherently demeaning and suggests that disability is a tragedy needing to be eliminated.[23] Conceiving of disability as tragedy provides theological justification for attitudes of pity and exacerbates practices of healing that can alienate people with disabilities.[24] Thus, talk of disability and sin can become unhelpful and even damaging.

Nevertheless, sin can remain a useful theological construct when talking about disability as a social phenomenon. The label "sin" serves a vital purpose when it identifies the way people with disabilities are marginalized and disempowered. As Thomas Reynolds, responding to his autistic son's question, "Why did God make me this way?" writes, "I am compelled to inquire into the social conditions and theological premises that bring this question to his lips. Perhaps in another family, another society, his condition would be seen as a gift, a strength, and not a liability."[25] The suffering of people with disabilities, then, may indeed result from sin, but this is not the whole story.

SUFFERING AND GREATER GOODS

Neither Augustine nor Aquinas uses the concept of evil as privation as a theodicy, since God allows, or could prevent, any evil that we commit or that is inflicted upon us.[26] As Aquinas explicitly observes, "whatever happens on earth, even if it is evil, turns out for the good of the whole world."[27] The question of precisely what that good might be lies at the heart of most philosophical theodicies. One of the more blunt (and seemingly self-contradictory) suggestions is that suffering is central to God's loving plan to rescue us from the consequences of our sin; that to be reunited with God, "human beings must know what it means to be separated from [God]. And what it means to be separated from God is to live in a world of horrors."[28]

A more nuanced proposal that takes a similar direction draws on Aquinas' theology of love. Aquinas understands love as constituted by two desires; the desire for the good of, and union with, the beloved.

Love of others requires love of self, which is the desire for one's own good and living with an integrated will (an internal union). But the consequence of the fall is a "willed loneliness" that results from the internal disintegration of the will, and that creates a distance from others and shuts out God. In this light, suffering serves God's justifying grace, by "bringing [one] to surrender to the love of God and, through that surrender, to the act of will in faith constitutive of justification."[29] Suffering allows a person to see his or her shallow and temporal desires for what they are, to long for the greater good, and ultimately to surrender to the loving help of God. Here, Aquinas sets out a scale of values, which prioritizes some goods over others, with the highest goods being relational—love of God and neighbor. This highest good is worth the sacrifice of lower goods. Love outweighs suffering.

Another proposal draws on the spiritual tradition to identify the contribution of suffering to spiritual transformation, compassion, and empathy.[30] From this perspective, suffering is capable of moving people away from self-interest and sensitizing them to the needs of others.[31] The spiritual significance of suffering is grounded in the suffering of Christ, which is more than a mere remembrance but is a creatively reconstructed symbol of solidarity and compassion made possible through sacramental practice and the experience of the Spirit. In this context, one's own suffering is never forgotten but is "transmuted into an ongoing active concern for others."[32]

A final example comes to the question of theodicy by focusing on horrendous evils, defined as "evils the participation in which (that is, the doing and suffering of which) constitutes prima facie reason to doubt whether the participant's life could (given their inclusion in it) be a great good to him/her on the whole."[33] These evils would include the rape, torture, and murder of women and children, the accidental running over of an infant son, a degrading death by cancer, and so forth.[34] Horrendous evils result in both the victim and perpetrator of horrors experiencing an irreversible and dehumanizing degradation, such that no good in this life seems capable of making the suffering worthwhile.[35] In response, it is argued that God defeats and transforms horror in Christ by the power of the Spirit. First, God shares in our degradation by Christ's experience of horror on the cross—horror participation. Second, God transforms horror by investing it with the meaning of the cross—horror transformation. And third, in Christ's resurrection, God promises a future in which we are no longer vulnerable to horrors—horror defeat.[36] While such a defeat may be partially realized in this world, the horrendous nature of some evil makes no sense and cannot be vanquished except in the afterlife, especially since death itself can be a horror. It is only in the resurrection and renewal of every life that a balancing of horrors is possible. In the glories of the afterlife, all the horrors (and joys) of life are invested with meaning,[37] from which vantage point victims of horrors will recognize even the worst of their experiences "as points of identification with the crucified God, and not wish them away from their life histories."[38] In fact, the importance of belief in an afterlife for theodicy is emphasized by many of the scholars advocating the proposals outlined above. In greater-good theodicies, without reference to the afterlife the paradox of suffering cannot be resolved. It would be like trying to understand "the pattern of suffering in a hospital without reference to life outside the hospital."[39]

Providing a comprehensive response to this vast array of twenty-first-century theodicy would be nearly tantamount in scope to offering a compelling response to evil in general. What is possible in the scope of this work, however, is to reflect on the potential of theodicy to provide insight into the experience of spinal cord injury and to offer implications for the struggles involved with disability more generally. I should note that I am reluctant to equate my own experience to the type of horrendous evils described above, although, as I have already said, every experience of suffering is incomparable, and the losses I have had to deal with have at least caused me to question life's value.[40]

In this light, it was a surprise to me to meet high-level quadriplegics who claim that if they could live their life over, they would not change a thing; that disability has enriched their life in multiple ways.[41] The possibility of this enrichment is borne out in research into the well-being of people with spinal cord injury. While quality of life is negatively impacted by the injury, studies show that many people eventually discover that their disability is a catalyst for self-discovery; that it can deepen family relationships, help and encourage others, become a source for new meaning in life, and encourage spiritual growth (see chapter 6 for an overview of this research).[42] In my short time of living with quadriplegia, I have experienced staggering generosity, heartfelt compassion, courageous determination, and exemplary care. I have been enveloped in self-sacrificing as people have *walked* with me in and through difficult times. And in my darkest hours, I have sometimes found comfort in the presence of the Spirit and resilience in the power of hope—a resurrection dance outside the constraints of my bed and wheelchair.

Many in the Deaf community and others with any number of different types of disability understand their seeming impairment as a gift;[43] and more broadly, it can be argued that disability enriches society. Almost every human virtue arises as a response to hardship, so that the virtues of the Spirit—love, joy, peace, patience, kindness, goodness, faithfulness, gentleness, and self-control (Gal 5:22-23)—are potently manifest in communities enriched by people with disabilities. In terms of faith, disabled people have unique opportunities to learn about grace (if only through having frequently to extend it to others), to appreciate that God's judgment about them matters more than the prejudgment of others, and to know that God's love is not dependent upon stature or success—even though they do contribute substantially to communal life.[44] As Jean Vanier, founder of L'Arche communities, observes, "People with disabilities have profound lessons to teach us. When we do include them, they add richly to our lives and immensely to our world," not because disability provides able-bodied people the opportunity to be charitable, or because people with disabilities are especially virtuous, but because virtue is best worked out in the midst of the vulnerabilities of life.[45] Reynolds similarly observes:

> Living out our interdependency is a source of genuine good. It entails caring for others—represented by a range of disabilities—as essential not only to our own flourishing but also to the common good of the communities in which we flourish. Human solidarity is not found inside the cult of normalcy, but rather in sharing space and welcoming each other vis-à-vis a condition of vulnerability.[46]

Reflecting upon the various ways to conceive of the good that might come from suffering has provided me with resources for imagining ways of transcending my losses and pains.

However, that good can come from disability does not necessarily justify its troubles or excuse God. Disability does not always lead people closer to God or elicit personal and communal growth, and it is as capable of degrading a person as it is of elevating her. The danger of arguments for the greater good, including those that defer resolution to the afterlife, is that they can trivialize both disability and evil. It is vital that we never lose sight of what is at stake in theodicy—that suffering can be unfathomable.[47] This was brought home to me by correspondence I received from Jay McNeill (sometime earlier than his more mature reflections in the previous chapter):

> I don't think God is good. I suffered abuse from a Christian min-ister father and God didn't rescue me; I had to rescue myself. My daughter suffers cerebral palsy and no matter how many thousands of people prayed nothing changed. The recent death of my brother-in-law from cancer was one in thirty-nine cases recorded in the world since 1968. He was a good man. All these things force me to conclude there is no method, reason or consequence because there is no cosmic justice on this earth. If God professes to be just, then how could he endorse things that are unjust?[48]

The problem of greater-good theodicies is that it is indecent to "acquire goods at the expense of the victims of evil."[49] A good paid for with the price of an abused child is corrupted, and no amount of postmortem compensation or retrospective consent is enough.[50] In fact, we should never consent to evil. Thus far I have made no distinction between so-called moral evil and natural evil, since theodicies generally recognize the horror of all types of suffering, and since both are seem-ingly allowed by God. The distinction is important, however, because it is one thing to embrace our vulnerability and another thing altogether to accept and justify evil. Because evil is privation—the human decision not to pursue truth, goodness, and beauty—it is the absence of meaning and goodness, unintelligible, and so it defies comprehension. "And what is unintelligible cannot be understood, even by God."[51] Consequently, to suggest that God permits evil for a subsequent greater good—as each of the theodicies discussed seems to do—becomes an implicit justification of evil when "in fact, God repudiates evil; God forbids evil."[52]

It is sometimes assumed that free will, which is central to our ability to love and be loved, is itself the greater good that makes the suffering of the evil that follows worthwhile.[53] But that assumption conflates a human capacity with the good to which that capacity is intended. Free will does not justify evil, but, since it is central to our identity, it does explain evil's existence. Without free will, we would not be who we are—"To repudiate the conditions from which we have emerged is to repudiate our own existence."[54] Whether the fact of evil is sufficient reason to deny the existence of God will then be a matter of perspective. Lonergan contends,

> Without faith, without the eye of love, the world is too evil for God to be good, for a good God to exist. But faith recognizes that God grants men their freedom, that he wills them to be persons and not just his automata, that he calls them to the higher authenticity that overcomes evil with good.[55]

FRAGILITY AND VULNERABILITY

Of course, the problem of suffering is not limited to the consequences of sin but is inherent to the very nature of the creation itself.[56] My quadriplegia, for example, is the product of dumb luck and the constitution of the human neurological system and spine. I broke my neck and destroyed my nervous system because I landed badly when jumping a bicycle—an admittedly regrettable decision, but not a sinful one. Jay's daughter was born with cerebral palsy, one of the many risks of childbirth, and his brother-in-law's cancer had its origin in processes of genetic mutation that have shaped the evolution of life.[57]

One of the problems with all these approaches to theodicy is that they focus almost exclusively on primary causation, paying almost no attention to the "perfections" (the creative and causal power) of secondary causes. It has been asserted that "the distinction between primary and secondary causation does not explain anything at all,"[58] but such a view arises only when the focus is on primary causation without adequate reflection on secondary causation and its implications. And that is to miss the fact that nature has its own reasons for the flow of events, and our fragility and vulnerability go hand in hand with creaturely existence in a material universe.

The focus on secondary causation raises the question as to whether it makes sense for a theist to explain disability and illness as being a product of natural contingency. There is a tendency to presume that providence and chance cannot go together (no less than Einstein famously declared that "God does not throw dice"), but "what God wills to happen through the unfolding of chance, will occur through the unfolding of chance."[59] This assertion is not a capitulation to metaphysical mystery (as tends to occur in Reformed conceptions of providence that see God as the primary cause of good and evil acts, but as not responsible for the latter), but recognizes that creation in its totality is contingent upon the will of God. Indeed, God transcends time and space, and God's will grounds the totality of the universe's past, present, and future, establishing and foreknowing its laws. This includes the laws of chance apparent in natural processes such as evolution and quantum physics, and in the contingency that frames everyday life. The key point is that contingency, both good and bad, is real and yet also encompassed by the divine will.

This insight has been especially important to my own experience of suffering. In response to the question, "Why me, God?" I have come to the view that the only reasonable answer is that injuries such as mine are a part of what it is to be a creature of the earth. In the midst of the experience of suffering, the search for a deeper explanation will inevitably fall short, since it is difficult to see how the challenge of quadriplegia (or cerebral palsy, or any disability or ongoing experience of suffering, loss, and grief) can be imagined to be worth the subsequent benefits that might accrue, however many they might be. I am a quadriplegic because to be human is to be subject to the vulnerabilities of finite life. It is this contingent finitude, inherent to the cycles of cosmic and quantum physics and the evolutionary processes of biological life and death, that gives rise to the wonders of creation, including the emergence of the human species in general and my personal consciousness in particular. And if I can recognize the goodness of God in creating and sustaining the laws and processes of nature, might it also be possible for me to trust the gracious providence of God in the midst of the suffering that results from the way things are—in my case, the misfortune to have broken my neck? If I were to frame this problem in terms of the greater good, then it is not what is achieved by suffering that tips the scales; it is the wonder of life itself that is worth the suffering that accompanies it.

It is sometimes argued that God could have created things differently, setting up a universe without pain, suffering, and death, and without disability. But whether or not that is possible (and how could we know?), it would be a universe without the glories of the one we inhabit, without the beauty of the earth, without humanity, and without our own personal consciousness, since these are all products of the laws of physics and evolutionary biology that have made things the way they are. To wish for a universe without suffering is thus to wish away our own existence; and "there is an absurdity in putting an end to human life to spare us the suffering it involves."[60]

One problem of modern society, even with all its medical and technological wonders, is its implicit demand that we should live forever in perfect health. We keep our dead and dying out of sight; we abort babies that do not match our ideals of normalcy; we worship photoshopped images of beauty. In consequence, suffering, disability, and fragility come as a complete and utter shock. We just do not know what to do with them. In reality, however, there is no theological reason to assume that we should be immune to the consequences of biological existence.[61]

JESUS: MAKING MEANING OUT OF SUFFERING

Earlier, I defined suffering as ongoing and meaningless pain, which suggests that the answer to the problem of pain might be found in the pursuit of meaning. In this light, Christian theodicies generally draw on Christology as the source of meaning, focusing particularly on Jesus' sharing in and transformation of the experience of suffering.[62] Describing the life and ministry of Jesus, they identify his healings, natural miracles (such as walking on water), and resurrection as "downpayments on and signal of divine power and intention to follow through with horror defeat" (cosmic re-creation).[63] From this perspective, Jesus' story provides us with hope, and ends "the power of matter to ruin personal meaning."[64] In healing, Jesus reverses horrors; on the cross, he is in solidarity with our suffering, sharing the horrors; and in the resurrection, he promises the complete defeat of horror, including the universal horror of death.

Notwithstanding the centrality of Christology to Christian theodicy, there is a tendency to ignore the more ambiguous elements of the gospel stories, particularly about the treatment of disability. We will return to this issue in the next chapter, but for now, it is enough to say that the gospel narrative evokes liberation and inclusion; it is first and foremost about Jesus' compassion for and embrace of those who suffer illness and social exclusion. The gospel stories serve to establish a basis of hope for those trapped in intractable suffering; indeed, by locating oneself in these narratives, Jesus' encounters with various impairments take on new significance.

The cross is especially important for theodicy. In the context of my own disability, Nancy Eiesland's oft-quoted connection between the broken body of Jesus and a quadriplegic is significant:

> I saw God in a sip-puff wheelchair, that is, the chair used mostly by quadriplegics enabling them to maneuver by blowing and sucking on a strawlike device. Not an omnipotent, self-sufficient God, but neither a pitiable, suffering servant. In this moment, I beheld God as a survivor, unpitying and forthright.[65]

This follows a long tradition of identifying the crucified Jesus with marginalized people: the black Jesus, the female Jesus, and now the disabled Jesus. If we move beyond identification to theological conceptions of the atonement—such as satisfaction and penal theories of the atonement—it is the action of God that is normally in view. What is too seldom emphasized is the fact that the crucifixion is, first of all, an experience of contingent evil and human fragility. That the Messiah is crucified, after proclaiming a message of healing, liberty, peace, and reconciliation, is utterly incomprehensible.[66] In the face of the injustice and horror of the crucifixion, we understand the urgency of Jesus' prayer, "Take this cup from me," and the soulful depth of his final cry on the cross, "My God, my God, why have you forsaken me?" Indeed, we should not move too quickly past Jesus' form of the question, "Why me, God?" or the silence that constitutes the Father's response.[67]

Within the logic outlined thus far, there is analogical significance in thinking about the cross in terms of the distinction between primary and secondary causation. On the one hand, the crucifixion of Jesus cannot be explained, other than to say that he experienced the blunt end of human finitude (and evil). We miss the point if we think there is something unique about his suffering and death—as though the pain he experienced was of a magnitude different from countless others who have been crucified, tortured, or subject to the innumerable types of suffering that go hand in hand with life on earth. We also miss the point if we declare that God crucified Jesus; indeed, since his crucifixion is evil, it has no substantive cause and no explanation. Still, we can say that God's providence encompassed the cross, a fact made clear by God's creating meaning out of the unintelligibility of the cross event.[68]

The disciples—and the risen Jesus—experienced this meaningfulness retrospectively. In the midst of suffering there is no meaning to be had—no adequate explanation. Only on looking back does it become apparent that God, in his providential grace, has imbued the cross with meaning.

The meaning of the cross is complex and multifaceted, but at its most profound the cross transforms evil into good and meaninglessness into meaning. As for the predicament to which the cross is a response, God wills the good, but sin has consequences: the deprivation of the good; evil (and its attendant suffering), which is the penalty of sin. As the incarnate Son, Jesus proclaims the good news of the kingdom of God, the defeat of evil, the overcoming of poverty, captivity, and sickness—a message most fully embodied on the cross where Jesus offers satisfaction for human sin. But satisfaction is not to be understood as divine retribution inflicted on the Son. Rather, it is the Father's acceptance of the sacrifice of the Son and Jesus' choice to submit to evil and transform it into a good.[69] And this is the key point: the cross is a symbol of transformation because the evil done to Jesus is not reciprocated but answered with love and forgiveness. Furthermore, resurrection follows Christ's self-sacrifice: a vindication of his message of love and a promise that suffering is not the end of the story.[70]

So the cross has the potential to transform evil into good, but is it of relevance to the broader problem of suffering—to the pain, sickness, disability, and ultimately death that are inherent to life? The case can be made that the gospel of Jesus has always been about more than sin. The incarnation is a celebration of life in all its wondrous fragility; and the cross and resurrection challenge the idea that the cycle of life and death is meaningless—nothing more than cold-hearted chance. Further, the gospel narrative invites imitation: not a masochistic embrace of suffering, but the deliberate choice to work for the defeat of evil and the minimization of suffering, whatever its cause. For the disciples, the hopelessness and godforsakenness that accompanied the grief of the persecution and death of Jesus—and that was part and parcel of Jewish life under the brutal Roman occupation—was replaced by a new sense of faith, hope, and love (1 Cor 13:13; 1 Thess 1:3). This did not eliminate suffering, but it did give meaning to life and enabled the Christian community to flourish.

SUFFERING AND FAITH, HOPE, AND LOVE

If the incarnation, cross, and resurrection are capable of transforming suffering by actively creating meaning out of meaninglessness and horror, this transformation is instantiated in the present by faith, hope, and love. These are described by Aquinas as the theological virtues, because they are gifts of grace infused by God, enhancing the human capacity by transforming and enriching the intellectual and moral virtues that enable a person to flourish over the course of the ups and downs of life.[71] Thus far, I have focused on primary and secondary causation and their implications for theodicy, with particular emphasis on the latter. In terms of transforming meaningless suffering—in making a go of life in the struggle with disability and impairment—the theological virtues become the bridge between God's action and our own, since God works not principally by supernatural intervention, but through cooperative grace, empowering us to have faith, hope, and love. But what does this have to do with theodicy?

Beginning with faith, defined in Hebrews 11:1 (KJV) as "the substance of things hoped for, the evidence of things not seen," we are confronted with the fact that the problem of suffering leads to the potential emergence of doubt. In contemporary church circles, the embrace of doubt and uncertainty has become fashionable, but the experience of doubt in the midst of suffering is no small matter.[72] I am sometimes asked whether the accident and its aftermath have changed my theology, a question that is difficult to answer, largely because I have worked out my theological positions through many years of study. This experience has, however, confronted me with the question of whether God exists at all. When you are trapped in bed, staring at the ceiling and unable to move, the line between "Why me, God?" and "Am I praying to myself?" is thin indeed.

In the face of intractable suffering, how does one persist with faith and, equally important, why bother doing so? An initial answer to both questions is that faith is as much a gift as a choice, an idea that again relies on the distinction between primary and secondary causation. Aquinas differentiates between the proofs of God's existence—the products of intellectual virtue—and faith in the existence of God, a gift pertaining to both the intellect and the will. Faith is a virtue, a habit both of the mind that pursues the truth found fully in God, and of the will that hungers for the good, and so is oriented to God as the ultimate good. Faith is not opposed to reason, but transcends and illuminates it.[73] Of course, Aquinas wrote in an era in which the existence of God was largely taken for granted, and for him, suffering did not undermine faith but, rather, sharpened and directed it, reordering a person's priorities so that he is focused on God rather than on material and temporal pleasures.

But does Aquinas' treatment of faith still make sense? Earlier, I cited Lonergan and his argument that "without faith, without the eye of love, the world is too evil for God to be good, for a good God to exist."[74] Arguments for the existence of God that are grounded in the intelligibility and beauty of the natural world are offset by the hardship of earthly existence. Theodicies such as those I outlined are intended to help make sense of this conundrum, but without faith they remain ambiguous. However, even with faith this ambiguity persists. While living with a disability, I have been unable to regain my once-held certitude that Aquinas associates with faith.[75] I have struggled to know whether I have experienced or simply longed for "God's love poured into my heart through the Holy Spirit" (cf. Rom 5:5). That longing is grounded in the hope that we live in a friendly universe, one in which the effort to address individual and social hardship matters. In any event, faith, even faith as uncertain as my own, provides motivation to resist the paralyzing despair that threatens to cause us to give up when pain and trouble become overwhelming. And even uncertain faith, if it is a longing for the good, is still ultimately faith in God.[76]

The difficulty of faith is concerned not just with God's existence but with God's continued work in the world. The question "Why me, God?" is shorthand for "Why, God, don't you intervene?" The theological challenge of disability is its permanence and God's failure to respond to countless desperate prayers for healing. In previous work I have criticized Pentecostal/charismatic theology and practices that focus on miraculous physical healings.[77] Instead, I argued for an understanding of well-being that seeks the flourishing of people with a disability, and that is able to hold together the fact of suffering and the possibility of the good life. Indeed, so-called supernatural physical healing is no answer to the problem of pain—not only is it extremely rare (and inherently unsubstantiable), it is also inevitably arbitrary. Until there is no suffering in the world, theodicy remains. Yet, while prioritizing prayer for physical healing is a distortion of faith, denying the presence and activity of God in the world (for example, by the practical atheism of Deism) eliminates faith altogether. Catholic and Orthodox practices of sacramental healing provide a more balanced and nuanced conceptualization, since they seek to mediate the presence and grace of God in the midst of suffering and in the face of death, and stress "efficacious wholeness rather than focusing solely on physical cure."[78] That is to say, faith, expressed and built up through prayer, looks to God to infuse life with a meaning that embraces and transcends its hardships.

Faith gives birth to hope. This is vital in the case of spinal cord injury (and any acquired disability or permanent form of suffering), which, by its very nature, has the potential to lead to hopelessness. Wide-ranging evidence now available shows that hopeful individuals tend to be more resilient, more likely to establish and achieve goals, to have better psychological health, and to have a greater overall well-being and life satisfaction than those who tend toward pessimism.[79] Interestingly, the grounds of hope can be varied (e.g., personal experience, religious teaching, technological advancements, etc.) and more or less substantive. Studies have found that even unrealistic hope (such as for miraculous healing) helps people cope, at least in the early stages of recovery.[80] The theological virtue of hope, though, has a longer term capacity, since it looks beyond the vicissitudes of daily life, and grounds hopefulness in the character and promises of God. It is more than mere wishful thinking, because it makes a difference to life here and now. As Benedict XVI noted in his encyclical *Spe Salvi*, "Faith draws the future into the present, so that it is no longer simply a 'not yet.' The fact that this future exists changes the present; the present is touched by the future reality, and thus the things of the future spill over into those of the present."[81] Theodicies that concentrate on the afterlife as the means of rectifying present horrors go awry if they merely look to the future. The real power of hope is that it transforms the present.

While hope in God can be unlimited—is anything impossible for God?—in application to living with a disability, it exists in the mean between naive optimism and nihilistic despair. Thus hope enables a person to be realistic about their situation—knowing that fragility and hardship are always companions to the joys of life—but not defined by it. Hope transcends the limits of dependency, paralysis, and a wheelchair; the virtue reaches for a future that defies the constraints of the present.

Finally, this transformation is possible only because of the theological virtue of love—of self, others, and God. The problem of pain raises questions about the love of God, since the cry "Why me, God?" might equally be framed, "Don't you love me, God?" Again, God's love is mediated through secondary causes. I spoke earlier about the possibility of retrospectively imbuing suffering with meaning. Only love makes this a possibility. In this light, the meaning of my spinal cord injury is found in the constant love of my wife and children, in the ways my parents put their life on hold to care for my family, in the hospital-bed conversations with close friends, in the wisdom and compassion of doctors, in the attentiveness of nurses, and in the encouragement of occupational therapists and physiotherapists. I return this love when all these people experience the joy of my rehabilitation (a process facilitated by faith and hope), when I respond to their felicitation with gratitude, and when I encourage them not to lose hope. Over the long run, and even in the face of permanent disability, continued pain, and the loss of many of my heart's desires, it will nevertheless be possible for me to contribute to others in both small and substantive ways, and so to live a life of meaning, transforming the problem of pain into a narrative of the goodness of God.

It seems appropriate to finish this chapter by returning to Jay's legitimate complaints arising from his experience of abuse, disability, and grief. I hope it is not glib to suggest that I can perceive God's grace at work in the life of his family, even while understanding why he might conclude that there is no cosmic justice and that God is not good. Certainly, there is no justification for the abuse he suffered. It was not allowed by God, nor does it serve any purpose. Yet the evil done to him by his father is transformed (though never forgotten) by his choice to walk the difficult road of forgiveness (following the example of Jesus and empowered by the grace of the Spirit), and therein to learn a very different way to be a loving father to his children.[82] Likewise, the death of Jay's brother-in-law to cancer, while explainable in terms of the biological cycle of life and death, is not explained by some imagined greater good. But this suffering was given significance by the resolute love and care of family and friends over the long period of travail until his passing, sharing in grief, and hoping for a reunion in the life to come. Lastly, while it might seem impossible to fathom how God could allow the hardships of his daughter's cerebral palsy, the beauty of her smile and the delightful sound of her laughter shows us all how wondrous this terrible life can be.

3

Disability, Virtue, and the Meaning of Happiness
A Disabled Reading of the Virtue Tradition

Faith, hope, and love are labeled by the influential thirteenth-century theologian Thomas Aquinas as the theological virtues. Aquinas' reference to virtue arises as part of the virtue tradition that was central to his theological project. This tradition had its origins in the writings of the Greek philosopher Aristotle, whose treatises on ethics shaped Aquinas' thinking and have been central to Catholic moral teaching ever since. Although falling out of favor with secular scholars as a result of the Enlightenment critique of religious authority (since religion and virtue were thought to be intertwined), the tradition has been reappropriated by a number of contemporary moral philosophers and theologians.[1] Its longevity is testimony to the coherence of Aristotle's and Aquinas' thought, and to the fact that it speaks to themes that continue to be central to our self-understanding—in particular, our pursuit of happiness and the good life.

Since this book claims to be a work of Christian theology, it is perhaps necessary to justify my reliance on Greek sources. It is still common for Protestant and Evangelical theologians to lament the supposed Hellenization of Christianity, but the appeal to Jerusalem over Athens tends to be both anti-intellectual and totalizing, presuming that the Hebrew way of thinking is the high point of the history of ideas and that everything that follows the biblical canon is corruption and decline.[2] But such lament forgets that the New Testament itself brings Jewish thought into interaction with Greco-Roman worldviews, and thereafter the task of mission demanded meaningful exploration of dominant cultural values. In fact, a strong case can be made that the engagement of the church fathers with Greco-Roman thinking was more the Christianization of Hellenic thought than the other way around. It would be arrogant to say that Christians had nothing to learn from the Greeks, just as it would to ignore the history of ideas in the development of knowledge.[3] Certainly, Aquinas did not blindly follow Aristotle but utilized his philosophical schema as a way of systematizing a Christian theology substantially rooted in the scriptures. Because my goal is to reflect upon the flourishing of people with disabilities, I choose to draw on helpful sources from diverse strands of the Christian tradition (including its philosophical interlocutors) and hope that the exploration itself will bear fruit for future theological, and even doctrinal, thinking.

ARISTOTLE

Ethics may be understood to be seeking to answer the question, "What is the right thing to do?" but the virtue tradition's concern is the question "What is the best way to live?"[4] It answers that we live to attain *eudaimonia*, which is normally translated as happiness. But what is happiness?

In *Nicomachean Ethics,* Aristotle begins his response by identifying what *eudaimonia* is not, namely wealth, honor, and pleasure. People seek wealth, not for its own sake, but for what it can buy. This is not to say that money is irrelevant to happiness, since people need resources sufficient to meet their basic needs. Studies have found, for example, that wealth buffers happiness after the onset of a disability.[5] Aristotle's point, though, is that if money does contribute to *eudaimonia*, it does so by facilitating some other good—in the case of disability, money purchases social and technological supports that enable a person to negotiate their environment better. Similarly, Aristotle notes that we do not desire honor for its own sake but for the virtue that earns it.[6] This is why inspiration porn (outlined in the introductory chapter of this volume) is so galling; because it elevates the everyday activities of disabled people, and so implies that they are incapable of substantive virtue and achievement.[7]

Aristotle aims his harshest criticism at the conception of *eudaimonia* as the pursuit of pleasure. To live for pleasure is to be trapped by one's passions rather than directed by reason, and so to choose the "slavish" life of "fatted cattle."[8] We shall return to the value of pleasure in chapter 6 when we consider the scientific insights of positive psychology, but for now, it is enough to note that while the good life will have its pleasures (and virtue itself should be enjoyable), pleasure is a fleeting and insubstantial emotion. *Eudaimonia,* by contrast, is earned over the course of a lifetime. As Aristotle notes, "For one swallow does not make a spring, nor does one day. And in this way, one day or a short time does not make someone blessed and happy either."[9]

As developed by Aristotle, *eudaimonia* is teleological—it is the end we pursue for its own sake and nothing else.[10] We act for many reasons, with many ends or purposes in mind, but all of these ends aim for the ultimate purpose of living a good life, which is *eudaimonia*—happiness. In modern parlance, the term "flourishing" may capture best what Aristotle is talking about. There are many dimensions to the good life, and many ways to achieve it. But they all share a common thread, which is that we intend to live a rich and fulfilling life, seeking to make it count, to invest it with meaning.[11]

What it is for a thing to flourish depends upon its nature. We share with other animals many natural needs and capacities, and as with them, our flourishing encompasses our physical health, connection to the environment, need of nourishment, sexual pleasure, the raising of our young, social organization, and so forth.[12] For Aristotle, though, what makes us distinctly human is our capacity for reasoning, so that only a person who lives wisely (wisdom is practical reasoning) can be said to have lived a fully human life.[13]

While animals live according to their nature, what is characteristically human is that our rationality enables us radically to transform (although never transcend) our basic naturalistic structure.[14] Because this is so, our capacity for reasoning transforms every part of our life. Even our basic passions, such as our need for food, are altered by the exercise of reason, so that we are able—within certain limits—to decide how, why, when, and what we eat. To take another example, where the females of other species closely related to humans often live "rotten" lives compared to their male counterparts (anthropologically speaking), feminists have shown us that women—notwithstanding millennia of seemingly natural subordination—are capable of living differently, of living better:

> Our concepts of "a good human being" and "living well as a human being" are far from being completely constrained by what . . . biologically specialized members of our species actually, or, at the moment, typically, do; we have room for the idea that we might be able to be and to live better. . . . This is a major part of the genuinely transforming effect the fact of our rationality has on the basic naturalistic structure.[15]

It is noteworthy that what is most characteristic of the treatment of people with disabilities throughout history is the assumption that they lack the capacity for proper reasoning, and so are unable to interpret their own experiences, or speak for and decide for themselves.[16] In this way, they are treated as though they are less than fully human. Above all else, what the disability rights movement has insisted upon is that people with a disability, whether it be physical or intellectual, are human, and so as capable as anyone of self-understanding and self-determination. Indeed, it is disabled people themselves, and those who know and love them, who have reasoned that they should be able to live better lives, and so have banded together to advocate for change, transforming the seemingly naturalistic structures that for far too long have kept them marginalized and oppressed.

If *eudaimonia* is understood as the flourishing life, Aristotle argues that it is virtuous activity that achieves it. A virtue is a characteristic or trait—a habit of character—that enables a person to succeed in their undertakings and, more broadly, to flourish in life.[17] As noted, wisdom is the fundamental virtue that enables a person to decide what the virtues are and how to exercise them at any point in time. Taking his readers through the process of practical reasoning, Aristotle distinguishes between two types of virtue, moral and intellectual.

Moral virtues require a balanced character and are generally found in the mean between two vices, excess and deficiency.[18] Courage, for example, is the midpoint between the vice of excess, recklessly rushing into battle, and the vice of deficiency, cowardly refusing to

fight. In *Nicomachean Ethics* Aristotle identifies eleven moral virtues
as follows:

Vice of Excess	Virtue	Vice of Deficiency
Recklessness	Courage	Cowardice
Licentiousness	Moderation, Self-Mastery, Temperance	Insensibility
Prodigality	Liberality	Stinginess
Vulgarity and Crassness	Magnificence	Parsimony
Vanity	Greatness of Soul	Smallness of Soul
Ambition	"Ambition"	Lack of Ambition
Unreasonable Anger	Gentleness	Passivity
Obsequiousness or Flattery	Friendliness	Surliness and Quarrelsomeness
Boastfulness, Exaggeration	Truthfulness	Falsehood, Reservation
Buffoonery and Crudity	Wittiness and Tact	Boorishness and Dourness
Injustice of excess	Justice	Injustice of deficiency

Aristotle's list is not meant to be definitive, and since his frame of
reference is a context very different to our own, I will leave it to others
(and Aristotle himself) to provide a detailed analysis of the virtues and
vices he describes.[19] Regarding the broader logic, one way to understand
what Aristotle is on about is to consider particular activities or practices.[20] To succeed as a musician, for example, it will be necessary to
exercise ambition, patience, discipline, and the like, and the apathetic,
impatient, and ill-disciplined person will never progress. Virtues, then,
are the habits that enable a person to achieve the happiness that comes
with excellence, in this case the joy of becoming an excellent musician.
Virtues are taught and modeled by our parents and leaders, and we
learn them both through instruction and practice; practicing a virtue
enables it to become a habit, internalized as a part of our character. To
say that virtue is habitual explains why a person can be relied on to act
in particular ways—at least most of the time. From this perspective,

happiness is not a single thing but a way of living.[21] Virtue is both rational and pleasurable, bringing together our reason and our emotion. Virtue facilitates our achievements but is also its own reward. In his seminal work on the trajectory of the virtue tradition, *After Virtue*, Alasdair MacIntyre notes:

> Although the virtues are those qualities which tend to lead to the achievement of a certain class of goods, nonetheless unless we practice them irrespective of whether in any particular set of contingent circumstances they will produce those goods or not, we cannot possess them at all.[22]

Courage, for example, is the preparedness to give one's life for the sake of another, and the courageous person understands that the happiness derived from courage goes hand in hand with self-sacrifice. The virtue tradition presupposes a "distinction between what any particular individual at any particular time takes to be good for him and what is really good for him as a man [*sic*]."[23] Again, virtue is its own reward, the internal satisfaction of living wisely.

The recognition that there is an internal reward that comes from acting virtuously leads Aristotle to differentiate between a person who is self-controlled (or continent) and one who is fully virtuous. The former knows what to do and does it, even though it is contrary to her desires, and so exercises self-control when she acts.[24] The latter knows what to do and *desires* to do it, and so acts with full virtue. Aristotle goes on to praise the fully virtuous person over the self-controlled person, which is somewhat counterintuitive, since we normally imagine that self-control is praiseworthy. And it is. But more praiseworthy is the longer term self-control that is the product of developed character, which has transformed a person so that they delight in virtue.

Transcending the moral virtues are what Aristotle describes as the "intellectual capacities of the soul."[25] Aristotle draws on an ancient epistemology, distinguishing between the practical and theoretical operations of the intellect. The former incorporates knowledge specific to particular disciplines, as well as prudence, which, as noted earlier, is the practical wisdom that acts as the linchpin between the intellectual and moral virtues, helping a person to decide how to apply the virtues to any particular circumstance. The latter, theoretical intelligence, takes a person beyond the intellectual virtues of daily life, and enables her to contemplate the world, reaching for transcendent knowledge (even knowledge of the gods). It is this contemplative capacity that Aristotle believes is most distinctly human, and so for him, it is the intellectual virtues of the philosopher that facilitate complete happiness.

Virtues are taught, modeled, and highly contextual, and so sustained by cultural tradition. To participate in a practice is to join a community and a tradition with a purpose, and so "to enter into a practice is to enter into a relationship, not only with its contemporary practitioners, but also with those who have preceded us in the practice."[26] The best practitioners are those who embed themselves in the tradition, learning its habits and values, who then transcend the tradition, taking it forward.[27] To continue the musical illustration, the best musicians are those who are deeply embedded in the world of music theory and historical practice, but who also challenge and creatively transform that world. It is perhaps noteworthy that in my own case, acquiring a disability brought me into a community of disabled people, with its own history, values, attitudes, and practices. The research underpinning this book represents my attempt to understand its virtues and actions—to learn, for example, that sometimes rage is a virtue and not a vice, needed to deal successfully with discrimination. And as the book unfolds my goal is to reflect upon all I have been taught and shown about the virtues needed to flourish with a disability, and in however humble a way, to help take the community forward.

What is true of the particular practices is true for our moral life as a whole. Social embeddedness frames our conception of the virtues and our understanding of the good life but does not control it. Rather, we learn from living traditions, and are also capable of challenging and transforming those traditions. That is precisely what the disability community has achieved in its advocacy to transform cultural attitudes, political policies, and social structures so that disabled people are included, and their contributions recognized (notwithstanding that there is still more work to be done).

Finally, it is readily apparent that in Aristotle's conception of *eudaimonia* the social virtues loom large—gentleness, truthfulness, wittiness, and friendliness—and in *Nicomachean Ethics* he provides an extended discussion of friendship, distinguishing three forms: the useful, the pleasant, and the good. The first two are friendships in which the parties "do not love each other in themselves, but only insofar as they come to have something good from the other," such as between the wealthy and the poor, between work colleagues, and in the myriad of other relationships that make up our social life.[28] The best friendships are only possible between people of equal virtue and, according to Aristotle, equal advantage, and are characterized by the joy of living together. Such relationships enable people to achieve their own good by acting in the interest of the other.[29] The importance of friendship for the flourishing of people with disabilities warrants further attention, especially given Aristotle's view that true friendship is only possible between people of equal advantage. For now, though, it is enough to state the obvious fact that our happiness is dependent upon the quality of our familial and friendly relationships, which in the context of disability are too often framed as unidirectional, with the person with a disability the recipient of care. What is needed, though, is the formation of friendships with and between disabled people that are characterized by mutual giving.

In sum, then, for Aristotle *eudaimonia* describes the flourishing life, achieved by virtuous activity. The good life is most fully realized between friends, and in the exercise of intellectual virtue and the contemplation of transcendent truth, goodness, and beauty. This is an objective rather than subjective understanding of *eudaimonia*, but a person's flourishing can only be judged teleologically, at the end of life. From that vantage point, even crisis and hardship can be seen to have facilitated happiness, if faced virtuously, together with friends, in the pursuit of meaning.

This may seem a dispassionate way of conceiving happiness, although Aristotle recognizes that virtue alone is not enough for *eudaimonia*, and that we need certain bodily and external goods for true happiness, especially because a minimum level of wealth, health, and intelligence is the prerequisite for philosophical contemplation. Reflecting the prejudices of his day, Aristotle thus concludes that women and slaves are unable to be happy, in the fullest sense of the term, because they lack the freedom to make their own decisions, which restricts their exercise of virtue. "The slave is completely without the deliberative element; the female has it, but it has no authority."[30] More than just the cultural blindness of this position, what is noteworthy for our purposes is that this logic is extended by Aristotle to people who are chronically ill, mentally deficient, and even "ugly."

> For it is impossible or not easy for someone without equipment to do what is noble: many things are done through instruments, as it were—through friends, wealth, and political power. Those who are bereft of some of these (for example, good birth, good children, or beauty) disfigure their blessedness, for a person who is altogether ugly in appearance, or of poor birth, or solitary and childless cannot really be characterized as happy; and he is perhaps still less happy, if he should have altogether bad children or friends or, though he did have good ones, they are dead. Just as we said, then, [happiness] seems to require some such external prosperity in addition. This is why some make good fortune equivalent to happiness, and others, virtue.[31]

For Aristotle, ill health, mental deficiency, and ugliness—characteristic ways of describing disability—are not only undesirable for their own sake (how could anyone consider the disabled life to be a good life?) but necessarily restrict the full exercise of virtue. The key issue is the extent to which disability makes a person the recipient of rather than the benefactor of virtuous activity. The fully virtuous person—described by Aristotle as the person with greatness of soul—"is also the sort to benefit others but is ashamed to receive a benefaction; for the former is a mark of one who is superior, the latter of one who is inferior."[32] There is also the problem of capacity, since Aristotle considers slaves and women to be "naturally" incapable of virtue, particularly intellectual virtue, a judgment that would inevitably apply to a person with a disability.

And so we come to the crux of the matter. For Aristotle it is impossible for the disabled person to be truly happy. This prejudice cannot be brushed aside, since it indicates one of the problems of virtue ethics, which is the tendency for virtue to be conceived of in ways that entrench the status quo. Aristotle understands human nature and virtue in such a way as to entrench his own superiority, privileging Greek philosophy and political culture, and keeping women, slaves, disabled people, and every minority group in their place. In turning to the scriptures, there is some hope for a more inclusive perspective, although as we shall discover, the treatment of disability and flourishing in these authoritative texts is relatively ambiguous.

THE HEBREW BIBLE

As we seek to make sense of the resources the Bible offers for thinking about human flourishing, we are immediately faced with the problem of the size of the task: a book comprised of many books and multiple authors (many of them invisible and lost to time), writing from diverse perspectives, sometimes in agreement and other times in dispute, written and redacted over tens of centuries, the most recent two millennia ago, after which it became the most studied book in human history. What follows, then, cannot be a thoroughgoing biblical theology but, rather, an overview of scriptural conceptions of flourishing and virtue, read critically, once again using the lens of disability.

The Hebrew Bible's primary conception of the good life emphasizes covenant and obedience to divine laws, but at key points Israel's scriptures do encourage ways of thinking that reflect the virtue tradition and, more importantly, that challenge it.[33] Immediately, the Bible opens with the affirmation that God created a good world and commanded its constituents to flourish; "to go forth and multiply." Humanity is made in God's image, which has traditionally been associated with our rationality, morality, and relationality. In both Hebrew and Christian theologies of creation "our flourishing involves the authentic fulfillment of our natural inclination to know what is true, to love what is good, and to be rightly related to God," and rightly related to one another and the whole creation.[34] Throughout the remainder of the Hebrew Bible, and especially in the Psalms, Proverbs, and other wisdom literature, there is an emphasis both on prudence (practical wisdom, which flows from divine wisdom) and moral formation; "the purpose of the whole collection is moral training."[35] While the Hebrew Bible does not emphasize reason to the same extent as the Greeks, there is still a firm commitment to knowledge of truth, especially the truth of God, as well as the transformation of the heart that flows from that knowledge.[36]

In Hebrew moral instruction there is also an emphasis on narrative, both at a personal and national (or tribal) level.[37] Narrative is not central to Aristotle's conception of virtue, but I shall argue that it should be, since human life is its history, and, therefore, narrative provides the means of describing, judging, teaching, and challenging conceptions of the good life.[38] This is certainly true for the moral teaching of the scriptures. Covenantal law was not about blind obedience or legalism but grateful obedience as training in holiness. Israel learns what it is to flourish and live virtuously by narrating the stories of its history; small- and large-scale accounts of the events that followed the wise and the foolish decisions of the nation's forebears. In critically reading the biblical stories, Jews and Christians throughout the ages have sought to understand the positive consequences of virtue and the negative consequences of sin (the biblical equivalent of vice), and to exercise wisdom; translating the lessons of history to the choices they faced in their present situations. The great advantage of narrative is that it encourages multivocal readings, so that conceptions of the good life are subject to debate and ideological criticism. In making narrative central, telling stories that embrace complexity and ambiguity, and incorporating alternate and sometimes contradictory perspectives, the Bible "makes provision for its own critique."[39]

The story of Israel's exodus from Egypt, more than any other, is the central narrative of the Hebrew Bible, and grounds the covenantal promise. It is the preeminent symbol of divine grace, and its memory is a promise of justice and deliverance intended to provide hope in the context of suffering.[40] Its promise applies to the nation as a whole, and also to local communities, families, and individuals, including the disabled. In the Decalogue, Yahweh describes himself as "the LORD your God, who brought you out of Egypt, out of the land of slavery" (Exod 20:2), and thereafter the commands set out the pattern of life that Israel is to follow if it wants to flourish. Covenantal obedience is not about law keeping but is oriented to establishing values and habits of living—self-mastery—and thus facilitating personal well-being and the common good.[41] As with the virtue tradition, character and flourishing go hand in hand.

The Hebrew scriptures also emphasize the problem of sin, the need for repentance, and the transformative power of forgiveness.[42] In respect to the resonance with virtue ethics, there is a clear overlap between the concepts of vice and sin, as both have negative consequences for flourishing, and are indicative of poor character and behavior. The biblical construction of sin is often concerned with actions rather than character, but the scriptures also talk about corruption of the heart. In comparison to Aristotle, the biblical tradition gives sin extra significance because it is considered an inclination and action against God, God's people, and creation as a whole. But as serious as is the problem of sin, more potent is the offer of divine forgiveness that is made possible by repentance and atonement. Sin is both a serious problem and a reason for divine compassion and grace (e.g., Joel 2). The Hebrew scriptures encourage regret for past sin and an offer of grace that facilitates reform. In this way, they set out a concept of flourishing that is intended to overcome sin (or, said another way, to transcend vice).

The Hebrew Bible maintains a careful tension between two constructions of flourishing, and this can be illustrated in the wisdom literature and, in particular, in the comparison between Proverbs and Ecclesiastes. Proverbs follows the *eudaimonistic* pattern, where the exercise of wisdom and righteousness (virtue) leads to a vital, healthy, and long life, and folly and wickedness result in suffering and death.[43] By contrast, Ecclesiastes finds that "the act-consequence relationship is unreliable"; that good and bad things happen to the righteous and unrighteous alike.[44] In this case, all a person can do is take life as a gift from a mercurial sovereign, enjoying to the fullest extent possible whatever comes one's way:

> [7]Go, eat your food with gladness, and drink your wine with a joyful heart, for God has already approved what you do. [8]Always be clothed in white, and always anoint your head with oil. [9]Enjoy life with your wife, whom you love, all the days of this meaningless life that God has given you under the sun—all your meaningless days. For this is your lot in life and in your toilsome labor under the sun. [10]Whatever your hand finds to do, do it with all your might, for in the realm of the dead, where you are going, there is neither working nor planning nor knowledge nor wisdom. (Eccl 9:7-10)

In this way, Ecclesiastes presents an essentially hedonistic approach to life. It is not arguing against virtue or hard work ("whatever your hand finds to do, do it with all your might"), but that both should be enjoyed for their own sake. While Aristotle might decry the emphasis on pleasure, he would at least concur that virtue is its own reward. But Aristotle, as an elite Greek, is unable to see the dark side of life with the same perspicuity as the authors of the scriptures, and this is important for disability. The author of Ecclesiastes speaks to the disempowered condition, and "the hedonic joy he describes could be seen as an important act of resistance against oppressive conditions, since he refuses to let the human spirit be crushed."[45] This refusal gets to the heart of what disability pride and empowerment are all about.

Even so, the Hebrew Bible is not without its difficulties in the ways in which it understands the relationship between flourishing, sin, and disability. Indeed, the text shares in the ideological biases of its ancient context, a fact that should not be surprising (the social model of disability is a very recent insight), but which becomes problematic today when people treat those ideologies as unquestionably authoritative. Although rarely acknowledged by biblical scholars, disability is ubiquitous throughout the Hebrew Bible, even if this occurs as part of the backdrop to the more obvious themes in the text.[46] Disabilities— understood as defects—excluded a person from the priesthood, and were understood morally; the external defect was symbolic of an inner character flaw, and evidence of divine curse. In Deuteronomy 28, for example, disability is the consequence of disobedience:

> [27]The LORD will afflict you with the boils of Egypt and with tumors, festering sores and the itch, from which you cannot be cured. [28]The LORD will afflict you with madness, blindness and confusion of mind. [29]At midday you will grope about like a blind person in the dark. You will be unsuccessful in everything you do.

The stigmatization of disabled people often occurs by way of dualistic comparison, where people are classified as either favored/ disfavored, whole/defective, clean/unclean, honored/shamed, blessed/ cursed, beautiful/ugly, wise/mad, loved/hated, and so on.[47] Israel's laws about purity (clean/unclean) are multifaceted and complex, having various impacts upon a person's capacity to participate in cultic rights. Deuteronomy 23:2, for example, excludes a person with mutilated testicles from entering the sanctuary, a ban that related to the lack of reproductive capacity.[48] To be excluded from the sanctuary was to lose access to the heart and soul of the social life of the community, and the marginalizing effects cannot be understated. Indeed, people with particular skin diseases were excluded from the community altogether (Lev 13:45-46), which is to be treated as symbolically dead.[49] While such laws ostensibly respond to disability, the truth of the social model is readily apparent—religious rules such as these are themselves disabling.

Biblical authors also use denigrating metaphors ("a blind man gropes in darkness"), and disability is often associated with "weakness, vulnerability, dependence, and ineffectuality" (e.g., Isa 6:9-10; 56:10; Ps 38:14-15).[50] Disabled imagery is used to describe the falsity of idols: "They have mouths, but cannot speak, eyes, but cannot see. They have ears, but cannot hear, noses, but cannot smell. They have hands, but cannot feel, feet, but cannot walk" (Ps 115:5-7).[51] Seemingly less problematic are the eschatological texts that promise to heal people of their impairments (e.g., Ps 146). But while these arise out of a compassionate impulse, they assume that disability is abnormal, and that flourishing is impossible without the "healing" of the "defect."[52]

Taken altogether, this treatment of disability in a sacred text is not just an abstract historical curiosity. Consider the full text of Leviticus 21:16-23:

> [16]The LORD said to Moses, [17]"Say to Aaron: 'For the generations to come none of your descendants who has a defect may come near to offer the food of his God. [18]No man who has any defect may come near: no man who is blind or lame, disfigured or deformed; [19]no man with a crippled foot or hand, [20]or who is a hunchback or a dwarf, or who has any eye defect, or who has festering or running sores or damaged testicles. [21]No descendant of Aaron the priest who has any defect is to come near to present the food offerings to the LORD. He has a defect; he must not come near to offer the food of his God. [22]He may eat the most holy food of his God, as well as the holy food; [23]yet because of his defect, he must not go near the curtain or approach the altar, and so desecrate my sanctuary. I am the LORD, who makes them holy.' "

I have a visceral reaction to this text. I know that it is anachronistic to judge historical attitudes based on present-day values, but this passage is talking about my "defects." SCI has rendered me lame, deformed, with a crippled foot and hand, hunchbacked, and with damaged testicles, and I am the one told that I cannot enter the temple, that I am unholy and impure, and that I am unfit to meet with or represent God. That I can eat food outside of the house of God is a measly compromise. As a person with a disability I inevitably see this text—and others where disablement is less obvious but equally oppressive—differently than my nondisabled colleagues. I have learned from feminists the importance of looking at a text with disabled eyes and so I am enraged by the attitudes and assumptions of Leviticus 21, and of other biblical texts like it, because I know that over the millennia the disabling attitudes of the Bible have functioned to marginalize people with disabilities. John Wesley's explanatory notes in response to this passage are emblematic:

> The reason hereof is partly typical, that he, might more fully represent Christ, the great high-priest, who was typified both by the priest and sacrifice, and therefore both were to be without blemish; partly moral, to teach all Christians and especially ministers of holy things, what purity and perfection of heart and life they should labour after, and that notorious blemishes in the mind or conversation, render a man unfit for the ministry of the gospel; and partly prudential, because such blemishes were apt to breed contempt of the person; and consequently, of his function, and of the holy things wherein he ministered. For which reason, such persons as have notorious defects or deformities, are still unfit for the ministry except where there are eminent gifts and graces, which vindicate a man from the contemptibleness of his bodily presence.[53]

Contemporary readings are rarely so explicit in their prejudice, but especially in evangelical scholarship, there is a tendency to gloss over disability discrimination within the biblical text. The prominent Word Biblical Commentary series, for example, explains, "To serve at the altar, a priest has to be whole in body. . . . The wholeness of the priest, just as the wholeness of an animal acceptable for sacrifice, corresponds to and bears witness to the holiness of the sanctuary and the holiness of God. . . . This is another indication of the higher standards placed on a priest."[54] The problem is not the entirely unsurprising attitude of an ancient text, but that contemporary scholars not only fail to recognize prejudice, but try to justify it. Even more disabling is the Interpretation commentary's explanation:

> Ancient Israel's concern that physical deformity can impair a priest's capacity to serve [is] of course expressed in different terms than we would use today, but there is good reason to believe that we view the requirements for our own leaders in much the same way. One has only to recall the great care that was taken to hide President Franklin D. Roosevelt's paralyzed legs from public view, presumably on the assumption they might have signaled a physical weakness that was politically damaging.[55]

But while the Hebrew scriptures more or less inevitably reflect ancient attitudes to disability, they can also surprise with their inclusiveness and compassion.[56] This is especially true when Israel's attitude to the poor, the widows, the fatherless, and refugee aliens is contrasted to that of surrounding nations. And although explicit references contesting the oppression and stigmatization of disabled people are much rarer, they do exist.[57] Isaiah 56:3-7, for example, specifically responds to the Deuteronomic exclusion of men with mutilated testicles, noting that "to the eunuchs who keep my Sabbaths, who choose what pleases me and hold fast to my covenant—to them I will give within my temple and its walls a memorial and a name better than sons and daughters; I will give them an everlasting name that will endure forever."

There are also biblical narratives that exemplify disability, such as Jacob's limp after wrestling with God (Gen 32). Here Jacob's lameness can be understood as a sign of courage and persistence (although it might also be read as emblematic of his weakness).[58] The narrative of the book of Samuel includes King David's honoring of the "crippled" Mephibosheth, and sympathetically describes the disablement of David later in his life.[59] Messianic texts also make positive use of disability, as epitomized in the description of the suffering servant in Isaiah 53:1-4:

> [1]Who has believed our message and to whom has the arm of the LORD been revealed? [2]He grew up before him like a tender shoot, and like a root out of dry ground. He had no beauty or majesty to attract us to him, nothing in his appearance that we should desire him. [3]He was despised and rejected by mankind, a man of suffering, and familiar with pain. Like one from whom people hide their faces he was despised, and we held him in low esteem. [4]Surely he took up our pain and bore our suffering, yet we considered him punished by God, stricken by him, and afflicted.

It is noteworthy that this text is rarely understood by biblical scholars to be referring to disability, but whatever conclusions historians arrive at in respect to the explicit intention of the author (or redactor), it is surely significant that the messianic promise incorporates descriptions characteristically used to disparage disabled people—ugly, undesirable, despised, rejected, familiar with pain, turned away faces, punished by God.[60] That disablement (in the broadest sense of this term) is placed at the center of the messianic promise is a potent counterpoint to concepts of flourishing that exclude disability (including those encountered in the Bible itself).

THE NEW TESTAMENT

In the previous chapter we considered the significance of the gospel, and in particular the cross of Christ, for the problem of suffering. Without wishing to repeat what has already been said, in the following section the goal is to explore the significance of the New Testament for our conceptions of happiness, flourishing, and virtue. While its themes are both continuous with and distinct from the Hebrew Bible (its primary source), the New Testament was written after Aristotle in a Jewish society ruled by Rome. As a result, its authors both appropriate and critique Greco-Roman cultural values, including those established in the virtue tradition.

Like virtue theory, the Christian scriptures are teleological in orientation, and relate human flourishing to virtuous living. But while there is a common shape to the two traditions, the Christian vision is thoroughly differentiated by the countercultural life and message of (the Jewish) Jesus Christ. Jesus summarizes his own vision and mission in Luke 4:18-19 (citing Isa 61):

> [18]The Spirit of the Lord is on me, because he has anointed me to proclaim good news to the poor. He has sent me to proclaim freedom for the prisoners and recovery of sight for the blind, to set the oppressed free, [19]to proclaim the year of the Lord's favor.

Jesus' fundamental message is the good news of the kingdom of God, which is a vision of human flourishing (the Lord's favor) that is personal, social, and cultural in scope. In so doing, it intends to fulfill the liberatory promise of the Exodus narrative that frames the Hebrew Bible. It is a promise of friendship with God the Father, through the Son, in the power of the Holy Spirit, and the formation of a new and loving community, aimed especially at people living on the margins (a fact mostly forgotten by middle-class Christianity in the West today). The barriers to the flourishing of the poor, the oppressed, and the disabled (symbolized in Luke 4 by blindness) are the injustices perpetrated against those groups, so Jesus' preaching of and action toward the kingdom launches "an all-out attack on evil in all its manifestations."[61]

Happiness is a prominent theme in the gospel narratives, and Jesus' teachings on the topic were socially and culturally radical. The Beatitudes potently illustrate the point:

> [20]Looking at his disciples, [Jesus] said:
>   "Happy are you who are poor,
>   for yours is the kingdom of God.
>   [21]Happy are you who hunger now,
>   for you will be satisfied.
>   Happy are you who weep now,
>   for you will laugh.
> [22]Happy are you when people hate you, when they exclude you and
> insult you and reject your name as evil, because of the Son of Man.
> [23]Rejoice in that day and leap for joy, because great is your reward in
> heaven. For that is how their ancestors treated the prophets." (Luke
> 6:20-23)

The blessings (happy are you) sound a reversal in fortunes, in which the
poor, the marginal, the powerless, and the despised (and reference to the
excluded, insulted, and rejected resonates especially for disability) are
declared to be happy, while the rich and powerful who have inflicted
injustice and suffering are promised woe (vv. 24-26). The promise is
not merely of future happiness, but describes how things are now. As
Joel Green observes:

> [The blessings and woes] define the life-world disclosed in the com-
> ing of Jesus. To be sure, it is a topsy-turvy world when, for example,
> the poor can be declared "happy" rather than "down on their luck" or
> even "cursed." But this only underscores the degree to which Jesus's
> vision of the world is eschatological—not a vision of life relegated to a
> future bliss, but to the present disclosure of God's kingdom.[62]

Christianity is sometimes understood as offering happiness in
heaven and stoicism in the present, but the eschatology of Jesus looks
to the future, and in so doing brings joy to the present day, notwithstanding its ups and downs. As Green says, people "who orient their
lives to the divine purpose disclosed in the Messiah will experience the
pleasure and meaningfulness associated with human flourishing within
this eschatologically determined world."[63] Happiness, then, transcends
the pursuit of pleasure, is teleological (eschatological), and derived from
living meaningfully in service to Jesus.

Where Aristotle focuses on virtue, Jesus is especially concerned with
the devastation of sin. Jesus confronts the glaring problem of both the
virtue tradition and standard religious piety, which is that flourishing
seems to have nothing to do with virtue or vice; unjust people do well,

and the virtuous suffer. Aristotle is not unaware of the problem, and so admits that a certain amount of luck is needed for a person to flourish, but this understates the consequences of vice. The Hebrew Bible takes a firmer stance on the issue, challenging sin and unmasking injustice, and the wisdom literature is really an extended exploration and lament on the problem. Jesus teaches and then embodies a solution to the problem of evil: the divine choice to submit to the injustice and suffering of the cross, and transform the evil done to him into a good by responding with love and forgiveness. These were the issues addressed in the previous chapter, and there is no need to repeat them here.[64] What is important is the recognition that the life and teachings of Jesus are not abstract transactions focused on whether or not a person gets to heaven, but, rather, that they are intended to make a difference in human history. It does so by orienting people to meaning, the meaning of the story of Jesus, which gives life purpose. And this purpose is achieved by exercising virtues (charity, hope, faith, forgiveness, mercy, and so on) in the formation of a new community (the church), which is a vessel of the good news of the kingdom of God (God's just rule) for the wider world.

It is noteworthy, once again, that narrative is central to the New Testament framing of the good life. All four Gospels narrate the story of Jesus' life, and Jesus' characteristic way of teaching was through parabolic stories.[65] In emphasizing narrative, the New Testament embraces objective and subjective constructions of the good life. We make judgments about whether or not a person has flourished based on the story of his life. It is not individual episodes that matter as much as the character that emerges through the highs and lows that define a person's life. This is why funerals are occasions for deep reflection about the nature and purpose of life. In the same way, the Gospels are eulogies of the life of Jesus, intended to provide people with the opportunity to evaluate his life, and make sense of its message and meaning. And while these judgments have a certain objectivity, what a person does with that in respect to the meaning and actions of her or his own life is thoroughly open-ended and subjective.

To the central questions of virtue ethics, "What is the best way to live?" and "Who am I to become?" the Christian vision answers, "Imitate Christ."[66] As St. Paul says, "Have the same mindset as Christ Jesus: Who, being in very nature God, did not consider equality with

God something to be used to his own advantage; rather, he made himself nothing . . . [and] humbled himself by becoming obedient to death—even death on a cross!" (Phil 2:5-8). In a deliberate interplay with philosophy, St. Paul regularly contrasted the foolishness of the gospel with the wisdom of the Greeks. That foolishness was a seemingly upside-down vision of the good life that took the form of self-sacrificing love for God and neighbor, and more radically again, love of one's enemies (an impossibility for Aristotle).

To imitate Christ is not merely to act as he did, but to be transformed into his likeness, to have a changed heart and renewed mind. Jesus taught clearly that virtue and vice, while manifest in our actions, flow from the state of the heart (e.g., his teaching on anger in Matt 5:21-22), and so are a matter of character. But good character is the problem as much as it is the goal, as St. Paul understands with tragicomic clarity:

> [14]We know that the law is spiritual; but I am unspiritual, sold as a slave to sin. [15]I do not understand what I do. For what I want to do I do not do, but what I hate, I do. [16]And if I do what I do not want to do, I agree that the law is good. [17]As it is, it is no longer I myself who do it, but it is sin living in me. [18]For I know that good itself does not dwell in me, that is, in my sinful nature. For I have the desire to do what is good, but I cannot carry it out. [19]For I do not do the good I want to do, but the evil I do not want to do—this I keep on doing. [20]Now if I do what I do not want to do, it is no longer I who do it, but it is sin living in me that does it. [21]So I find this law at work: Although I want to do good, evil is right there with me. [22]For in my inner being I delight in God's law; [23]but I see another law at work in me, waging war against the law of my mind and making me a prisoner of the law of sin at work within me. [24]What a wretched man I am! (Romans 7:14-24)

St. Paul's response is that we should give up the impossible fight against our sinful nature (in Aristotle's language, our passions), embrace our brokenness, and accept the grace of God, who has shown us on the cross that we are loved as we are. With the foundation of grace in place, St. Paul insists that the Spirit of God will help to set our minds on Christ (Rom 8:1-17), so that imitating his self-sacrificing love becomes habitual. Indeed, the fruit of the Spirit (Gal 5:19-25) is not ethical rule-keeping but a transformed character, and love, joy, peace, patience, kindness, goodness, faithfulness, gentleness, and self-control (vv. 21-22) are virtues. And like Aristotle's fully virtuous man, the virtuous life modeled on Jesus becomes something that Christians do gladly (2 Cor 12:9, 15), so that happiness and virtue go hand in hand.[67]

The New Testament contains some striking contrasts with Aristotle's analysis of virtue. In particular, it praises virtues that Aristotle knows nothing about—faith, hope, and love—and counts as virtues qualities that Aristotle treats as vice, such as humility. And while Aristotle argues that the luck of wealth is necessary to attain happiness and exercise virtue (magnanimity, generosity, and friendship, he thinks, can only be exercised by the wealthy), the New Testament tends to be of the view that riches make it harder to live virtuously, whereas key virtues are more readily available to the poor, slaves, outcasts, and the disabled.[68] MacIntyre holds that Aristotle would not have admired Jesus Christ, and would have been horrified by St. Paul.[69] Even so, there is a logical and conceptual agreement between Aristotle and the New Testament, since both emphasize the importance of virtue to achieving the human telos.

Jesus, Disability, and Healing

As with Aristotle and the Hebrew Bible, the New Testament is steeped in the perspectives of its day, so it is important once again to attend to the text with the critical lens of disability. As has already been observed, Jesus' biographers reveal that he frequently addressed disabled people, whose importance to his ministry was made explicit in those passages in which he summarized his own purpose (e.g., Luke 4:18-20).

But his dealings with disability are not without potential ambiguity. All three of the Synoptic Gospels, for example, recount Jesus' healing of a paralyzed man lowered through the roof of the building; a healing predicated by Jesus forgiving the paralytic's sins (Matt 9:2-8; Mark 2:1-12; Luke 5:17-26). These accounts, which suggest a causal relationship between disability and sin, are echoed in John's narrative when, after Jesus had healed the paralyzed man who lay by the pool of Bethesda, he said to him, "See, you are well again. Stop sinning, or something worse may happen to you" (John 5:14). But while it might seem that Jesus assumed a causal relationship between sin and disability, in fact, Jesus' typical response to every person he encountered was to show them grace and then charge that they "sin no more." When asked an explicit theological question as to whether Galileans murdered by Pontius Pilot were worse sinners than all the other Galileans, he insisted that they were no guiltier than anyone else (Luke 13:1-5). Jesus was an equal opportunity judge and forgiver.

Jesus arrived at the same theological conclusion in John 9 when asked whether a man was born blind because of his sins or those of his parents. Jesus' response, "neither, but this happened so that the works of God might be displayed in him," is followed by the man's healing, and thereafter an extended discussion of the spiritual blindness of the Pharisees and Jesus' identity as "light of the world." While Jesus here clearly separates sin from disability, the story seems to assume that the display of God's work occurs "not in disability but in its overcoming," a conclusion reinforced by the seemingly negative metaphorical reference to blindness.[70] The impression given is that blindness and flourishing are antithetical. There are, however, alternate ways to read this passage. From a disabled perspective, Amos Yong argues that far from denigrating blindness, Jesus here honors the blind man because he was able to see what Jesus' opponents could not. On this reading, the metaphorical reference to blindness is not a denigration of disability but, rather, a celebration of the spiritual capacities of the blind man.[71]

That the Gospels place healing at the heart of Jesus' identity and ministry creates the more substantive difficulty. Consider Jesus' response to the doubts of John the Baptist:

> [20]When the men had come to him, they said, "John the Baptist sent us to you to ask, 'Are you the one who is to come, or should we expect someone else?'" [21]At that very time Jesus cured many who had diseases, sicknesses and evil spirits, and gave sight to many who were blind. [22]So he replied to the messengers, "Go back and report to John what you have seen and heard: The blind receive sight, the lame walk, those who have leprosy are cleansed, the deaf hear, the dead are raised, and the good news is proclaimed to the poor." (Luke 7:20-22)

It is Jesus' love and compassion for marginalized people, including those with a disability, that is the standout feature of his life and ministry, especially when compared to the secular and religious powers of his day (and with philosophers such as Aristotle). But that his solution to the problem of disability and terminal illness seems to have been to heal whoever sought him out is problematic, especially from the perspective of the social model of disability. It is a problem exacerbated in the context of ancient beliefs about evil spirits, since Jesus' compassion sees him exorcise people suffering what today would likely be diagnosed as mental illness (Luke 4:31-41) and epilepsy (Luke 9:42).

It is sometimes difficult to explain to people, especially Christians, why the healing ministry of Jesus can be problematic for disabled people. One way to illustrate the issue is to take a step back from the sensitivities of the story of Jesus, and reflect upon the experiences of people with disabilities in the context of modern healing ministries. Particularly with the rise of Pentecostal/charismatic spirituality, the twentieth century has seen renewed emphasis on supernatural faith healing, which is promoted as being an imitation of the miraculous ministry of Jesus. Healing is central to Pentecostal identity and practice and some have argued that this is one of the key reasons for the movement's growth.[72] That much of this growth has occurred in the Global South strongly suggests that the offer of healing meets the felt needs of people experiencing the hardships of global poverty and crisis. But there is an underside to the ministry of healing, which is the impact it has on those who are not healed. Take the example of Joni Eareckson Tada, whose perspective merits quoting at length. Reflecting on the confusion she felt attending a healing rally, she writes:

> One time, years ago, I too had been desperate to get healed. My sister Jay and I heard that Kathryn Kuhlman, a famous faith healer, was coming to the Washington, D.C., Hilton ballroom. Stories had reached us about cancer-ridden people who'd been cured in Philadelphia, Pennsylvania, at one of her crusades. I wondered if I should go to the healing service in Washington, D.C.
>
> One morning, when Jay was putting my legs through my range-of-motion exercises, Ernest Angley came on television. He was an odd sort of man who wore a bad toupee and ill-fitting suits, and Jay and I enjoyed his antics. My sister and I stopped and watched as people dropped their crutches or got up out of their wheelchairs, many raising their hands and declaring they were free from pain. "Do you think God could heal you?" Jay asked, staring at the screen. "Maybe it *is* time," I replied. And so, wondering if this might be an answer to the prayers of many, we found our way to the Washington Hilton and the packed healing service in the big ballroom.
>
> I remember the night so well, Miss Kuhlman breezed onto the stage under the spotlight in her white gown, and my heart raced as I prayed *Lord, the Bible says You heal all our diseases. I'm ready for you to get me out of this wheelchair. Please would You?* But the spotlight always seems

to be directed toward some other part of the ballroom where apparent healings were happening. Never did they aim the light at the wheelchair section where all the "hard cases" were; quadriplegics like me; stroke survivors, children with muscular dystrophy, and men and women sitting stiff and rigid from multiple sclerosis.

God answered. And again, His answer was no.

After the crusade I was number fifteen in a line of thirty wheelchair users waiting to exit at the stadium elevator, all of us trying to make a fast escape ahead of the people on crutches. I remember glancing around at all the disappointed and quietly confused people and thinking, *Something's wrong with this picture. Is this the only way to deal with suffering? Trying desperately to remove it? Get rid of it? Heal it?*[73]

This powerful image of the "disappointed and quietly confused" is telling, unmasking the effect the healing message can have on people with a disability. Rather than liberating people, healing ministry can burden them, adding failed faith to the challenge of living with a disability. There is something terribly unjust in the idea that God heals some people (often those with relatively trifling problems), but ignores the cries of others seeking similar remedy.

From the perspective of the social model, healing ministry can be disabling because it makes a spectacle of illness and disability—a contemporary version of the freak show. But the deeper problem is that modern healing ministries claim to imitate the supernatural ministry of Jesus. How, then, do we deal with the fact that the Gospels seem to show that Jesus' primary response to disability, sickness, and mental illness was healing and exorcism?

Admittedly, we face the problem of anachronism, of judging Jesus and the New Testament authors by standards entirely alien to their context. There is also the challenge of biblical interpretation, since our efforts to understand the scriptures are informed by a diverse range of interpretive strategies and competing claims about the meaning and intent of the Gospels. Disability scholars have drawn from a wide range of approaches, finding particular alignment with the insight of feminist scholars. Central to the logic of the social model of disability is that disabling attitudes and structures are often embedded in cultures and authoritative texts, and especially in the way in which those texts are interpreted and used to frame and direct contemporary behavior. In this light, feminist theologians have suggested that the Bible should come with a warning, "Caution! Could be dangerous to your health and survival."[74] Accordingly, we need a number of reading strategies that help both to unmask ideology and reframe an inclusive interpretation.[75] In the context of disability, these strategies include highlighting the experience of disabled people in the interpretation of these key passages, reading with a hermeneutics of suspicion, and rereading with the spirit of creative imagination. For Christian readers, reading the biblical text suspiciously is psychologically confronting, especially when it comes to reading the Gospels. But the goal of suspicion is not to undermine the liberating message of the gospel but, rather, to liberate that message so that it can speak to and for disabled people.

I have loosely employed these reading strategies in the analysis taken thus far. But to consider another example, we need only look to the story of Jesus' healing of the woman who had suffered from twelve years of hemorrhaging (Mark 5:21-43; Matt 9:18-26; Luke 8:40-56). A reading strategy that highlights disabled experience not only identifies the physical hardships associated with long-term bleeding, but explores the marginalization that results from religious and social ideologies that considered menstruating women to be impure (Lev 15). A suspicious reading might question the gospel account for its focus on healing, judging it as a concession to the purity laws. As presently written, the story has the woman reaching out and touching Jesus, an action perceived as shocking precisely because she was impure. A creative reimagining of the story might treat the woman as the real hero of the narrative for her bravery in defying cultural convention. We might even reimagine the story with Jesus shocking the onlooking crowd by giving the woman a long hug. Having employed these strategies, it might then come as no surprise that historical-critical exegetes do raise the importance of the social implications of this passage.[76] In praising the woman for the faith she exercised in reaching out and touching him, Jesus is rejecting any suggestion that she is impure, and the consequent healing is an expression of his compassion for the long hardship she has endured.

Reflecting on the Gospels as a whole, there are a number of features about the narratives that encourage a more nuanced response than simple literalism allows. First, for the gospel writers, healing and exorcism pointed to Jesus' messianic vocation; they are symbols of the good news of the kingdom of God. The Gospels communicate this truth metaphorically. This is apparent in Jesus' usage of fictional parabolic stories to challenge the thinking of his readers, as well as in his descriptions of himself as "light of the world," "bread of life," and so forth. Further, the authors of the Gospels not only recount parables by Jesus, their accounts can be understood as parables *of* Jesus; as stories with metaphorical meaning. This does not mean Jesus did not heal people. Indeed, Jesus' reputation as a healer and exorcist was a consistent feature of first-century testimony about him. It was his reputation as healer and exorcist that attracted crowds to his teaching, and even his enemies regarded him as possessed of power (which they attributed to Jesus being in league with Beelzebul).[77]

But the gospel writers are doing more than simply recounting history. Their narratives are deliberately theological and symbolic, and they tell the stories of Jesus with deliberate metaphorical intent. At least some of the stories, such as Jesus walking on water, have a symbolic purpose that supersedes debates about historicity; in this case, the intent is not to encourage Christians to imagine they can defy gravity, but to seek out Jesus in the midst of the storms of life. Indeed, "to argue about whether the stories narrate what actually happened most often distracts us from the meaning of the stories."[78] Taken as a whole, the meaning of Jesus' message, healings, and exorcisms is the good news of the coming kingdom, which, as already noted, is an attack on evil in all its manifestations. Jesus' message and actions were subversive, and posed "a serious threat to the social, cultural, and religious world of his day," a threat that ultimately led to his crucifixion.[79] And Jesus makes a specific point that this attack especially includes the social, cultural, and religious evil done against people with disabilities.

Second, throughout the ages, faith in Jesus, and through him the possibility of healing, has offered hope to people subject to pain, disability, and grief. As is apparent throughout the New Testament, the promise of healing is normally fulfilled eschatologically (every biblical character experiences the full gamut of human growth and decline, and fragility, suffering, and death are the one universal reality, even for Jesus). As we live in hope of the eschatological vision, we are graced with the Spirit as the firstfruits or deposit of the future (Rom 8:23). In this way, hope transforms the present, not by eliminating hardship, disability, or even death, but by giving us the fortitude to persevere and live constructive and meaningful lives.

What this means for people with disabilities today is that it is up to them to exercise hope according to the desires of their own heart. One of the problems of "models" of disability is that they tell disabled people what they should and should not want. In the case of the medical or "healing" models, what they should want is to be "normal" and rid of their defect. But for good reason, many people with disabilities are content with their selves, and rather than hoping for a technological or miraculous intervention, they long only for a social environment that enables them to flourish as they are. In the case of the social model, disabled people are supposed to want inclusion, not to be rid of their impairment. But many people with disabilities (especially those incurred later in life) long for both social inclusion and bodily restoration—even if, realistically, the latter is only an eschatological hope. The biblical witness of the New Testament suggests instead that Jesus responds with compassion and grace to people as they are, without demanding anything of them.

Third, if the life and ministry of Jesus are paradigmatic, it is not the miraculous and supernatural that are in view but, rather, his modeling of the love of God and neighbor. As has already been stated, the stand-out feature of Jesus' ministry is his promise of the coming kingdom of God, categorized by the embrace of people society normally excludes: the poor, women, sinners, children, the meek, the sick and disabled. The cures of Jesus are not described as miracles (a modern word), but as signs that reconstitute the people of God:

> Jesus' mighty works could be seen as the restoration to member-
> ship in Israel of those who, through sickness or whatever, had been
> excluded as ritually unclean. The healings thus function in exact par-
> allel with the welcome of sinners, and this, we may be quite sure, was
> what Jesus himself intended.[80]

That social inclusion reaches to disabled people is made explicit by Jesus in Luke 14, which recounts Jesus' telling of a parable that likens the kingdom of God to a banquet in which the poor, crippled, blind, and lame are invited, not to be healed, but to come as they are and feast in the kingdom. The countercultural edge of this parable is located in the common Greco-Roman social practice of using people with physical deformities as public entertainment, subjecting them to mockery and insult. As one commentator observed at the time, "laughter has its basis in deformity."[81] But while Romans invited the disabled to banquets as freaks, Jesus invited them to the banquet of the kingdom to participate as honored guests.[82]

Jesus, Disability, and the Problem of Submission

There is beauty in this description of the ministry of Jesus, who loves sex workers and banquets with the disabled; who celebrates meekness, mercy, and purity; who teaches his followers to let go of anger, love their enemies, turn the other cheek, and go the extra mile; and who lives out his message of self-sacrificing love by submitting to a Roman death on the cross. But our interest in this story is not to do with piety, but the good life, and the logic of submission is potentially dangerous, especially when directed at people with a disability. As feminist theologians have observed, theologies that insist on the necessity of Jesus' suffering and death and, thereafter, its paradigmatic role for Christians, inevitably justify and sustain female oppression and domestic abuse.[83] It is a logic that also applies to people with a disability, especially because theologies of submission are taught by those in power to sustain the meek acquiescence of people without power.

But while the Gospels do incorporate the message of submission and nonviolence, the narrative of Jesus is not so readily contained. The Jesus who condemns anger is the same man who enters the temple and turns over the tables of the money changers (Matt 21:12; John 2:15). The supposedly meek and mild Jesus condemns religious hypocrisy in the strongest terms, and declares woe upon the teachers of the law who reject justice, mercy, and faithfulness (Matt 23). Among those commentators who treat the four Gospels as parabolic histories, what John Dominic Crossan calls "an unnerving mix of fact and fiction," this violence becomes problematic. Crossan laments what he calls the "rhetorical violence" that is increasingly apparent in the latter dated gospel accounts (especially Luke/Acts and John). He defines rhetorical violence as speech that involves dehumanizing others: "crude caricatures, derogatory stereotypes, . . . and nasty name-calling"—hypocrites, brood of vipers, evil and adulterous generation, and so on.[84] His concern is that violent speech inevitably leads to physical violence, and the consequence of the violent rhetoric in the Gospels was a long history of anti-Semitism culminating in twentieth-century genocide. Crossan's conclusions are disputed, and it goes too far to lay the blame of anti-Semitism and genocide on a first-century social and religious dispute.[85] But from the perspective of disability, the problem with Crossan's construction is that he fails to appreciate that injustice demands an angry response. During his ministry, Jesus was subject to increasing abuse by religious and secular authorities because his elevation of society's outcasts challenged the religious and civil status quo. That he employed strong rhetoric in response to that power is a vital counterpoint to any misreading of his message of nonviolent love. Jesus sought to end the cycle of violence by self-sacrificing love, but this love was far from being passive.

Throughout this discussion of Jesus, I have been searching for some flexibility in the reading of the biblical narrative, and have found it in open and sometimes ambiguous and contradictory readings of the Gospels. Narrowly conceived stories are of little use in an unfathomably complex world, especially when drawn from authoritative sources. It is precisely for this reason that feminists have asked of Christianity, "Can a male savior save women?"[86] There are competing answers to that question, but it is at least true that many women from many different contexts have answered positively, although they have needed to be wise and creative in doing so. We might equally ask, "Can the story of a nondisabled man teach a disabled person how to live the good life?" Again, I think we can answer, "yes," provided we appreciate the need to be flexible in doing so. It would help to bring the insights of this narrative into conversation with those of disabled people. We need more than one story when contemplating the good life, but more on this in the next chapter.

I focused this brief overview on the story of Jesus set out in the Gospels. No doubt there is further insight to be had from a similar analysis of the remainder of the New Testament canon. But it is sufficient for now to conclude with the observation that the Bible does not simply include marginalized people, it sets out to empower them. One of the prominent themes of the gospel and the writings of St. Paul is the idea that the seemingly weak things of this world are declared powerful in Jesus Christ. This idea is inherent to the elevation of the cross; the ultimate symbol of defeat and humiliation transformed into a sign of (nonviolent) victory. St. Paul, similarly, repeatedly claims that his power is made perfect in weakness, a theme that he illustrates by reference to the thorn in his flesh (2 Cor 12:1-10). Whether this thorn is a disabling illness or some other burden, St. Paul's point is that the gospel intends to overturn existing power structures and elevate people traditionally marginalized by their apparent weaknesses.

In summary, the New Testament sets out a vision of the good life modeled on the story of Jesus. It highlights the problem of injustice, and so insists that movements toward happiness will require political action—that individual flourishing, especially for those suffering injustice (including disabling injustice), is dependent upon social, cultural, and religious transformation. It affirms the importance of character, labeling virtues as fruits of the Spirit. But it also appreciates that people are trapped in sin (the habits of vice), and are in need of the transforming power of God's grace. It claims that happiness—the fullness of life—is achieved by loving God and one's neighbor, and seeks to make this love concrete in the formation of a new community, the church, the body of Christ.

AQUINAS

In exploring the message of the New Testament, we have traveled a long way from Aristotle's virtue theory. The Bible touches on some similar themes, but does so from a very different frame of reference and arrives at its own unique conclusions. From the ministry of St. Paul, and increasingly through the second and third centuries as the mission of the church took it from Jerusalem to Greco-Roman society, theologians were involved in apologetic interaction with Greek philosophy. By the time of Augustine (354–430 A.D.) the church found itself at the center of social power, and apology had given way to a systematic and philosophical explanation of Christian faith. While agreeing that the goal of human life is *eudaimonia*, Augustine criticizes the "pagan" philosophers for their description of happiness as the life spent pursuing truth (i.e., philosophizing); "he isn't happy who doesn't have what he wants . . . and if the Academics are always seeking truth without finding it, it follows that they don't have what they want."[87] Instead, Augustine insists that happiness comes from acknowledging Jesus Christ as both teacher and redeemer, and is fulfilled only by immortality, when we are united with the truth, goodness, and beauty of God. Similarly, he concluded that because of the depravity of the human will, "pagans" are incapable of living virtuously. He defines virtue as "rightly ordered love," which is rooted in the love of God and neighbor.[88]

It is not until Aquinas (1225–1274 A.D.) that the particularities of Aristotle's virtue theory come to influence Christian tradition. As noted earlier, while Aristotle and the New Testament have very different views about the good life and virtue, they share a logical and conceptual structure that identifies virtue with the achievement of the human telos (flourishing) and vice (sin) with its destruction. It was this parallelism that allowed Aquinas to synthesize Aristotle and Christianity, structuring his anthropology and ethics in Part II of his *Summa Theologica* by Aristotle's logic.[89] He thus begins with a discussion of humanity's ultimate end, which he identifies as happiness, and then goes on to discuss the will, the passions, and the habits of virtue. Like Aristotle, he distinguishes between intellectual and moral virtues (the contemplative and active life), and locates virtue in the mean between the vices of excess and deficiency. Aristotle gives Aquinas a systematic way of thinking about *eudaimonia* and the habits of character, but Aquinas' subsequent explanation of virtue is thoroughly grounded in his theological commitments.

Aquinas synthesizes Aristotle's emphasis on happiness as contemplation with the Christian emphasis on union with God, arguing that final and perfect happiness consists in the contemplation of God (a view that reflects the tradition of metaphysical theology more than it does the New Testament). In coming to this conclusion, Aquinas understands happiness to consist in activities of virtue, "as engaging in and enjoying a genuinely good activity."[90] Perfect happiness, then, is engaging in the very best and most enjoyable activity, which for him as a Christian is knowing and enjoying God in God's essence, an activity only possible in heaven.[91] Imperfect happiness, which is all that is available this side of heaven, is engaging in and enjoying the good activities accessible in our daily lives. Departing from Augustine, Aquinas understands imperfect happiness to be available to all irrespective of faith, as every person is made in the image of God with rational and moral capacity. Imperfect happiness, for Aquinas, is episodic, and so can be gained and lost; only perfect happiness is permanent.

Aquinas' conception of happiness is "a hybrid of the objectively good activity and the subjectively grounded enjoyment of the actor."[92] The happy person does the objective good, which is judged by the goodness of the ends or purposes for which the activity is done, and subjectively enjoys doing so. This hybrid objective and subjective conception of happiness recognizes the universal aspects of the human good, but also appreciates the distinct and diverse desires, loves, and joys of individuals. It also leads to the assertion that neither the vicious nor continent person can be happy. The vicious person might enjoy his activities, but if those activities are not genuinely good, then he is not genuinely happy. Conversely, the continent person might do the good, but if she does so unwillingly (without pleasure), she also is not genuinely happy (note Aquinas follows Aristotle in this conclusion, but also the New Testament.[93] The book of Hebrews even speaks of the pleasure of Jesus, who "for the joy set before him . . . endured the cross, scorning its shame, and sat down at the right hand of the throne of God"; Heb 12:2). This is not to suggest that a virtuous person always feels pleasant sensations when she acts. A virtuous action might be painful, but the higher pleasure is the delight in acting courageously, even in the face of death.[94]

Because imperfect happiness is an activity, Aquinas understands that it can be impeded by illness or severe disability, which is capable of undermining contemplation (for him the highest of pleasures) and virtuous activity. He goes on to insist, though, that perfect happiness is free of the body and available equally to all.[95] He thus adopts the long history of nondisabled prejudice, assuming the inferiority of disability, but at least is thoroughly inclusive in his explanation of perfect happiness, which for him is what matters most.

In addition to illness and disability, the impact of sin means that we are unable to live perfectly virtuous lives, so Aquinas argues that we need supernatural help. God graciously gives to us the theological virtues faith, hope, and love (the significance of which we considered in the previous chapter). And because perfect happiness is achieved by grace, it is not dependent on luck (on being born a wealthy, free, nondisabled, philosophical man) but is available to all, imperfectly in the here and now, and perfectly in God's presence after death.

Particularly important for Aquinas is love, which is not just a theological virtue, but also the greatest of all the human passions. His preferred term for love is the Latin *caritas*, charity, which, as noted in the previous chapter, has two interconnected desires: first, the desire for the good of the beloved, and second, the desire for friendship or union with the beloved.[96] Following the biblical injunction, he notes that to love others, one has to love oneself, which also involves these twin desires. To want one's own good is to want to flourish, but what does it mean to desire union with oneself? Here, Aquinas notes that sin causes us to be double minded, lacking internal integration, so that we are at war within ourselves (cf. Rom 7:14-26). Internal integration, for Aquinas, is ultimately a result of the love of God, since one is at peace with oneself when loving God wholeheartedly, and thereafter is able to love others fully.[97]

For Aristotle, friendship was only really possible between equals, since we can only really be friends with a person who is integrated toward the good. But Aquinas notes that God loves us despite our inadequacy, and the love that God has for us represents the nature of the friendship that we can have with others.[98] Love is most fully embodied in the self-sacrifice of Christ, and his embrace of us as friends. To this end, Aquinas cites John 15:12-15:

> [12]My command is this: Love each other as I have loved you. [13]Greater love has no one than this: to lay down one's life for one's friends. [14]You are my friends if you do what I command. [15]I no longer call you servants, because a servant does not know his master's business. Instead, I have called you friends, for everything that I learned from my Father I have made known to you.

Friendship, then, is central to happiness. A happy person, Aquinas notes, does not need friends for personal advantage but for shared virtuous living.[99] Mutual self-giving is central to friendship, but love can extend beyond relationships of "equal advantage" (as per Aristotle) to reach toward the poor, the outcast, and even one's enemy (following the injunctions of Jesus).[100] Love as charity encourages the virtues of mercy and pity, and in so doing intends to support the vulnerable and (presumably) the disabled:

> Mercy is heartfelt sympathy for another's distress, impelling us to succor him if we can. For mercy takes its name misericordia [pity] from denoting a man's compassionate heart for another's unhappiness.[101] . . . One grieves or sorrows for another's distress, in so far as one looks upon another's distress as one's own.[102]

The principal reason that Aristotle gave for the impossibility of friendship outside of relationships of equal status was his view that it is shameful to receive. For good reason, disability advocates are similarly critical of both charity and pity, since these sentiments presume the superiority of the so-called able-bodied and make the disabled acutely aware of their inferior status.[103] The difficulty may be one of translation. Aquinas' use of the term charity is synonymous with love and friendship, and is thus a term of mutual generosity. *Misericordia* (normally translated as pity) refers to that sorrow which treats another's distress as one's own, a notion that also resists any sense of the superior/inferior dichotomy. Yet whatever the intention, the expression of pity inevitably creates and sustains unequal power relations, as does the assumption that the pitied are unhappy. Pity is little more than the projection of one's fears and insecurities onto another. "Pity oppresses . . . because it raises walls of fear between the public and us."[104] It too easily leads to top-down intervention—to "ferocious standardizing benevolence"—and cements the superiority of the powerful by reinforcing their certainty that they live in a good society.[105]

One final difference between Aquinas and Aristotle is Aquinas' reference to the four cardinal virtues (following both Plato and Augustine)—prudence, justice, fortitude, and temperance—as central virtues, under which other virtues emerge and are classified.[106] Fortitude, for example, includes ambition, patience, perseverance, and the like as subsidiary virtues, and temperance contains abstinence, sobriety, chastity, humility, and so on. Whether structuring virtues in this way adds much to our understanding of virtue theory is debatable. MacIntyre, for example, argues that exhaustive classificatory schemes of virtue ought always to arouse our suspicions.[107] Indeed, the problem with structuring hierarchies of virtue as Aquinas has done is that those hierarchies are inevitably established to buttress the existing structures of power. This is perhaps nowhere more apparent than in Aquinas' elevation of temperance as one of the four key virtues. In emphasizing *self*-control in the way that he does, his ecclesial priorities function to keep people *under* control—an insight Western culture learned from Friedrich Nietzsche.

IS THE VIRTUE TRADITION OF ANY USE TODAY?

In *After Virtue*, MacIntyre traces the waning influence of virtue ethics from the time of the Reformation through to the Enlightenment, with

Nietzsche as its ultimate critic. Nietzsche argued that constructions of happiness and virtue are ideologies used by people in power (religious and secular) to control individuals and keep them in their place:

> All these morals directed at the individual person to promote what people call his "happiness"—are they anything other than recommendations for constraint, in proportion to the degree of danger in which the individual person lives his life? Or cures for his passions, his good and bad tendencies to the extent that they have Will to Power and want to play master?[108]

I have already identified the tendency of virtue ethics to sustain the status quo. This occurs primarily because fixed notions of an ideal human nature frame the historical constructions of what it is to flourish, and thereby preserve the so-called natural order of things: man as head of woman, rich as better than poor, master (and white) as superior to slave (and black), Christian as more righteous than pagan, straight as normal and gay as abnormal, and the disabled silenced and rendered invisible at the bottom of the pile.

In the same way, closed and hierarchical lists of virtue direct behavior deemed to be appropriate to particular groups of people: encouraging the submissiveness of wives to husbands (and congregations to priests and pastors) keeps victims of abuse in their place; celebrating the patience of the ailing and aged prevents them from complaining about poor treatment; demanding the obedience of soldiers and employees sees them follow immoral orders; and praising disabled people for positive thinking (focusing on ability rather than disability) stops them from complaining about injustice. Virtue, if wielded as a form of social control, can cause as much harm as vice.

It is only reasonable, then, to ask whether a seemingly outdated theory of virtue is of any use today? I think it is, or at least can be, and the growing interest in neo-Aristotelian virtue ethics among philosophers, theologians, and (surprisingly) scientists indicates that I am not alone.[109] A vision of the good life that emphasizes the enjoyment that comes from pleasurable, virtuous, and meaningful activities carried out together with friends and loving communities still resonates. But for virtue theory to be useful to people with disabilities, it is essential to distance it from any constraining assumptions about a theorized ideal of human nature and hierarchy of virtue. More on that later.

4

Disability, Advocacy, and the Good Life
Mark Tonga's Story

In the previous chapter I established the logic and key concepts of the virtue tradition. I have also emphasized the importance of stories for expressing a vision of the good life and teaching virtue. Stories are central to self-identity. The stories we tell about ourselves—the events, achievements (and failures) we narrate and the interpretations we take—frame our self-understanding and make a vital contribution to the shape of our future.[1] In this light, it is noteworthy that the occurrence of a disability (whether faced by parents who give birth to a disabled child, or by an individual who acquires a disability later in life) will impact our storied self-understanding: "Like a novel that loses a central character in the middle chapters, the life story disrupted by loss must be reorganized, rewritten, to find a new strand of continuity that bridges the past with the future in an intelligible fashion."[2]

In the early years of living with spinal cord injury, I found it difficult to envisage a worthwhile future. The possibility of rewriting the story of my life came when I met with people who had lived well with the disability over the medium- to long-term, and heard about their challenges and achievements. So encouraged was I by their stories, that I decided to collaborate with researchers from the Centre for Disability Research and Policy at the University of Sydney to undertake a study entitled "Quadriplegia and the Good Life." This study collected and examined the narratives of people who have flourished with the injury.[3] "God's Hammer" was one of those stories, and Mark has graciously allowed me to share it. By attending to the words of one who has narrated a life story disrupted by loss, we may find that the arguments offered in the previous chapter take on new and deeper intelligibility.

In 2008 thirty-five-year-old Mark Tonga broke his neck while training with his amateur rugby union team in the suburbs of Sydney. He was rendered a C3/4 complete quadriplegic, without any function or sensation below the neck. Unsurprisingly, the severity of Mark's injury had a drastic impact on his life, and rehabilitation and recovery were lengthy and extremely difficult. Mark says that he only got through this trauma by God's grace. He had been born into a committed Christian family in Tonga, but after emigrating to Australia while a teenager he deviated from his faith. While in intensive care, scared and in a dark place, he had a series of visions, in which he felt God tell him everything was going to be okay. It took some time, though, for that to come true.

Transferred from intensive care to the nearby spinal unit and rehabilitation center, he learned how to get about in a "sip and puff," chin-controlled wheelchair, but due to the severity of his injury, he would require twenty-four-hour care the remainder of his life. Before returning home, he spent one month in Weemala nursing home, which accommodated residents with severe disabilities (brain injury and SCI). I asked him how it felt, as a young man, to be placed with the elderly:

> It was an utterly depressing place to be, but I reframed it—it helped me to realize how lucky I was. The nursing home was the bottom of the barrel, but it was good, because it made me focus. But clearly the system had let me down. I'd fallen through the cracks. I couldn't believe they were still dumping people in these nursing homes—this happened in the 60s and 70s, and now it was 2008, and it was still happening to me. And I said no way; this is not for me.

Here Mark reveals the tension between the horror of his situation and the value of retaining a sense of positive hope. We are used to hearing stories about heroic people who overcome their disability—and we are right to label Mark a hero. But Mark does not shy away from his struggles and failures. This was particularly apparent when he described his eventual return to the home that he shared with his long-term partner. He noted that "you go from the trauma and injury, to the trauma of a nursing home, and then the trauma of getting home." Part of the problem was the message he felt was communicated by rehabilitation medical staff, which made him fearful. Their message to him was:

> If you had a catheter blockage, you could die, or have a heart attack or stroke. I thought, dude, give me some positive language. I was scared to go home, but I did because I had no choice.
>
> This time of my life really tested me. There is no book on these things. You just play it as it comes, as the landscape unfolds in front of you. You make decisions, and you don't know if it's right or wrong. It was a steep learning curve. 2008–2011 was a really dark period. I was just absorbing the injury and its consequences. I had struggles breathing, and eating was a chore. I had bad health, I got pneumonia every winter. I had pressure sores, one keeping me in bed for nine months. Everything was coming at me from all corners, and there were too many variables.

Mark's relationship with his partner suffered; indeed, spinal cord injury can burden families as much as it can the injured person. He says:

> She was working in a pressured job full-time, spending late hours in the hospital, getting home at 11 o'clock at night. She got extremely depressed, and something had to give. Before, she had someone who is looking after the house, mowing the lawn et cetera, and all of a sudden her life was turned upside down. I couldn't contribute anything, so the pressure came on her. When I got home, she stayed with me, and filled the gap where my family wasn't supporting me.

The relationship broke down, and Mark remembers:

> I tried to win her back. But it's just so hard to do that with your mouth only. To win someone back, you need action, and I couldn't do it—all I could do was talk. It was hard for her. It was hard for both of us. Half of me felt that I couldn't put the pressure back on her, but the other half of me wanted her back. I didn't want to be alone, and I was scared.

Spinal cord injury is a severe disability, and its consequences are not limited to the function of the body; in Mark's case it affected his family life and career (he never returned to accounting). But loss was not the end of his story. In 2011 he met up with a peer support worker who listened to his traumatic experiences, and suggested he consider moving to a group home for people with SCI in Chatswood on Sydney's North Shore. He notes:

Moving to Chatswood was an adventure. It was a fresh start. I thought, well, if I don't like it, I can go back to Fairfield. I was initially scared—I had to deal with new carers, and I had a lot of mixed emotions, because I was still holding onto the past. But when I moved in it felt like I'd left all my troubles on the other side of the bridge. Here I was a new person, starting a new life. No one knew me here, so I could start again. I had a sense of excitement—I'd left darkness behind me, and sensed new things on the horizon.

It is noteworthy here that friendship and peer support were key to turning Mark's life around. His later accomplishments are not just the fruit of his own character—although he does deserve the credit. Not long after moving to Chatswood, Mark met a representative of the Spinal Cord Injury Association (SCIA), and they talked to him about being involved in advocacy. This ignited in him a desire to fix the system that had been so brutal to him in previous years. He got involved in some advocacy projects, such as helping a disabled mother get ramps put into a school so she could visit her daughter. He also advocated for increases in the New South Wales (NSW) taxi subsidy scheme, a project that came to fruition in 2016 after many years of lobbying, when the NSW government doubled the subsidy. These activities did more than just occupy his time: they gave him a new sense of purpose, a realization that he could make a valuable contribution to his community.

Mark notes that in addition to his disability (which itself has a currency—it is hard to say no to a request that comes from Mark when he confronts you in his chair), he brought a number of preexisting skills into his advocacy. Only three months before his accident he had graduated from a university in Sydney with a degree in business, and commenced work as an accountant at the Returned Services League. This was a notable achievement since he had left school early (aged fifteen) and went to work as a laborer in a slaughterhouse, before deciding to return to study as a mature age student. After completing his degree, he started his professional training to become a chartered accountant—and then he broke his neck. When asked why he didn't return to accounting he replied:

> At first, everything was too out-of-control, but when I got to Chatswood, and my life was starting to refocus and get back on track, I thought about accounting, and then I thought, do I need money, do I need a career? I don't need all that shit; I need a purpose in life—to do something good with my life. I want to change things, make things

better for people. I'm not going to waste the little time that I have punching calculators all day, just so people can turn around and say, I made a profit this year. What's the purpose in that? Knowing that I could go anytime and that my health was vulnerable (every year I end up in the hospital with pneumonia), meant that I had no interest in going back to accounting. I looked back at my own situation, and didn't want people to go through what I'd gone through—so I wanted to spend my time fixing the system.

Presently, Mark is a Director of the Paraplegic and Quadriplegic Association of NSW (ParaQuad), and acting Secretary (after serving as Director) of People with Disabilities Australia (PWDA). Also, he is a member of Willoughby City Council's "Access" Committee and has been appointed an Ambassador for charities Lifestart (Kayak for Kids) and the Hearts in Union Rugby Foundation. In 2016 he was appointed as the chair of the Disability Council of NSW, which reports directly to the NSW State Government. He regularly speaks at schools and other events. Indeed, Mark leads a full life, spending his days on projects that are meaningful and enjoyable.

Mark credits much of his positive attitude to God and the church:

> The Church always encourages me. It gives me strength and courage to stay focused. Every Sunday I get a message that reinforces what I'm doing, that encourages me, that fills up my soul.

When asked what he does for fun, Mark says that he likes to roam around Sydney's fish markets. Otherwise, he says, "I just get out there and get involved. I'm never bored." He enjoys watching rugby, and given his injury was incurred playing the sport, he is regularly invited into the inner sanctum of the Australian team. He spends as much time as he can with friends. He says that when he had his accident, he lost a lot of friends:

> But I've met more, better friends. I have this mindset, you just do things, and you don't know where it will take you and who you will meet. People come out of the woodwork. I'm not lonely—I'm fighting people off.

Mark says that he wasn't always a friendly person, but that his injury has made him friendlier.

I need help. I can't do anything for myself, so the only skill that I have is to form relationships with people. It was hard, at first, to ask people to do things for me, but I've come to realize that everyone has got something to contribute—to help—and generally they're willing to do so. It might sound like I'm devious, like I'm manipulating people, but I'm not. Sometimes I get carers who get grumpy. Once, when I asked the nurse for something, she said, "say please." That hit home. On the one hand, I think it's pathetic that a person needs to get a please out of a quad. But even so, I learned early on that it makes a difference if I say please. The old Mark would fight it. But the new Mark that I'm developing now is about cooperation, collegiality, and team effort.

This feeds into my advocacy work and my board work. It might seem like a cliché, but making sure I'm positive really works. Massaging the situation is what I call it. I've got great confidence that doors will be open to me because I'm working for the right outcomes, and I'm doing so positively. I don't go in and scream at anyone—but I form relationships and friendships.

What Mark is suggesting is that the demands of his disability required him to develop virtues that he did not need prior to his injury when he was a typically independent and self-sufficient man. And these new virtues helped him establish new relationships. Indeed, not long after moving to Chatswood, Mark developed a close friendship with Juno. Originally employed as a care worker, she kept in contact with him after changing jobs, and their friendship has deepened. Given the hardship of living with the injury, and its impact on his previous relationship, Mark is somewhat nervous about what the future holds:

That's just another thing in my life I've got to deal with. Everything is working well now. A relationship means I'd have to move out, go through the whole care plan again. It would distract me from my goals. You're taking on another person in your life, and maybe I'm selfish, maybe I'm scared. I'm just surprised that she is interested in me. When you're in a relationship, you're always doing something for the girl; now it's the other way round. All I can do is maybe take her out for dinner. It seems like I've always got to rely on somebody to do something for me. It just seems, not genuine—I always need to get help. But I'm still adjusting. It's just like adjusting to the chair.

Juno doesn't share his fears. She says:

> I'm really happy to be with him. I'm so glad I can be one of his helpers. I don't think of him as a quad. I'm really happy. He's just a normal guy. Much smarter and cleverer than others. He's smart and caring. He's a guy with a good sense of humor. He is always ready to help others, and that's what attracts me to him. In our relationship, it's 50-50. He gives more than 50-50, actually. He gives me a lot, especially sharing out of his experience. He is always ready to help, and give me new ideas. I don't think giving and taking is a problem. I'm getting more from him than I'm giving to him. He shares his deep experience, which really helps me. Not only me, but everybody.

Mark's concluding reflections on the good life are worth quoting in full:

> I was lying in bed in the hospital, and I thought, this is the bottom of the barrel, so it was time to climb out. The only thing you can do now is climb. Suddenly I had a thirst for life. Before the injury, I lived carelessly. I just didn't think about life. I'd had a couple of car accidents, bike accidents. All these things reinforced to me the grace of God.
>
> I had the accident, and I thought, I want to live, I don't want to die. I don't care if my arm[s don't] work or my legs don't work—I just wanted to live. Most people think they'd rather be dead, but I was the opposite. Things just became clear to me. I didn't know my purpose yet, but I didn't want to die. You think people would just want to top themselves, but I knew I wanted to live. I had to find a way to get out. Find a way to get help. Find a way!
>
> Whatever happens, I'll be able to say to myself that at least I tried.
>
> I've not said this to many people, because it's embarrassing to say it, but this is the best thing that could have happened to me. You might say, "Oh what, you'd rather be in the chair?" Don't get me wrong; I've got difficulties. Like last night I couldn't sleep, my blood pressure was up; my bowels were going off. Who'd want that? But for me, what I've gone through now, what I've achieved, where I'm going, and my goals—I never had that before—I wasn't that focused. A lot of good things have happened to me, really good things. And it's all happened because I'm in the chair. It's the best thing that's happened to me. It's brought me closer to God, it's given me purpose, it's given me focus, it's brought lots of people around me. To say that to someone who is able-bodied, it's hard to comprehend. Does that make me sound crazy?

Who wants to sit on the toilet for an hour every day, and have a PR [per rectum] every day? Who wants to sit there and their nose is itchy all day, and they can't scratch it? Me! I do. It's the bigger picture.

I know God has been talking to me all my life. He saved me during all of those accidents. He gave me a lot of warning signs, but did I listen? He's called me to come back—many times. He said, this is it, no more chances—and that's why I want to live. So this is it. I'm listening now, God. Guide me. I'm your hammer. [What an awesome self-description by a person who can't move their arms.]

My life is changed. There are things I've done before that I can't do now. Go for a walk in the National Park. Go for a swim. Don't get me wrong; I miss it all. But those are just small pleasures—small things that will give you an endorphin rush. But I'm getting a bigger buzz now. To not be able to embrace Juno, hug her, take her in my arms, stroke her hair. I'm giving up a lot, to get this gold. But I'm willing to do so—it's worth it.

MARK AND THE VIRTUE TRADITION

For Mark, Christian faith provides consolation, encouragement, and a sense of vocation that coalesces with his passion for advocacy. From his perspective, the good life involves serving God through efforts to transform society so that people with disabilities can access services and live well. It is his passion for this purpose that enables him to view his postinjury life as superior to his preinjury life; his days have meaning and purpose that they previously did not. It might be thought that Mark is in denial;[4] that his claim of happiness is a psychological strategy to help him cope. But such judgments are little more than thinly veiled paternalism. After all, who would know more about the hardship and joy of living with a serious disability, the outsider looking in or Mark himself?[5]

Mark has a justified pride in his achievements. Even the traumatic years immediately following his accident were marked by a determination to live, to climb out of crisis one step at a time, and "to find a way." He has directed his focus to advocacy (as "God's hammer"), and to shaping his skills and capacities to enable him to navigate the constraints of his disability, utilize its advantages (his disability is visually obvious and compelling), and make substantive contributions to his local community. Mark's story is a textbook case of the flourishing envisaged by the virtue tradition.

Mark is impressively self-aware. He takes responsibility for his shortcomings, and is quicker to blame himself than to criticize or judge others. His telling of his personal story takes a particular shape: preinjury recklessness and meaninglessness, injury and rehabilitation trauma, and postinjury personal growth and purposeful living. These categories color his interpretation of events, and help him to remain positive while dealing with the hardships and constraints of quadriplegia. Mark's positivity should not be confused with the positivity myth. He has not overcome his disability, and he readily admits that life with quadriplegia is hard, and subject to limits. Life is up-and-down, but he judges it to be more up than down.

Mark has obvious interpersonal virtues. He is open, generous, humble, funny, and immediately likable. It is likely that these are natural characteristics, but he insists that living with the injury forced him to develop personal skills. He had to learn to be appreciative and positive so as to get the help he needs to navigate daily life. The injury creates challenges for some friendships, particularly for intimate partnerships, in which case mutual self-giving is complicated. But as Juno asserts, Mark brings to his friendships strength of character and virtues that count for more than the loss of his physical capacity, and despite his need for constant help, he gives more to relationships than he takes. The most important dimension of mutual self-giving is not physical but intellectual, emotional, and social, and it's precisely in these areas that Mark excels.

5

Disability, Psychology, and the Science of Happiness
Measuring Happiness in Hedonic Science

Recent developments in the psychological sciences have done much to overcome the frequent yet regrettable divides that separate the fields of philosophy, theology, and the sciences. Particularly in the fields of hedonic and positive psychology, there is now significant empirical support for the logic of the virtue tradition. Moreover, these scientific studies also have something to tell us about the happiness and resilience of people with disabilities. The findings of the psychological and behavioral sciences are not the standard fodder of theological and ethical reflection, but engaging them invariably aids the virtue tradition and religious faith as both contribute to the flourishing of people with disabilities. By remaining open to the insights of sciences as well as philosophy and theology, we are in the best possible position for testing a real vision for human flourishing—one that chastens any account not rooted in the real lives of those who live daily with disability.

THE DISABILITY PARADOX

In its variety of manifestations, and in comparison to the life of a nondisabled person, disability will limit physical or intellectual function (or both), will result in social and environmental exclusion, and may involve pain, ongoing medical intervention, and in many cases reduced life expectancy. It would be surprising if these various struggles did not diminish happiness, but that is precisely what the psychological sciences tell us. The so-called disability paradox describes the difference between the seemingly inescapable conclusion that disability negatively impacts happiness and the reality that many people with serious disabilities report having a good life.[1]

The theory most often proffered to explain the paradox is the hedonic treadmill, which asserts that, although positive and negative events temporarily impact happiness, people quickly return to hedonic neutrality—to a baseline (or set point) of happiness that is substantially determined by personality traits.[2] Lottery winners, for example, ride an emotional high for much less time than might be imagined before returning to their pre-win level of happiness. By a similar logic, the intense ache of grief fades with time.[3] Hedonic adaptation is an evolutionary capacity that prevents us from being overwhelmed by either positive or negative emotion, enabling us to retain our sensitivity to subsequent events and so respond appropriately to the continued ups and downs of life.[4]

In fact, hedonic adaptation is not a perfect mechanism. Recent longitudinal studies have shown that people who suffer a life-changing disablement do experience significant and permanent reductions in happiness.[5] Interestingly, hedonic adaptation is faster and more complete in response to positive circumstances, so that euphoria dissipates quicker than depression—"bad is stronger than good."[6] It is the impact on our expectations that explains why hedonic adaptation is faster for positive than for negative experiences. We attend more to negative events, our emotional reactions are stronger, and we find it harder to explain why bad things happen to us. In evolutionary terms, our survival is more dependent on our paying attention to danger than it is on passing up opportunities for pleasure.[7] This also suggests why, in the context of faith, the problem of pain (where is God when we suffer?) is more urgent than the gratefulness we feel when life goes well.

The extent of a person's hedonic adaptation to the challenge of disability is affected by various factors. People born with a disability are generally happier than those who incur one later in life, and younger people tend to adapt more easily to a disabling condition than do the middle-aged.[8] Individual psychological characteristics have also been found to affect resilience.[9] Taken altogether, hedonic research is converging on the conclusion that happiness is both heritable and changing, with personality traits establishing a stable baseline, which

is then influenced by conditional factors such as an individual's environment, activities, relationships, choices, and so on.[10]

It is noteworthy that hedonic psychological research has found that
disabled people, like most people, are happy most of the time, and even
those whose disability has resulted in reduced baseline levels are happier
than might be imagined by people looking from the outside.[11] To make
sense of this conclusion, we need to clarify the various ways in which
the psychological sciences conceive of and measure happiness. The first
distinction is between objective and subjective measures. The former
refers to indicators that can be judged from the outside; factors such as
health, education, vocation, income, relational status, and so forth.

The distinction between objective and subjective measures has
become especially important in debates between bioethicists and
disability rights activists. In relation to the issue of prenatal testing,
for example, one of the arguments used to justify the abortion of a
fetus with an impairment is that its quality of life will be lower than
that of a fetus without an impairment—in which case prenatal testing
and legalized abortion are said to be good policy, since they serve to
reduce the suffering and increase the net quality of life in the general
population (setting aside, for the moment, theological and philosophical
perspectives on the status of the fetus). Peter Singer makes a similar
argument on the allocation of health funding, asserting that limited
funds are better spent on nondisabled people than quadriplegics:

> Health care does more than save lives: it also reduces pain and suf-
> fering. How can we compare saving a person's life with, say, mak-
> ing it possible for someone who was confined to bed to return to an
> active life? We can elicit people's values on that too. One common
> method is to describe medical conditions to people—let's say being a
> quadriplegic—and tell them that they can choose between 10 years
> in that condition or some smaller number of years without it. If most
> would prefer, say, 10 years as a quadriplegic to 4 years of nondis-
> abled life, but would choose 6 years of nondisabled life over 10 with
> quadriplegia, but have difficulty deciding between 5 years of non-
> disabled life or 10 years with quadriplegia, then they are, in effect,
> assessing life with quadriplegia as half as good as nondisabled life.
> (These are hypothetical figures, chosen to keep the math simple, and
> not based on any actual surveys.) If that judgment represents a rough
> average across the population, we might conclude that restoring to

nondisabled life two people who would otherwise be quadriplegics is equivalent in value to saving the life of one person, provided the life expectancies of all involved are similar.[12]

Such shockingly utilitarian arguments are predicated on the assumption that the quality of life of a person with a disability is substantially lower than that of everyone else; however, they carry far less weight if it can be shown that disabled people have a good quality of life. And that is precisely what subjective measures of happiness have discovered.[13] Indeed, we inevitably overestimate the horror of a disability, or at least misjudge its hardships, overstating some aspects while being completely ignorant of others (e.g., people are fearful at the thought of being "trapped" in the wheelchair that actually enables freedom, but know nothing of the nerve pain that goes with SCI). This overestimation occurs not only because we fail to account for hedonic adaptation—most of us are more resilient than we expect we will be—but because people looking from the outside tend to focus narrowly on a person's disability, ignoring other aspects of a life, such as a quadriplegic's happy marriage (or, conversely, the lottery winner's divorce).[14]

Even so, bioethicists such as Singer insist that subjective measures of happiness are inadequate in determining quality of life for the purpose of public policy. From this perspective, subjective assessments are subject to the bias of lowered expectations:

> Individuals who suffer serious disability often come to accept their limitations in function in a way that makes possible a higher level of satisfaction or happiness than the nondisabled person correctly expects that he would have, given his current aims and expectations, if he suffered that same disability. In the extreme case of complete accommodation to the disability, disabled persons may have sufficiently changed their aims and values so as to have as high a degree of success (or even higher) in pursuing their new aims as they had with their old aims before becoming disabled, and to have as high a level of satisfaction or happiness (or even higher) as they had before becoming disabled. Should we then say that the disability has produced no reduction in their quality of life?[15]

The hypothetical example of the happy slave can be used to make the point: if a slave has a high degree of subjective life satisfaction, would we be compelled to agree with him?[16] The following typology provides a helpful overview of the different ways objective and subjective assessments can relate to one another:

PARADISE: People's living conditions are good (objective), and they accurately perceive their living conditions as good (subjective).

REAL HELL: People's living conditions are bad (objective), and they accurately perceive these conditions as bad (subjective).

FOOL'S PARADISE: People's living conditions are bad (objective), but they inaccurately perceive their living conditions as good (subjective).

FOOL'S HELL: People's living conditions are good (objective), but they inaccurately perceive their living conditions as bad (subjective).[17]

It would be easy enough to locate individuals within the rubric of such a typology, but it is another thing altogether to assert that disabled people as a whole are happy slaves living in a fool's paradise, which is essentially what Singer concludes. The happy slave (if there really is such a person) may be ignorant of the delights of freedom, but the person with a disability is not ignorant of the difference between a nondisabled and disabled life, not least because many have experienced both states, and everyone with a disability is constantly confronted with the able-bodied norm. Indeed, do those arguing that we should ignore the subjective perspective "really want to claim that nondisabled people know better than disabled people what the different lives are like?" Sadly, the answer appears to be "yes," since "the testimony of disabled people about their lives has been dismissed in favor of that of nondisabled 'experts' for a very long time."[18]

What this fraught discussion highlights is the importance of taking the disabled perspective seriously. But is there a middle ground? In an earlier chapter, I outlined Aquinas' synthesis of Christian theology and the virtue tradition, and his argument that happiness is both objective and subjective. The happy person does the objective good, which is judged by the goodness of the ends or purposes for which the activity is done, and subjectively enjoys doing so. Aquinas' logic is informed by Christian anthropology, which understands people as made in the divine image with rational and moral capacities, and so tasked—within the constraints of the circumstances of their life—to choose their own future, but also given the responsibility to choose the good. Aquinas draws on Aristotle to argue that the vicious and continent person is not genuinely happy, because happiness requires a person both to do good and to delight in doing so. This conception of happiness demands that we take the desires and joys of the individual seriously, and also that we recognize the individual's own judgment about the goodness of the activities of their life. At the same time, it understands that individual perspectives can be both limited and distorted, and so invites the outside judgment, since human nature elicits at least a minimum set of objective dimensions of the good life.

As the discipline of hedonic psychology developed, it came to a similar conclusion, expanding its measures to include both subjective and objective accounts. In the new millennium, the various scientific measures of happiness have come to be shaped by the emergence of positive psychology.

POSITIVE PSYCHOLOGY AND DISABILITY

Positive psychology marks a shift of focus in the discipline, away from psychological deficits, and toward the nurturing of happiness and strength—a transition that mirrors (and follows) that which has occurred in disability studies, away from impairment and handicap and toward strength and empowerment.[19] In its earliest incarnations, proponents identified three distinct but mutually reinforcing types of happiness in ascending order of importance: (1) positive emotion, which references mood and defines happiness as maximizing pleasure and minimizing pain; (2) gratification/flow, which describes the satisfaction achieved by engaging in valued activities such as sport and work; and (3) meaning, which recognizes the deep joy that comes from living for more than just oneself.[20] They also argued that the happiness of gratification and meaning (specifically referencing *eudaimonia*) is achieved by exercising virtues and strengths. In the years following the presentation of the original theory, two other dimensions of happiness have been added—positive relationships, and achievement—which together form the summative acronym PERMA: flourishing consists of positive emotion, engagement, positive relationships, meaning, and achievement. The goal of positive psychology was not just to theorize about happiness, but to ground the *eudaimonic* conception of flourishing and psychological strength in the rigors of empirical science: "in statistical tests, validated questionnaires, thoroughly researched exercises, and large, representative samples."[21]

The debt owed by positive psychologists to the virtue tradition is obvious (even if it is not always adequately acknowledged). Indeed, in arguments reminiscent of Aristotle, proponents criticize the tendency to equate happiness with pleasure, asserting that "positive emotion alienated from the exercise of character leads to emptiness, to inauthenticity, to depression, and, as we age, to the gnawing realization that we are fidgeting until we die."[22] And like Aristotle, they recognize the pleasure—gratification—of virtue, and assert that *eudaimonia* is found in the pursuit of transcendent meaning: "just as the good life is something beyond the pleasant life, the meaningful life is beyond the good life."[23] Conversely, positive psychology provides invaluable empirical support to the philosophical conclusions of virtue theorists. There is a tendency among philosophers to be suspicious of science, but "empirical studies show us that [virtue ethics] is an ethics for us."[24]

Pleasure

In respect to happiness as pleasure, hedonic psychology measures subjective well-being by scoring positive and negative affect, so that a person who has a high level of subjective well-being is one whose positive emotions (such as ecstasy, contentment, or pleasure) outweigh negative emotions (such as sadness, depression, or anger).[25] It is this type of happiness that is most subject to the hedonic treadmill and, as noted above, people with a disability score as well as anybody else, or, more to the point, their measures of subjective affect are as diverse and as stable as the rest of the population. It is sometimes suggested that people with particular disabilities, such as Down syndrome, are characteristically cheerful, easygoing, and affectionate, but such stereotypes have not only been shown, empirically, to be false, they create social expectations that pigeonhole individuals.[26] They underplay the significance of the full gamut of individuals' emotional capacity—especially their right to be angry at the stereotypes that constrain them:

> The popular view that all children with DS are happy, affectionate, mischievous and good mimics who love to sing and dance does not stand up to scientific investigation. In real life encounters, children

with DS soon demonstrate that they have the right to be viewed as individuals, with their own unique personalities, just like other children.[27]

While it is assumed that disabled people are less happy than "normal" people, as I have said, the horror of disability is much less than might be expected. In fact, there is no normal person, if what we mean by that is someone free from functional restriction, social exclusion, pain, medical intervention, and death. All of us, to one degree or another, are *cripples* next to Usain Bolt, slow learners compared to Stephen Hawking, excluded from the power of the political elite, and short-lived in the context of the age of the earth. As I have argued throughout, to be human is to live with fragility, vulnerability, dependence, and the likelihood of disability and certainty of death, and thus our mood adjusts to our expectations, which are themselves informed by our particular embodied experiences and context. This goes some way to explaining why some people who have faced serious illness, loss, or disability report high levels of subjective well-being; they have learned that struggle and joy can go together, and so are well placed to appreciate life's consolations.

The logic of hedonic stability might lead us to conclude that, in terms of our overall well-being, pleasure is unimportant. But that would be to misunderstand both Aristotle and the science of positive psychology. In the virtue tradition, pleasure is a good, even if *eudaimonia* subsumes it. Aristotle recognizes, also, that joy attends to virtuous living, so that a person who lives the good life will also experience pleasure. Positive psychology reverses the equation, arguing that an overriding positive mood—having a greater balance of positive over negative emotions—contributes to virtuous activity and meaning.[28] The broaden and build theory asserts that positive emotions have adaptive value; where negative emotions focus and narrow attention, triggering specific actions (e.g., attack and flight), positive emotions open the mind and stimulate thought and expansive activity. In this way, pleasurable experiences, although transient, build personal resources that are durable.

In humans and other species, for example, juvenile play facilitates physical, cognitive, and emotional developments, stimulates creativity, and teaches individuals how to cope with the unexpected twists and turns of life.[29] Laughter and joy, similarly, serve a multiplicity of functions; improving mood, mitigating stress, acting as a social lubricant, dampening friction between individuals, building community bonds, and so on.[30] Contentment facilitates the savoring of life and builds self-esteem, and the positive emotion of curiosity creates the urge to explore the world and increase knowledge.[31] The emotion of gratitude has been referred to as "the moral memory of mankind," and found to provide the basis for reciprocal altruism, establishing the debt we owe to individuals and social networks, and thus motivating prosocial behavior.[32] There are many other positive emotions—empathy, compassion, hopefulness, awe, and so forth—which serve a multitude of functions. And they all come together to help us experience love and be loved. Happy people are easy to love, and love itself is the greatest and most potent of positive emotions, and so encompasses them all.

The various positive emotions serve all people in much the same way, so that there is no real need to speak about disability in the context of each. There are some emotions, though, that might be said to have a unique place for disabled people. Laughter, for example, has a dark side, and there is a long history of disabling comedy that extracts humor from impairment.[33] And while traditional freak shows may be a thing of the past, television and film are today's mediums of disabled othering (e.g., the Farrelly brothers' *Dumb and Dumber* and its mockery of intellectual disability; Ben Stiller's *Tropic Thunder* and the character "Simple Jack"; Martin Scorsese's *Wolf of Wall Street* and its "tossing" of people with dwarfism; and so on). On the other hand, laughter can be a way of dealing with the absurdity of disabled bodies (and here I am thinking of no one else's but my own), and used by disabled comedians to unmask prejudice: humor as liberatory art.[34]

The positive emotion, pride, likewise has a special importance for disability. In Christian tradition, pride is understood as a vice set against the virtue of humility, but while pride can be egoistic and false, disability pride means that *I* am not (or need to learn not to be) embarrassed about my body and its unusual shape and function, that I refuse to accept that it is reasonable that I am excluded, that I defy the assumptions about what it is my life must be like, and above all that I am proud of disabled people, proud to be a part of the disability community, celebrating all that they have accomplished for themselves and each other.

Beyond specific emotions, research has found that positive emotion also reduces stress and facilitates resilience in times of crisis (such as acquiring a disability), and so enables people to return more quickly to their hedonic baseline.[35] And because positive emotion functions to motivate activity, creativity, social integration, and recovery from crisis, it has a circular effect. There is, therefore, potential for an upward spiral of happiness; positive emotions facilitate engagement and achievement, which leads to further positive emotion.[36]

It is one thing, however, to identify the benefits of positive emotion, and another thing altogether to know what to do about it. The problem is not only the constraint of our particular hedonic set point—the genetic lottery of emotional happiness—but that circumstances are often beyond our control. And the challenge of disability is that its impact upon physical, cognitive, and emotional capacities is such that it can generate a downward spiral of unhappiness that is difficult to reverse. In the case of SCI, for example, the losses are multifaceted and, at least at first, utterly overwhelming. Sporting activities once done for play are likely to be suddenly out of reach, and it may not be easy to find alternatives that stimulate equivalent passion. The injury permanently affects sexual pleasure. And the general balance of one's mood is subject not just to the loss of function and sensation (you do not realize the joys of touch until they are gone), but to the nerve pain that often replaces that pleasurable sensation—and pain is negatively associated with mood. The injury also has the potential to impact virtuous activity (such as vocation), and undermine meaning (consider the discussion of theodicy in chapter 1), all of which takes its emotional toll.

In my previous work, I argued that journeying through the experience of SCI is analogous to grief, and this is likely to be true of any acquired disability.[37] Certainly, some parents of disabled children grieve for what looks like the lost potential of their child, and people born disabled may well lament their situation from time to time. One of the potential limitations of positive psychology is its tendency to diminish the importance of the full range of human emotions, and to judge positive emotions positively, and negative emotions negatively. However, the journey of "grief, like death itself, is undisciplined, risky, wild," and anger, sadness, frustration, and the like are a normal part of life.[38]

In fact, though, positive psychology does not deny the role of negative emotions, but argues,

> People should cultivate positive emotions as a regular feature of their lives without giving up their ability to react to good and bad events as they come. Negative emotions help us respond to threats, avoid risks, and appropriately mark losses, while positive emotions help us to take advantage of everything life has to offer.[39]

Strategies for such cultivation are multifaceted, and as diverse as are the objects of human passion and play. Beyond the individual pursuit of pleasurable activities, we soon discover that "life is an ambiguous stimulus" (does acquiring an SCI mean life is over, or one is lucky to be alive, or both?).[40] Thus, positive psychologists have identified a number of psychological strategies that have been shown to build emotional resources, including practicing gratefulness (counting one's blessings), mindfulness meditation, self-compassion, savoring pleasure, and so on.[41]

It is noteworthy that mindfulness meditation has been the subject of substantive psychological research, a practice that has its origins in Buddhist spirituality. In a manner typical of Western approaches to the sciences, much of the research has divorced the meditative practice from its religious context, focusing on its capacity to moderate emotion, although there have been recent efforts to recontextualize mindfulness and draw from its Buddhist roots.[42] The spiritual disciplines of Christianity (and other religious traditions) have not received the same attention, even though we might imagine that formal and informal practices of prayer, praise and worship, confession, and the like could have a beneficial emotional effect. Studies have made it clear that religion contributes to the meaning-making dimension of happiness, but at present, we can make no substantive empirical claims about the emotional efficacy of Christian disciplines.

The strength of the psychological studies on positive emotion is their focus on subjective well-being, but that also is their limitation. Missing is the moral role of emotions, the extent to which our emotional intuitions, whether rational or irrational, just or unjust, predominantly positive or negative, inform our ethical horizons and actions. In this context, negative emotions serve a vital purpose, not only because unpopular emotions such as shame and guilt moderate behavior (sometimes for better and sometimes for worse), but because facing up to the dark side of life is the prerequisite for defeating the status quo. Frustration, boredom, loneliness, shame, embarrassment, uncertainty, guilt, and above it all rage—these are the negative passions that in one way or another inevitably accompany life with a disability, and they cannot be set aside by well-meaning talk about an appropriate balance of positive over negative emotion.

But rage is not the end of the story. Rather, life is moved forward by the variety and fluidity of our passions, which color the narrative of a person who, from the perspective of the end, can be said to have lived the good life. As stated in chapter 2, the virtue tradition argues that our flourishing is dependent upon virtues steering and moderating our passions; not eliminating them, but cultivating emotions that motivate virtuous activity, encourage friendship and build community, and drive us to live meaningfully. Positive emotions are not an amoral good, and neither are negative emotions inherently evil. Instead, our long-term flourishing demands the development of character and the exercise of wisdom.

Gratification and Achievement

Notwithstanding the importance of positive emotion, positive psychology mirrors the virtue tradition in holding that pursuing happiness by focusing on pleasure, in and of itself, is a trap. One of the consequences of the hedonic treadmill is that pleasure and pain are subject to habituation; activities that give extreme pleasure one day give less the next and eventually become routine, so that we require "bigger doses to deliver the same kick as originally."[43] Gratification offers a deeper and more lasting form of happiness, and is earned by engagement in activities in which we can achieve "flow" (the state of being absorbed in the challenge of what we are doing). While positive emotion can be experienced with little effort, there are no shortcuts to gratification. On the contrary, it is earned through discipline, by exercising virtues and strengths.[44] The exercise of virtue provides the internal pleasure of gratification irrespective of external reward, although there is a distinct happiness that comes with achievement. Further, virtue facilitates not just engagement but every aspect of happiness; virtue generates positive emotions, is the prerequisite for engagement and achievement, facilitates relationships, and enables a person to live meaningfully. It is noteworthy that this account resonates with the virtue tradition, although positive psychologists draw on ethical traditions across global cultures and temporalities. The following list is illustrative:

Virtues	Strengths (24)
Wisdom and knowledge	Curiosity, love of learning, judgment/critical thinking, ingenuity/practical intelligence, emotional intelligence, perspective
Courage	Valor, perseverance, integrity
Love and humanity	Kindness and generosity, loving and allowing oneself to be loved
Justice	Citizenship/loyalty, fairness, leadership
Temperance	Self-control, prudence, humility
Spirituality and transcendence	Appreciation of beauty, gratitude, hope/optimism, spirituality/faith, forgiveness and mercy, playfulness and humor, zest/passion

SOURCE: *Martin Seligman's virtues and strengths, from "Flourish," 264–66*

The twenty-four strengths listed in the above table are essentially virtues, and the distinction between virtues and strengths is equivalent to identifying cardinal and subsidiary virtues. It is noteworthy that positive psychologists generally fail to appreciate the relationship between virtue and vice.

For our purposes, though, what is important is positive psychology's intention to measure gratification and the contribution of various virtues to a person's well-being. Gratification is measured by adding life satisfaction to the notion of subjective well-being. Life satisfaction is a cognitive judgment of the circumstances of one's life (how do you feel about your life as a whole? Are you satisfied with the current circumstances of your life, with what you have accomplished, what you are doing, and where you are going?), and researchers have developed a number of statistically validated survey tools that are considered reliable measures.[45] As noted in our earlier discussion, the flourishing in view in the focus on gratification and achievement can be understood both subjectively and objectively, and, as a result, researchers have sought to measure quality of life (QOL) by accounting for both life satisfaction and objective indicators, such as an individual's financial and employment status, education, living conditions, relationship status, and so on.[46] More recent studies have sought to extend QOL indicators to include the capabilities framework described in the previous chapter.[47]

The results of the research on the QOL of people with disabilities validate the insight of the virtue tradition, although the studies are wide-ranging and beyond our capacity to summarize here.[48] Given the emphasis in the previous chapter on independent moral agency, it is noteworthy that significant attention has been given to researching the self-determination of people with disabilities, where self-determination is understood by reference to self-directed and goal-oriented attitudes and behavior. In respect to people with intellectual and developmental disabilities, while there is evidence that, on average, they score lower on self-determination than their nondisabled peers, studies have also found that people who live and work in community-based settings do better than those in restrictive environments, and that people provided with opportunities to learn appropriate skills and attitudes can become more self-determined. It is also the case that people with high levels of self-determination have substantially higher QOL ratings, both in measures of subjective life satisfaction and in respect to objective outcomes in education, employment, and independent living.[49]

A number of studies have investigated the factors that facilitate resilience in the face of an acquired disability, where resilience is understood to refer to the personal qualities that enable a person to adjust positively to significant adversity.[50] There is a myriad of factors that might be expected to contribute to adjustment: biological, demographic, environmental/social, and psychological. In respect of studies on the adjustment of people with SCI, it is noteworthy that biological determinants, such as level and severity of injury, have less impact than might be imagined, although there is some evidence that people with high-level quadriplegia, and those who suffer substantive pain, do have a lower QOL.[51] Demographics—age, gender, ethnicity income, education, and employment—have likewise been found to have a negligible impact on life satisfaction, although again the data are inconsistent, with some studies suggesting that income and employment improve the subjective well-being of persons with an SCI.[52] In terms of social environment, studies repeatedly found that the support of family and friends made an important difference to resilience, and, similarly, that spirituality and faith helped people make sense of their experience.[53] Finally, various psychological resources (virtues and strengths) were found to be significant. Foremost among them is self-efficacy, which refers to beliefs about one's capacity to exercise control and achieve desired outcomes.[54] Persons with high levels of self-esteem, likewise, showed higher life satisfaction, as did those with positive, hopeful, and optimistic attitudes.[55] In another study, bravery, kindness, and humor were found to lessen the impact of serious physical illness on life satisfaction.[56] To summarize:

> The bad news is that illness and disorder take a toll on both strengths of character and life satisfaction. The good news is that these effects only last until the crisis runs its course and recovery occurs. Recovered individuals may then show elevated strengths of character that contribute to renewed life satisfaction.[57]

This suggests that people with a history of physical illnesses and disability sometimes develop virtues and character strengths in response to their circumstances; such as "appreciation of beauty, bravery, curiosity, fairness, forgiveness, gratitude, humor, kindness, love of learning, and spirituality."[58] This is because bravery, for example, is needed to face illness and disability with equanimity; the experience of hardship is capable of heightening a person's empathy and capacity for kindness; and humor helps to deal with the absurdity of daily living with a disability, and so forth.[59]

One of the markers of resilience and well-being is employment, and given hedonic adaptation, it is unsurprising that there is some ambiguity about the relationship between employment and subjective well-being.[60] But when objective and subjective dimensions of QOL are both taken into account, there is overwhelming evidence that employed people with every type of disability are substantially better off than are the unemployed.[61] Within the framework of positive psychology, vocation is one of the key places in which people experience gratification, and employment also provides financial security, self-esteem, networks of social relationships, and so on.[62]

Sadly, employment levels of people with disabilities are low, and those who are employed are more likely to work part-time and be in low-paying occupations. In Australia, for example, 42 percent of the working age population with a disability is employed, compared to 72 percent in the overall population, a trend that is reflected around the world: Canada, 56 percent vs. 75 percent; India, 38 percent vs. 63 percent; Japan, 23 percent vs. 60 percent; Switzerland, 62 percent vs. 77 percent; United Kingdom, 39 percent vs. 69 percent; United States, 38 percent vs. 73 percent; and so on.[63] To illustrate the multiplying effect of the problem, one study found that employment rates for quadriplegics in Queensland declined from 78 percent preinjury to 29 percent post-injury, and that, on average, quadriplegics receive approximately half the mean annual earnings of able-bodied people living in the state.[64] It goes on to note that the situation is worse when the impact on families is taken into account, estimating that unpaid care provided by family members takes up more than 80 hours of their time per fortnight, a figure that also amounts to a substantial loss of income. On the other side of the equation, people with SCI spend approximately twice the community average on health care.

The relationship between net income and subjective well-being is subject to contradictory data. The most common perspective holds that happiness is dependent upon whether or not a person has enough income to satisfy their resource needs. Below this level subjective well-being is substantially less than average, in which case increases in income correlate substantively with increased life satisfaction. But beyond the safety net level, "making more money rapidly reaches a point of diminishing returns."[65] More recent analysis, however, has found that "richer people report higher well-being than poorer people; that people in rich countries, on average, experience greater well-being than people in poorer countries; and that economic growth and growth in well-being are clearly related, and the data show no evidence for a satiation point above which income and well-being are no longer related."[66] Whichever view prevails, higher levels of poverty resulting from unemployment and lower wages hit harder on the life satisfaction of disabled people.

Disabled unemployment has multiple causes, and while functional capacity does limit the options available—a blind person is not an ideal taxi driver, and a person with SCI is unlikely to make a good fireman, but both may excel in any number of other professions—the types of employment open to people, whether or not they have a disability, are framed by their particular capacities and skills. None of us can do every job. Further, studies have found that most people with a disability feel capable of working, are motivated to do so, but identify barriers to their employment.[67] These barriers include levels of education (the gap in educational attainment between those with and without a disability is substantial), inaccessible work environments, misconceptions and prejudices about the capacity of people with disabilities to perform the role required of them, and financial disincentives (employment income offset against pensions and resources, meaning that people end up working for marginal return).[68] For good reason, the focus of disability advocacy and government policy is on breaking down the barriers, but in terms of positive psychology's emphasis on virtues, studies have also found that an individual's psychological capacities (virtues) do contribute to the likelihood of gaining and sustaining employment: optimism, motivation, achievement orientation, internal locus of control, self-determination, work attitude, and so on.[69] This is not to blame disabled people for their unemployment. Optimism cannot overturn prejudice on its own, and pessimism, failed motivation, and despair result from prejudice and injustice. But to the extent that character strengths can be taught and encouraged, it will help individuals to defeat the barriers they are likely to confront in the workplace.

Studies have found that people with disabilities who participated in adaptive sports have significantly higher QOL compared to those who did not, and, similarly, involvement in community-based choirs substantially increased QOL.[70] And while there is much more that might be gleaned from the wide-ranging empirical research on QOL and disability, for our purposes it is enough to note that these sorts of activities require focused effort and the exercise of virtues and strengths, and so provide gratification, along with the social benefits of team sports and group undertakings.

Before moving on to positive psychology's final category of happiness, it is important that we do not lose sight of the sobering reality that, when QOL is focused on objective rather than subjective indicators, there is overwhelming evidence that people with disabilities are substantially worse off than those without. A global study on the QOL

of disabled children, for example, concluded that they were significantly more likely than their nondisabled peers to be living in socially
deprived areas, in households characterized by income poverty, material
hardship, and overcrowding, and that they are worse off in terms of
health, education, and social relationships.[71] As noted above, adults with
disabilities, likewise, are subject to substantially higher unemployment,
lower average wages, and higher costs of living, and are more likely to
experience food insecurity, poor housing, and lack of access to adequate
health care, as compared to the nondisabled.[72] The study goes on to note
that "these observations stand in stark contrast to those of studies which
have conceptualized quality of life as subjective well-being, where the
disadvantage does indeed look muffled and muted."[73]

Meaning and Relationships

Finally, positive psychology recognizes that pleasant experiences and
the activities that facilitate "flow" only enable us to achieve full happiness if we direct our lives to a larger meaning and purpose; "just as the
good life is beyond the pleasant life, the meaningful life is beyond the
good life."[74] Aristotle identified this meaning in contemplation itself.
Aquinas, like other people of faith, emphasized contemplation and
service of God. Considered the father of positive psychology, Seligman
provides what may be the limit case for the relationship of religion and
science—the deification of science itself. In response to the assertion,
"I thought you were a nonbeliever," he says:

> I am. At least I was. . . . I don't read theology literature, and when
> I come across theological speculations written by aging scientists, I
> suspect the loss of grey cells. I have wavered between the comfort-
> able certainty of atheism and the gnawing doubts of agnosticism my
> entire life, but . . . I feel, for the very first time, the intimations of
> something vastly larger than I am or that human beings are.

By "something vastly larger," Seligman does not point to a traditional
deity but, rather, to a God created by the multigenerational success of
science. Yet, for him, there is a transcendent reality present. He writes:

> A process that continually selects for more complexity is ultimately
> aimed at nothing less than omniscience, omnipotence, and goodness.
> This is not, of course, a fulfillment that will be achieved in our life-
> times, or even in the lifetime of our species. The best we can do as

individuals is to choose to be a small part of furthering this progress. This is the door through which meaning that transcends us can enter our lives. A meaningful life is one that joins with something larger than we are—and the larger that something is, the more meaning our lives have. Partaking in a process that has the bringing of a God who is endowed with omniscience, omnipotence, and goodness as its ultimate end joins our lives to an enormously large something.

Coming straight to the heart of this work's interest, he then distinguishes between the good life, which "consists in deriving happiness by using your signature strengths every day in the main realms of living" and the meaningful life. "The meaningful life," he continues, "adds one more component: using these same strengths to forward knowledge, power, or goodness. A life that does this is pregnant with meaning, and if God comes at the end, such a life is sacred."[75]

This odd mix of science, science fiction, and quasitheology invites the question, "Why reach for a religious construction of science?" The answer is likely to be pragmatic: research has led to the conclusion that religious meaning contributes to flourishing. In any event, meaning can be found in various places, in work and achievement, in family and intimate friendships, and most fully, in self-transcendence, in living for something beyond oneself. Religion offers a ready path to the latter, and studies have identified a number of associated (and sometimes surprising) benefits of religious practice. Religious people have higher levels of life satisfaction and better QOL scores than nonreligious people.[76] Those who gain religion increase life satisfaction over the long term, while those who lose religion record sustained decreases (in defiance of hedonic set point).[77] And people who attend church regularly are not only more satisfied with life, but are generally healthier and live longer than those who do not.[78] It is also noteworthy that the advantages of religion accrue irrespective of the particularities of religious practice: all major world religions achieve similar outcomes.[79]

The relationship between religion and QOL gives rise to the so-called religious paradox, which asks, "If religion makes people happy, why are so many dropping out?" Multinational and multireligious studies have found that the association between religion and happiness was stronger in nations and communities with more difficult life conditions, where religiosity was related to "social support, feeling respected, and purpose or meaning in life." Conversely, where living conditions are more favorable, religiosity is not only less prevalent, "but religious and non-religious people experience similar levels of subjective well-being."[80]

The association between religion and happiness holds true in the context of disability, where it has also been found that religious and/or spiritual people tend to be more resilient than those without faith, a finding that correlates with the evidence that religion is especially helpful when a person is dealing with difficult life conditions.[81] Theorists speculate that, where crisis gives rise to feelings of helplessness, religion and religious practices (such as prayer) provide people with an indirect form of control over their situation, while also helping them to make sense of their circumstances and providing a basis for hope.[82] But whatever the mechanism, rehabilitation specialists are encouraged to take a pragmatic approach:

> From a rehabilitation perspective, the specific mechanisms by which religion facilitates adjustment to disability [are] of relatively minimal importance, whether it is through divine intervention, the power of repetitive religious practices (e.g., individual or group prayer, chanting, laying on of hands, yoga, anointing ceremonies, sand paintings, etc.), or a placebo [e]ffect (which may be the perspective of non-religious rehabilitation professionals). If religion helps an individual cope with a disability in a positive manner, it should be used accordingly.[83]

This entirely pragmatic and value-free analysis of religion brings to the surface both the strength of the scientific analysis of happiness, and its weakness. On the positive side, there is no need for religious practitioners to shy away from practical and empirical analysis of faith. As noted in respect to the virtue tradition, empirical study of religion provides important evidence that faith and spirituality are not irrelevant metaphysical speculations, but make a difference to life in the real world. This insight resonates with modern theological conceptions of religious doctrine, which understand doctrines as "communally authoritative rules of discourse, attitude, and action" that function to shape individual and communal life.[84] That is to say, religions should make life better. Negatively, happiness is not an adequate basis for judging religious function, and the danger is that religion gets co-opted to keep disabled people in their place. Friedrich Nietzsche summarizes the issue with delightful sarcasm:

Finally, as for the common people, the great majority, who exist and are only *allowed* to exist to serve and to be of general utility, religion gives them an invaluable sense of contentment with their situation and type; it puts their hearts greatly at ease, it glorifies their obedience, it gives them (and those like them) one more happiness and one more sorrow, it transfigures and improves them, it provides something of a justification for everything commonplace, for all the lowliness, for the whole half-bestial poverty of their souls. Religion, and the meaning religion gives to life, spreads sunshine over such internally tormented people and makes them bearable even to themselves. . . . It refreshes, refines, and *makes the most* of suffering, as it were. In the end it even sanctifies and justifies. Perhaps there is nothing more venerable about Christianity and Buddhism than their art of teaching even the lowliest to use piety in order to situate themselves in an illusory higher order of things, and in so doing stay satisfied with the actual order, in which their lives are hard enough (in which precisely this hardness is necessary!).[85]

Nietzsche is wrong about religions, at least when they function according to their own ideals. Christian faith, for example, is (or should be) a protest movement that exists for the marginalized, providing people subject to poverty and living with disability the self-respect and purpose that is too often denied them by the wider society. But it does not always achieve this end: "Individuals, parents, and professionals who live and work with disability have far too frequently experienced attitudes and practices that are insensitive, theologically questionable, and at times simply spiritually abusive."[86] There is a dark side to contemporary Christian practices of faith and healing that result in the ultimate form of disability exclusion; when "God" fails to embrace the disabled as they are, exclusion is total.[87] Which is to say that empirical analysis of religion takes us only so far, and that theological reflection on the empowering and liberatory (or stultifying and imprisoning) content of faith for disability is vital.

In respect to positive psychology and the contribution of religions to flourishing, research has also considered the efficacy of virtues that are of particular importance to religious traditions. Scientific research on forgiveness, for example, has burgeoned in the last decade, with studies showing that it is positively associated with psychological well-being, physical health, and desirable relationship outcomes.[88] But as with other virtues, forgiveness is not an absolute good, and demanding that victims forgive victimizers, or that people with disabilities forgive individuals and social systems that have marginalized them, has the potential to entrench the status quo and exacerbate harm. Gratitude, similarly, is a virtue of importance to religious traditions that appreciate life as a gift of God; psychological research has shown that such traditions enhance mood, build character, and contribute to healthy friendships. But gratitude, too, can degenerate into obsequiousness, entrenching hierarchies of disabled subservience. Anger (and rage), pride, forgiveness, gratitude—these are character traits that, in the context of disability, demand a nuanced analysis that goes beyond the measures of empirical science.

Religion is not the only avenue to meaning. Meanings and purposes that transcend the self are many and varied, although they almost always coalesce in our communal life. Religion is always the love of God and neighbor, and most of the things we devote our lives to have friendship and community at their heart. Even environmental activism is the recognition that the earth is our home and not, as is sometimes assumed, the act of pitting nature against humanity. In the context of disability, there is meaning to be had in identifying with the disabled community. In the introduction to this book I cited Stella Young's letter "To My Eighty-Year-Old Self" in which she says,

> By the time I get to you, I'll have written things that change the way people think about disability. I'll have been part of a strong, beautiful, proud movement of disabled people in Australia. I'll have said and written things that pissed people off, disabled and nondisabled people. You will never, ever stop challenging the things that you think are unfair.
>
> By the time I get to you, I'll be so proud. The late Laura Hirshey once wrote about disability pride, and how hard it is to achieve in a world that teaches us shame. She said "you get proud by practising." Thanks to my family, my friends, my crip comrades and my community, I'm already really proud. But I promise to keep practising, every day.[89]

I am a relative newcomer to the disabled community, and I'm not sure that I've yet earned the right to the pride Stella Young so thoroughly deserves. But at the least I have glimpsed the wonderful enigma of the advocacy of the disabled community; the fight against injustice and exclusion has provided disabled people with a community and a purpose that at one and the same time rages against disablement and is deeply and joyously meaningful.

THE LIMITS OF THE SCIENTIFIC STUDY OF HAPPINESS

The width and depth of the scientific literature beckon for more theological inquiry; and all I have accomplished is an overview of a vast and escalating discipline. I have only rarely interjected with what would normally be considered theological content, and I make no apologies for focusing principally on what science has to tell us about happiness. If we hope to be able to use the insights of the virtue tradition in our own lives and when we are working with others as activists, pastors, counselors, and medical and rehabilitation professionals, then we had best be confident that what we have to say is evidence based. Indeed, it seems clear that the insight of the virtue tradition, as well as some key aspects of religious faith, holds up to the rigors of scientific study.

However, empirical science will never achieve omniscience. Leaving aside debates about the epistemological foundations of the scientific method, we can at least observe that "statistical tests, validated questionnaires, thoroughly researched exercises, and large, representative samples" cannot begin to capture the complexity and wonder of human life.[90] As I have said, flourishing emerges in narratives, which are not reducible to mathematics. Further, to speak of tendencies and averages and statistical reliability is inevitably to ignore the outlier that is most characteristic of disability. Disabled people are not normal (where this word means average), and will inevitably resist being treated as such. This is not to dismiss the insight of science altogether, but simply to recognize that we need to respond to its conclusions with a "yes, but . . . maybe . . . not always."

The "not always" is especially important. Positive psychology assumes a world in which an individual has control of her circumstances, and in which the exercise of signature strengths is efficacious. In our discussion of happiness in the Hebrew Bible, we noted that there were two constructions of flourishing. The first and the predominant view mirrors that of positive psychology, recognizing that the virtuous and wise person will flourish. The second, apparent in the psalms of lament and the book of Ecclesiastes, sees that the world does not always operate as it should, and that those who are disempowered are more likely to be subject to the vicissitudes of life. In such cases, a person's opportunity to exercise a "locus of control" may well be diminished, and positive emotions such as contentment, optimism, and hope be made much harder to achieve. In fact, the learning of virtue is itself a chancy affair, and people subject to disabling injustice are also likely to be stuck in conditions that undermine the development of the virtues and strengths that normally facilitate resilience and flourishing. In this context, balancing the positive and the negative is not enough. Rather, dissatisfaction, frustration, despair, anger, and conflict are the prerequisite to the social and cultural change that is needed for disabled flourishing. It is precisely for this reason that the gospel story faces up to injustice, and looks to grace as the ultimate response.

Finally, positive psychology focuses on virtues and strengths, but it does so in the absence of substantive discussion of vice, and there is no moral judgment built into its analysis. Indeed, it is entirely possible for a person to exercise signature strengths and be satisfied with their life, but for this to occur in the context of a criminal gang, a terrorist cell, or an abusive religious cult. The measures of positive psychology serve well for certain forms of analysis but fail to offer criteria that allow us to judge meaning and value. Science is at its strongest when it aids our ability to describe the world in which we live. Ethics, and particularly the rich tradition of virtue ethics, enables us to go on to deeper forms of judgment about that world, even as it attempts to transform it.

6

Profound Disability, Independence, and Friendship
Practical Reasoning and Moral Agency

The virtue tradition, as already noted, has an ambivalent history with respect to disability, declaring the good life to be impossible for the disabled and prioritizing virtues that may prevent people from challenging their marginalization. In *Dependent Rational Animals*, one of the few books on virtue ethics that specifically addresses disability, Alasdair MacIntyre critiques the entire philosophical tradition (including his own work) for its failure to face up to the fact of human animality, fragility, and dependency. Right from the beginning, Aristotle had elevated "the great-souled man," who disdains external goods and delights only in virtue, which he possesses fully. He (and it is always he) projects his greatness in all his attitudes and actions, shows equanimity through both good and bad fortune, lives to benefit others, and deplores asking for or receiving help, a sign of inferiority.[1] And while after Aristotle the ideal "man" shifted shape—from the contemplative philosopher, to the pious and celibate monk, to the scrupulous interpreter of the scriptures, to the objective scientist, and finally to the radical postmodern—that which was considered most distinctly human was the intellect, so that the fully flourishing man was one or another version of the independent intellectual. Certainly, such a person was never disabled.

In this light, the task before us is to redeem the virtue tradition for disability by building on the work of those few virtue philosophers who have attempted to account for our fragility and (inter)dependency.

Central to this assignment is exploring ways of talking about flourishing without deferring to hierarchical and exclusionary notions of human nature. I have ordered what follows logically rather than historically, exploring the work of three virtue ethicists (Garret Merriam, Alasdair MacIntyre, and Martha Nussbaum) and one theologian (Hans Reinders). Because independent reasoning is important for the virtue tradition's conception of flourishing, I focus largely (but not exclusively) on intellectual disability, since it is cognitive impairment that seems most vulnerable to a notion of flourishing that emphasizes reason.

DISPENSE WITH AN OBJECTIVE ACCOUNT?

I noted earlier Nietzsche's critique of virtue, which amounts to a rejection of objective accounts of human nature; of any notion of telos and purpose. In response, it has been argued that virtue ethics can contribute to our understanding of disability and flourishing only if we eliminate the notion of human nature altogether.[2] This follows the postmodern view that species essentialism was done away with by Darwinian evolution, after which we came to appreciate that "the species *homo sapiens*, like all other biological species, is dynamic, in flux. Accordingly, there is no single, absolute, metaphysical, archetypal human being by which the rest of us are to be measured."[3] From this perspective, rather than measure a person's flourishing against the species norm, we can only judge whether a person is living well or poorly based on the particular circumstances of that person's life.[4] To make such a judgment requires that we exercise *phronesis*—wisdom—to determine whether a person has done well and exercised virtue in relation to their unique physical, psychological, and social realities. While relying on practical wisdom means that there will not be definitive and clear-cut judgments about flourishing, to do so is to accept that we live in a complex and "fuzzy" world.[5]

But what does it mean to rely on practical wisdom without the use of objective categories? The proposed way forward is to identify and seek to understand relevant factors in a person's life, and then judge them accordingly.[6] Consider the example of Helen Keller as a paradigm case of flourishing. Keller, who became blind and deaf after contracting scarlet fever as an infant, learned to speak and read Braille in five languages, became the first deafblind person to earn a bachelor of arts degree, and among many other achievements, went on to become a famous advocate for people with disabilities, and co-founder of the American Civil Liberties Union:

> Her achievements were made, not so much in spite of her disabilities, but rather (at least in part) because of them. Given the circumstances of her life, what sort of judgements should we make regarding how well she lived? Keller's story is a paragon of several of the key virtues that we commonly think constitute a good life: courage, strength, resiliency, self-knowledge, compassion, and wisdom, to name but a few. Her life is a shining example of the best attributes of the human spirit. It was certainly a life filled with difficulty that most of us do not have to deal with, yet that struggle elevated rather than hindered her. When we think about what kind of persons we want our children to be, what kind of life we want them to live, we could do much worse than using Keller's life as an exemplar.[7]

It seems obvious that Keller flourished, and did so because she exercised virtue. It is noteworthy that you cannot judge Keller's life against an idealized norm, nor try to imagine what her life would have been like had she not contracted scarlet fever. In that case, she would not have become Helen Keller, and we can only contemplate flourishing against the concrete actuality of real life. When we do, what becomes more than clear is that Keller flourished, not only as a disabled woman, but as a person. In her case, disability did not inhibit her *eudaimonia*. On the contrary, it was the context that made her flourishing what it was.[8]

A comparative case, that of anencephaly, illustrates how practical wisdom might lead to a different judgment.[9] Anencephaly is a rare condition that occurs when a child is born without a cerebrum, and so normally dies before birth or within hours or days after.[10] In this situation, practical wisdom will lead us to conclude that there is no possibility for flourishing.[11]

In respect to the usefulness of this reworking of virtue theory, the argument suffers because the paradigm cases are extreme; virtually lifeless on the one hand and impossibly perfect on the other (or, at least, Keller's story is told in such a way as to give that impression, which is always the difficulty of narrative). That is to say, it is not clear that much is added to our understanding of how to conceptualize the flourishing of disabled people without reference to any particular telos. Without any notion of what it might be for a human to flourish, even the concept and practice of wisdom are vague and ultimately content-less. Yet, there is a way to say more about the content of that vision of flourishing without thereby setting up a totalizing and exclusionary vision of human nature.

"THE FACTS OF VULNERABILITY AND AFFLICTION"

Alasdair MacIntyre has been in the background of much of the argument of the previous chapters, not only because his publications were central to the reappropriation of virtue ethics among philosophers and theologians during the latter half of the twentieth century, but because he is one of the few virtue ethicists who explore virtue ethics in the context of disability.[12]

In drawing on disability, MacIntyre is attempting to reframe the virtue tradition, asking, "What difference to moral philosophy would it make if we were to treat the facts of vulnerability and affliction and the related facts of dependency as central to the human condition?"[13] Too often philosophers ignore fragility, rarely acknowledging the bodily dimension of existence and focusing instead on that capacity of human nature that makes us different from other animals, our rationality. But whatever our unique capacities, we should never lose sight of the fact that we are animals.[14] Identifying our animality highlights the fact that we flourish as animals. Even the brain, which is central to our uniqueness, is a creaturely organ. Post-Darwin, there is nothing surprising in this conclusion, except that it reminds philosophers and theologians that our physicality and connection to the environment, one another, and other species are central to any conception of flourishing. Sociobiology frames our nature as a teleological fact that must be taken account of in any analysis of flourishing.[15] And it is noteworthy that this realization becomes obvious after facing up to the fact of disability.

Just as *eudaimonia* is a whole of life vision of happiness, so is our flourishing connected to the various stages of our life, from the cradle to the grave. We are born vulnerable and utterly dependent on our parents, and this dependency frames infancy and childhood. If we live long enough, we become dependent again in old age, and throughout the rest of life, to greater and lesser degrees, we remain dependent on others and are always at risk of severe illness and disability.[16]

Particularly important for our moral development is the care and education we receive as children, a fact that normally goes unremarked in the philosophical focus on the rational "man," but that has rightly been brought to the fore by feminists.[17] MacIntyre learns from feminism the centrality of the parental bond, especially that of mother and child, and talks of the "ordinary good" of motherhood, a phrase meant to elevate the beauty of a mother's love and the impact that it has on the healthy psychosocial development of the child.[18] He asks, what virtues must mothers, fathers, and families embody to provide the loving security needed for a child's healthy growth? Of central importance are the commitments of unconditional love, which sees us give resolutely, without expectation of proportional receiving, and unconditionally even (especially) in the context of severe disfigurement, illness, and disability.[19] This unconditionally committed love of a parent for a child is not extraordinary, but wonderfully ordinary, because relationships of dependence are central to who we are as human beings.

The loving care and ongoing education children receive from families, friends, and schools are intended to help them make the transition into adulthood. It is a transition from complete dependence to becoming an "independent practical reasoner" and a person who exercises the virtues.[20] This is a key phrase of MacIntyre's, and describes the aim of raising children—that they take responsibility for the goals and actions that shape their life, that they understand what their flourishing entails, and that they exercise the virtues needed to bring that about.

Yet independence is never absolute. This is first because we learn about "the good" from others. We are born into families and cultural traditions, and so are never the sole authority on our own good, but are continually accountable to others. Our independence is always a balancing act, between slavishly following what we have been taught and dispensing with tradition altogether. As social creatures, our flourishing is intertwined with the networks of families, friends, and local and global communities. But, even so, the aim of parents raising children is for them to be happy, and what we mean when we say that is that we hope for them to become responsible people who live well over the course of the ups and downs of life.[21]

Independence and dependency go together. Because we have been and are likely to be again dependent, dependency translates to indebtedness. Because we have received, we have an obligation to give. This obligation transcends the normal rules of giving and receiving, since when we are dependent we receive from others out of all proportion to what we can repay. So when we have the freedom of independence, we have the responsibility to give to those dependent upon us in ways incommensurate to what we might hope to receive from them in return.[22] This responsibility is not just between parents and children, but extends to our broader social obligations, which especially include the care that we give to the disabled and others who are seriously ill or encumbered. And what this means is that the virtues that attend to dependency need to be cultivated for all of us to flourish together.

In respect to this social responsibility, MacIntyre is particularly concerned with political community. Politics involves the intersection of a person's individual good and the common good, and what should always balance egoistic self-interest is an underlying social contract that appreciates that the misfortune that befalls another could easily have been mine.

> And the kind of care that was needed to make us what we have in fact become, independent practical reasoners, had to be, if it was to be effective, unconditional care for the human being as such, whatever the outcome. And this is the kind of care that we in turn now owe or will owe. Of the brain damaged, of those almost incapable of movement, of the autistic, of all such we have to say: this could have been us. Their mischances could have been ours; our good fortune could have been theirs.[23]

I have cited MacIntyre in full here to highlight the strength of his argument—his emphasis on the universality of dependency—and to bring to the surface a key weakness. When he speaks of disability he almost always does so in terms of deficit and dependency, where disability is inevitably misfortune. At certain points, he recognizes that social structures impact the experience of disability, and rightly devotes substantive attention to the political and social structuring of the common good.[24] But he does not seem to have read much about disability itself and demonstrates no knowledge of the social model. His concern reflects the medical model's assumption that disability is about individual loss—in his argument, the loss of independence. The focus of the whole book is on caregiving, and the virtues needed to look after those who become dependent on us. This includes his prioritizing of the virtues of love, charity, pity, generosity, and the like. To understand another person's distress as our own, he says, is to recognize that other as neighbor, and in relieving another person's distress, I relieve my own distress at their distress.[25]

I have already considered the limitations and dangers of pity in the previous chapter, but the real problem here is not MacIntyre's valid concern that we exercise virtues of care, but his failure to consider these issues from the perspective of disabled people. He does briefly address the importance of the virtues of receiving, such as gratitude, courtesy, forbearance (toward an inadequate giver), and so forth.[26] But for the most part he speaks to caregivers (whether individual or society as a whole), and so assumes asymmetrical relationships between people who are supposedly independent and their dependents. His argument would have been richer had he recognized that the interaction between carers and disabled people is not the same as between a parent and a newborn, so that giving and receiving is a two-way street (as is parenting). To speak of *interdependency* is richer than to concentrate on independence and dependence as distinct terms. Indeed, to focus on vulnerability and dependency without an attendant concern for the potential powers of the dependent person is dehumanizing, and the logic of MacIntyre's project is best realized when the goal of care is to maximize the capacity of a dependent person to choose the shape of her own life, and to bring that about by interdependent virtuous action.

The swings and roundabouts of independence and dependence were brought home to me in the instant transition from forty-year-old nondisabled man to a quadriplegic. I vividly remember the early weeks in intensive care when there was not a single thing I could do on my own. Utterly dependent, I was fed, bathed, toileted, and moved about at the direction of others, without the power of choice or action. In the seven months of rehabilitation that followed, I regained some upper body movement, and learned new ways of navigating the world. I was transformed into a cyborg, benefiting from the technologies that gave me movement and access to the virtual world. I have regained some independence I once thought lost forever, but I am still woken by carers first thing in the morning, hoisted out of bed, showered, dressed, and given breakfast (that I can eat myself). With the freedoms and constraints of my electric wheelchair (and its sometimes difficult inter-action with the built environment), I have wide-ranging independence during the day, but it will still be necessary to ask for help constantly—I am a "please and thank you" machine. At night, my wife cooks dinner, and my children serve as carers, taking on the intimate responsibility of getting me to bed.

I am grateful for the immeasurable love and virtuous care of my wife, children, parents, brothers, and wider family and friends, without whose help I would be completely lost. They have answered the need of my vulnerability by giving without thought of return, exercising the virtues needed for my care in a myriad of ways. I am also full of praise for the professional solicitude of the doctors, nurses, physiotherapists, occupational therapists, and others who cared for me and encouraged my rehabilitation. They have responded to my dependency by providing care in such a way as to maximize my independence.[27] In this way, dependence and independence are not opposites, but mutually reinforcing.

As for me, to live as a quadriplegic, I have had to learn the habits that enable me to negotiate dependency. I need the gumption, wit, and tact to ask for help, sometimes from complete strangers, other times from those tired of my requests. I need to learn to express gratitude, and to do so willingly and without compulsion, while avoiding the vice of ingratitude, of presuming that I am owed assistance by dint of my disability, or the fact that a nurse is working for pay, or that my wife is doing her "duty." It is sometimes frustrating to be asking constantly for help, but I need to appreciate that Aristotle had it wrong: there is no dishonor in receiving.

But while I have known new forms of dependency, I have also had to discover new ways to give in return. This has been particularly challenging as a husband and father. Families are built on mutual self-giving, but mutuality seems to be undermined by asynchronous giving. Without the capacity to do the physical tasks of running a household, I have had to be creative in finding new ways to contribute while, at the same time, learning to accept my limitations. I have been able to continue my work, so my role as provider has not been destroyed by my disability (in this I am fortunate indeed). But bringing in a paycheck is not enough. My involvement in family life is supported by carers who act on my behalf and under my instruction, so that their caregiving empowers me as a husband and father. I have also realized that although my children have missed out on some of the things I would have liked to have done with them (I have been unable to teach them to surf, or show them how to make repairs on the house), their experience of my dependency has given them responsibilities that will enrich their character. Every interaction between us, even those that seem most asymmetrical (such as putting me to bed), is fundamentally about giving and receiving love, and in that, I can be a vital participant.

All of us touched by the realization of my vulnerability have needed to exercise the virtues relating to interdependency. Those that have cared for me have exercised pity and mercy—taking on my suffering as their own—but they have done so in such a way that they have neither diminished nor disempowered me. In this way, spinal cord injury has become an opportunity for us all to discover reserves of strength that we did not know we had (and wish we did not have to find), and within the constraints of disability and dependency, to take responsibility for living as well as we can. Such, at least, has been the goal. In practice, virtue and vice (especially my own) go hand in hand, and everyone does their best (and sometimes their worst) to get through the day, hoping that if we do so together and without giving up, over time we shall build meaningful lives.

INDEPENDENT PRACTICAL REASONING AND MORAL AUTHENTICITY

In the lineage of the virtue tradition, MacIntyre retains a focus on the importance of reason for the good life—on the goal of parents to raise their children to become "independent practical reasoners." While the virtue tradition had tended to elevate philosophical reasoning, MacIntyre deliberately shifts attention to practical reasoning—to individual moral agency in everyday life. Practical reasoning refers to the capacity of a person to judge well and act effectively in pursuit of desired ends, and so requires the acquisition of virtues, skills, and self-knowledge. Without knowledge of one's physical and mental abilities, temperament, character, and skills, a person is "unable to imagine that range of alternative possible futures that are, given their social circumstances and their own characteristics, futures that it would be realistic for them to attempt to make their own."[28]

The question we face in this chapter is whether it makes sense to elevate independent practical reasoning in the context of profound disability—an issue not taken up by MacIntyre. But before we can do so, we need a robust account of reason, since determining whether a person with an intellectual disability is capable of independent practical reasoning may well depend on whether we can describe what we do when we reason. To that end, Catholic philosopher and theologian Bernard Lonergan provides a helpful outline of reason and its relation to moral agency, inviting his readers to think about their thinking. He describes the processes of reasoning in terms of four levels of consciousness, which he identifies as experiencing, understanding, judging, and deciding to act. At the level of experience, our attention is drawn to the full range of data of human life: biological, aesthetic, intellectual, dramatic, practical, and mystical. At the level of understanding, "intelligence takes us beyond experience to ask what and why and how and what for"—what does the data of my experience mean?[29] Judgment takes us beyond intelligence to ask whether our understanding of what we have experienced is true or false. And finally, our conscience prods us to act upon the judgments that we have made. Lonergan labels these four processes as the transcendental precepts: "Be attentive, Be intelligent, Be reasonable, Be Responsible."[30] They are transcendental because the innate human drive to ask questions and seek answers moves us from ignorance to knowledge and then action, and so takes us beyond ourselves.

For Lonergan, a person "achieves authenticity in self-transcendence."[31] In asking what, why, how, and what for, we construct a worldview and explore what we could be and do. And in making critical judgments about our insights we determine whether our view of the world has substance. Thereafter, in acting on that determination, we become moral creatures, and so take responsibility for the shape of our future. Moral self-transcendence, Lonergan argues, creates the possibility for benevolence, honest collaboration, and true love, and so lies at the root of happiness.

Lonergan, writing as a Catholic priest, concludes that self-transcendence ultimately reaches toward God. He links the human pursuit of authenticity to our being made in the divine image. As God's creation of the world is the fruit of divine self-transcendence and an expression of benevolence and love, so our authenticity consists in self-transcending, in being origins of value, in being in love.[32] And the fruit of authenticity is joy:

That fulfilment brings a deep-set joy that can remain despite humiliation, failure, privation, pain, betrayal, desertion. That fulfilment brings a radical peace, the peace that the world cannot give. That fulfilment bears fruit in the love of one's neighbor that strives mightily to bring about the kingdom of God on this earth.[33]

In reality, authenticity is an ideal never achieved; "it is ever a withdrawal from inauthenticity, and every successful withdrawal only brings to light the need for still further withdrawals."[34] Inauthenticity is the product of the failure to be attentive, be intelligent, be reasonable, and be responsible. It occurs when individuals and traditions deliberately ignore relevant data, when they fail to ask what an experience means and what should be done in response, when they accept what they are told unthinkingly and without criticism, when they ignore the prod of conscience and take the easier path, when they rationalize bad behavior, and so on. The result of inauthenticity is decline, both individual and corporate. At its worst inauthenticity is judged to be authentic, and when that occurs self-improvement ceases. Again, this is why self-knowledge is so important, because to move toward authenticity we need to face our failures. And it is also why Christian and other religious traditions emphasize repentance and conversion.

Conversion is a change of direction, from inauthenticity to authenticity. Lonergan describes intellectual conversion, which is an orientation to pursue meaning and truth; moral conversion, which occurs when we act according to our values (rather than follow the herd); and religious conversion, which is being grasped by ultimate concern, an otherworldly falling in love. Lonergan notes that for Christians, this is considered to be a gift of grace, the love of God flooding the heart through the Holy Spirit, but he recognizes that grace is interpreted differently in different religious traditions, and his description of conversion is broad enough to have relevance beyond the formalities of religious conviction.[35] The fundamental issue is that reason is not principally about genius, philosophy, or scientific breakthrough (although it includes these things), but that it leads to moral responsibility and self-transcendence (love). Thus, reason's focus is communal; it is about our living and flourishing together.

INDEPENDENT PRACTICAL REASONING AND
PROFOUND DISABILITY

MacIntyre's elevation of the independent practical reasoner is an important reminder that the (relative) autonomy of disabled people must always be front and center. This affirmation is at its most complex in the case of intellectual disability, especially since the very nature of this disability seems to bring into question the possibility of independence.

The label itself is contested, with some preferring "learning difficulty" or "learning disability," although "intellectual disability" has gained wide acceptance internationally, and is the principal term used in Australia. As with other forms of disability, people with an intellectual disability have their lives affected by a cognitive impairment and by the social effects of their being labeled as such. Intellectual disability has been defined as

> a significantly reduced ability to understand new or complex information and to learn and apply new skills (impaired intelligence). This results in a reduced ability to cope independently (impaired social functioning), and begins before adulthood, with a lasting effect on development.[36]

Two aspects of this definition are relevant to understanding independent practical reasoners. First, a reference to "impaired intelligence" too often leads to the conclusion that a person with an intellectual disability is incapable of reason. There is a tendency in literature and policy to conflate intelligence and reason, and to limit the construction of both.[37] As Lonergan has helped us to see, intelligence is one part of our reasoning process, and it is subservient to moral authenticity. It goes without saying that a person with an intellectual disability is as capable as anyone else of living according to values. Further, intelligence is a multifaceted capacity. Intelligence responds to the data of our experience, but our experience is not limited to those things that are tested in schools or IQ scores (math and language). For example, we experience intersubjective meaning, and the capacity to understand the intention of a smile or a hug differs from that needed to make sense of an algebraic formula. It takes a different capacity again to create and to extract meaning from art and music. In this light, it is apparent that feelings and emotions are involved in intelligence, and we might say the same of other capacities, such as spirituality.[38] Intelligence comes in a variety of colors, and rather than measure it on a scale of high to low, and so weigh one person against another, we are invited to enjoy the variety of intellectual gifts that we encounter among our friends, and to celebrate each person's unique capacities and achievements.

Second, it is the stated impact upon a person's capacity to cope independently that is especially noteworthy. The problem with defining intellectual disability as "a reduced ability to cope independently" is that it exaggerates the difference between people with and without an intellectual disability, since independence and dependence go hand in hand for all of us—we are only ever relatively independent, and even then, only temporarily so.[39] More importantly, there is now substantial evidence that people with severe cognitive limitations can achieve significant independence given a healthy social and learning environment.

Consider, for example, the potentially fraught topic of parenting with an intellectual disability. Historically, and still, in most societies today, intellectually disabled people who hope to be parents face substantive barriers, even though creating a family is a basic human right. The stereotypical assumption is that people with intellectual disabilities are perennial children unable to take on the responsibility of adult roles such as parenting.[40] The effect of such prejudice has included forced sterilization, and even in countries where such practices are banned, intellectually disabled mothers announcing their pregnancy are likely to be met with dismay, and encouraged to have an abortion or give their child up for adoption. There is now, however, a body of research that shows that parents with an intellectual disability can raise healthy and well-rounded children.[41] While outcomes for such children can be negative, this is likely attributable to factors other than cognitive capacity, such as the disabled parent's personal history of maltreatment or childhood trauma, a lack of positive parenting models, an unsupportive social environment, and so forth. Of particular importance is the social environment. None of us parent alone, and the success of intellectually disabled parents is especially influenced by the support systems that frame their social networks. Support can be either "capacity promoting" or "capacity inhibiting," where the former helps parents to develop the skills needed to achieve for themselves, and the latter undermines confidence and denies a person opportunities to learn.[42]

What studies on the potential parenting capacities of intellectually disabled people reveal is that the goal of becoming an "independent practical reasoner"—a morally responsible adult capable of choosing the shape of one's own life—is as central to the flourishing of intellectually disabled people as it is for anyone else. This is only possible when we appreciate that independence is more about self-determination than self-sufficiency, so that support services (whether familial or institutional) aim to provide competence-promoting empowerment rather than competence-inhibiting care:

> Considering help to be a necessary step towards independence redefines the power relationship between people with intellectual disability and those who help them. It also defines independence as not necessarily meaning helping a person until they learn to do something on their own, but helping them take decisions, make choices and take control over their own lives, and continuing to do things with help where this is necessary. This is very much in line with how independence is understood by those disabled people who . . . conceptualize it in terms of autonomy and self-determination rather than mere self-sufficiency.[43]

There is a danger in using the language of "independence," which is too often interpreted as "doing things by yourself," in which case the elevation of independence in government policy could be used as an excuse to reduce support services. However, for people with an intellectual disability (or any disability), meaningful independence may require more rather than less support.[44] In this context, it may be that the language of "agency" and "self-determination" is preferable to that of independence. But properly understood, to speak of dependence, independence, and interdependence is to recognize that the human condition is always a balancing of strength and fragility, communal tradition and individual freedom, and ability and disability. The flourishing of every person, whether disabled or not, is dependent on others, on the support of our families, friends, communities, and social structures, as well as the cultural values given to us by religious and national traditions.

In the discussion thus far, I have focused attention on cognitive impairments that allow for at least some degree of independence, and I have done so deliberately to counter the prevailing tendency to underplay the capacities of people with an intellectual disability. But even as I make that case, Sunshine McNeill is front and center in my thoughts.

As her father Jay made clear, Sunshine is completely reliant on her parents and carers for all the activities of daily life: bathing, toileting, dressing, eating, and so on. One of the real challenges of parenting Sunshine is that there is presently no way to engage her in complex conversation, although she has been learning augmentative communication since age four, which Jay and Helena expect to continue to develop. It is important to note that she is still a child and most children continue an upward trajectory of learning. Now eleven years old, she was born both deaf and unable to talk, either verbally or using Auslan (Australian Sign Language) since she is unable to control either her tongue or hands. As a toddler, she was given a cochlear implant, which transformed her engagement with the world (the video of her joy at her first experience of hearing the sound of her parents' voices captures a deeply beautiful moment). She clearly understands some of what is going on around her, and communicates her emotional response by an infectious smile and many other expressions. But while she is unable to speak, the extent of her intellectual capacity is unable to be measured and therefore remains unknown—although her parents are working on the assumption that, as is normally the case with cerebral palsy, hers is a physical rather than an intellectual disability. But whatever the future holds for her, Sunshine is likely always to be extremely dependent on her parents and other carers. What, then, does this mean for the argument of the virtue tradition, and the claim that a person's emergence as an independent practical reasoner is foundational to her flourishing?

One potential response is to reject the value of independence. This is the approach taken by Eva Kittay, who writes as a feminist and carer (and it is noteworthy that carers are normally women), drawing on her experience of parenting her daughter Sesha, a young woman who has cerebral palsy and severe intellectual disability.[45] Although Sesha's "expansive, affectionate nature is a gift," she cannot walk, talk, or read. Thus, she is utterly dependent upon her parents and others. With this situation in mind, Kittay develops a dependency critique of the modern liberal notion of individual justice, with its elevation of individual independence and its attendant "ideological diet of freedom, self-sufficiency, and equality."[46] She says:

The point of the dependency critique is to show that, as long as the
bounds of justice are drawn within reciprocal relations among free
and equal persons, dependents will continue to remain disenfran-
chised, and dependency workers who are otherwise fully capable
and cooperating members of society will continue to share varying
degrees of the dependents' disenfranchisement.[47]

The launching point of her argument is similar to that of MacIntyre,
insisting that the tendency of liberalism to focus on independence fosters
the fiction that incapacity and dependency is an exception rather than a
normal part of human life.[48] In focusing on profound disability, Kittay
invites us to conceive of personhood by way of analogy to motherhood,
whereby a person's dignity is based not on their individual capacity for
independent action, but on the fact that each one of us is some mother's
child. Such a construction of personhood intends to ensure that "we
consider what is owed to a mother's child by virtue of its being vulnerable, to the extent that the child is dependent upon the mother for its
well-being."[49] That every person is "some mother's child" anchors an
approach to politics that takes social justice seriously, one that supports
the type of care that everyone needs at some point in life, and that is
too often forgotten and ignored in modern democracies and capitalist
economies.[50] The argument is philosophical and political, but it is also
theological. The nature of human personhood lies at the heart of theological anthropology, a topic we will consider at the end of this chapter.

Notwithstanding the importance of a political stand, to replace
independence with the idea of universal motherhood (rather than,
for example, to complement it), is unintentionally to elevate parenting
and caring over the dignity and agency of the disabled person. The
potential danger of this change in focus is poignantly illustrated in the
infamous case of the so-called Pillow Angel, in which a six-year-old
intellectually disabled girl, Ashley, was given high doses of estrogen,
and had her growth plates, breast buds, and uterus removed, all for the
purpose of making her care easier for her family as she transitioned into
adulthood.[51] Her parents argued that her smaller size "makes it more
possible to include her in typical family life and activities that provide
her with needed comfort, closeness, security, and love." The doctors
that performed the surgeries could not understand the visceral public
response to their actions, arguing that

this was not a girl who is ever going to grow up. She was only going to grow bigger. Some disability advocates have suggested that this course of treatment is an abuse of Ashley's rights and an affront to her dignity. This is a mystery to me. Is there more dignity in having to hoist a full grown body in harness and chains from bed to bath to wheelchair? Ashley will always have the mind of an infant, and now she will be able to stay where she belongs—in the arms of the family that loves her.[52]

The fundamental problem in this case is not simply the infantilizing of a disabled person, but that the changes to Ashley's body and reproductive capacity were done without her consent, and in a way that completely constrained her future horizons. Of course, we should not be too quick to judge specific cases, and Ashley's parents are the only ones in a position of being able to understand the intricacies of life with their daughter. But her story was made a matter of public record, and it is a terrifying thought that such cases might be seen to create a precedent for the treatment of people with disabilities. That is, in fact, what has occurred, with the *New York Times* describing very recent examples of growth attenuation therapy being used to keep disabled children smaller, lighter, and hence easier to care for, and referencing the "Ashley Treatment" in support.[53]

Growth attenuation therapy (a label that deliberately softens the actual nature of the intervention) is just another example of the long and sad history of legalized assault of disabled bodies, most poignantly apparent in the forced sterilization of disabled people. Reports such as the "Involuntary or Coerced Sterilisation of People with Disabilities in Australia" provide stark insight into the dehumanizing consequences of the failure to prioritize the bodily integrity and individual dignity of disabled people, and stand as a reminder that loving parents do not always know what is best for their child.[54] It seems likely that the "Ashley Treatment" is in breach of international law, and it is now generally recognized that "the principle of autonomy, expressed through full, free and informed decision-making, is a central theme in medical ethics, and is embodied in human rights law."[55] It is true that the complications of reproductive health and the challenge of determining exactly what constitutes consent for a profoundly disabled person are multifaceted, and hard and fast prejudgments should be avoided. But a prejudice toward personal agency should make us extremely reluctant to make decisions that will impact upon the bodily integrity of any person, especially those profoundly dependent on our care.

Returning to the principal point of this chapter, the insistence that maximizing a person's capacity to take independent responsibility for their choices and future is central to their flourishing is one that applies to all people. This is especially so for those who are severely disabled, since it is their agency that is most under threat. But again, what might this mean for a person as utterly dependent as Sunshine? I put the question to Jay, and he tentatively responded as follows:

> Yes, we think about the future and Sunny's independence as emotional energy allows. At the beginning our hope was that she would walk and be mobile but that was the dream of inexperienced parents . . . Now it is all about communication. If Sunny can even communicate yes or no, then she will have some level of independence and be able to regulate her immediate world. When Sunny is in high school most of the learning will be around practical things but if she shows interest in subjects and her communication becomes sophisticated enough, she has the resources to go as far as she would like. My feeling is this will be completely beyond her physical ability but we will have to negotiate that through once we create learning expectations/ plans with the teachers.
>
> Making her own moral choices is something I have thought about, not from a typical view (rage, bad behavior, truth telling, etc.) but from a spiritual perspective. Will she be interested in Jesus? Conceptually Jesus is probably beyond her ability to consider. Sunny's spiritual journey may simply be a global view which says, "there must be more"—her faith may be as basic as self-awareness and, therefore, purpose. Sunny's spiritual journey is why I question the idea about discipleship as a way to grow in faith. If it was that important, then in God's economy Sunny would be at a disadvantage and that seems unjust.
>
> Sunny only gives out love; she is not behavioral or naughty. I genuinely think she sees the good in people because of a lack of comprehending evil. This may change as she gets older of course—it is fascinating to watch.
>
> In regards to Sunny's independence, we will always have to help her. She may live in assisted accommodation at some point, but she needs all aspects of her life taken care of. We, of course, have the contrast of Jaz and Sunny growing in parallel. Jaz is

independent, and we are coaching her, as any parent would, to be a contributing adult, but for Sunny, the journey and approach to parenting could not be further apart.

Sunny shows will, preference, joy, and sadness, which are all attributes that will contribute to her reasoning and therefore the potential to make some "moral" choices. As to the extent, I'm not sure.

In reply, I asked Jay a clarifying question: "Is not her choice to be happy, to respond to you generously, itself an act of independence—a moral choice?" He responded:

It is a moral choice but her disposition, because of her brain injury, may make it easier to respond that way. If she doesn't understand people's motives or have to contend with skepticism, etc., she may have an easier pathway to show that generous spirit. In saying that, there is something very special that goes on inside her that is intimate and deliberate, and I will always attribute that to her choice to be uniquely loving. I hope one day that we will hear her thoughts clearly, but for now, all we can do is assume that she has all the potential in the world—it just may take time to unlock it.

Jay and his wife Helena are committed to Sunshine's care, a task that they expect to be lifelong, that is often intense and challenging, but one that flows from a deep reservoir of love. They are also committed to helping her to maximize her potential, and to that end long especially to "hear her thoughts clearly." Listening is at the heart of independence, since care is only empowering to the extent that it supports a person's flourishing in their own way. And whether or not Sunshine is ever able to communicate in complex sentences, it is already the case that her parents have learned to hear the voice of her heart, which has revealed a generous, joyous, and loving spirit. These are virtues, and their contribution to her flourishing, and that of others, should not be underestimated.

Sunshine experiences the good in people, and in so doing brings out the best in those with whom she comes in contact. I am reminded of a story Jay told me about her experience at the public school that she attends part-time with her sister Jazmine. Apparently, when Sunshine is pushed to the school gate in the morning, she is met by a gaggle of girls who lobby to take control of the wheelchair. Jay and Helena leave her in their care

and, thereafter, she is included in the activities of the school day, expressing her part in the proceedings by smiles and laughter. This interaction
enriches everyone. Sunshine earns the pleasure of being included. Her
school friends receive the joy of her responsiveness, and learn the virtues
that go with caring for a friend. Jay and Helena are helped to realize that
their dependent daughter has more independence from them than might
have once seemed possible, and are thereby encouraged to know that she
has a life that reaches beyond her family.

Jay speculates about whether Sunshine's responses are a product of
moral choice or merely a matter of disposition; that is to say, he wonders
whether her injury makes it easier for her to respond to people in the
generous way that she does (in fact, brain injury can often have the opposite effect). But this may be to underplay Sunshine's achievement and that
of her family. Consider Lonergan's summary of the process of reason as
it applies to her engagement with the world. Although her disability, and
particular family and social situation limit the data of her experience, her
varying responses to people and situations make it more than clear that
she notices much of what happens. This was especially apparent in the
advantage that came with her cochlear implant. Although these devices
are sometimes controversial, as they are seen by many deaf people to
pose a threat to the flourishing of Deaf culture, in Sunshine's case the
implant drastically widened her experience, in particular, opening her
horizon to the rich sound of voices and other environmental noises.[56]
While at present we cannot know exactly the level of her understanding
of what is said, she makes something of her insight clear in her emotional
responses to people, in her attention to what is going on, and so forth. And
thereafter, she chooses to respond in the way that she does. That this is
not merely preprogrammed by her impairment becomes clear when we
realize that she might well have responded differently. In another era and
another place, when in all likelihood she would have been taken from her
parents and placed in an institution, the manner of her experiences and
the things she might have learned from them would have affected her
character and disposition, and thus the nature of her chosen responses.
It may have restricted her capacity for moral agency and virtuous action
(although people can respond remarkably to negative experiences). And
it is difficult to conceive how she could have been as happy, and would
have flourished to the extent that she has and will continue to do as her

life unfolds. And this is to say nothing of the impact that she has on her parents and sister, and on her friends, who have all been transformed by her presence and the manner of her interactions.

Reflecting on Sunshine's situation may in fact help to clarify Lonergan's analysis of consciousness. We might imagine by his description that the effort to be attentive, be understanding, be reasonable, and be responsible is about individual thought. And it is—we should never forget the individual—but none of us attend to data, attempt to understand that data, make judgments about our understanding, and act in the light of those judgments on our own. Every process of consciousness is a shared interaction with our family and friends, teachers, and cultural traditions. Sunshine's parents support her reasoning agency, and where she is unable to grasp certain concepts and act on those in her own power (or at least we are unaware of her capacity to do so), they share in her agency. Jay and Helena provide Sunshine the support she needs, while also doing what they can to maximize her right to be herself and not merely an extension of themselves. She is more than her mother's child.

Having rightly celebrated Sunshine's wondrous beauty, we need to be careful not to idealize her (or any person with a disability), imagining that the life she shares with her family is pure joy. It is not. It is difficult, often painful, and messy, and neither she nor they are saints (at least Jay is not, thank God). But the happiness described by the virtue tradition is always achieved through struggle. It is best if I let Jay speak for himself on this point. The following was offered publicly, written in response to being asked whether it would have been better if his daughter had passed away:

> Here is how a benign conversation turned noxious. I was standing next to a man in a busy public space who I knew only by acquaintance. He asked me how my daughter Sunshine was doing. I delivered my usual rehearsed blurb that allowed me to congenially converse but stay emotionally aloof; a self-preservation technique that many reading this blog will relate to. Then I heard the sacred question roll off the tongue like a comment on the weather, *"Do you think Sunshine would have been better off if she had passed away?"* I coughed and spluttered through the conversation—I don't even remember what I said.
>
> Since that time (now ten years later) I have often contemplated that question and the motivation or values that man

may have held. The question told me a lot about him but also the status of society and even myself. Interestingly I wasn't angry at the time, and when I think about him now I actually feel sorry for him. Part of the reason I don't feel angry with him is I can't profess with a clean heart that I hadn't thought the same thing. In the early days when my two pound daughter would arch her back from excruciating pain I found myself conflicted. As the drugs refused to work and the heart apnoea continued on like a militant regime, I did wonder . . . I wondered if it was right that any human should suffer like this. There is no hiding the fact that the question should never have been asked of me, but the crass confrontation did prompt me to consider my own secret thoughts, albeit unwelcome and terribly confronting.

Insensitive questions like this irritate the disability community, but it simply reflects the tragic, modern belief that life is best when it's "perfect." In the early days I thought the same thing even though it wasn't a cognitive and verbally frequented belief. I am not sure it is worth getting angry at, but rather pitied. The reason I feel sad for the person who asked this question is they don't know what I know now. They don't know what love feels like when it has cost you emotionally, making it truly grounded and strong. They don't know what it feels like when a human being says a deep heartfelt "thank you," not with words, but with a look that reaches into your soul and spins your emotions like a fork in spaghetti. As much as I dislike it, the human struggle seems to give love substance; it reminds me of an Australian gum tree seed that only germinates when a bush fire burns it.

Not long after that man posed the question, I began seeing another side to life that contradicted all the useless lessons I had learned about what success was, and I am a far better person because of it. Sure, my daughter still suffers, but she is mostly happy and brings more than just joy to our lives, she brings balance, substance and offers character development to those around her that can only be realized on the foundations of pain and suffering.

I would give anything to change the journey my daughter has been on, but she has shown she wants to live and because of that, she has taught me what it means for me to live—a gift beyond measure. She has taught me that money means nothing and beauty is barely skin deep. The only reason I scoff at the world's vain striving for perfection is because Sunshine has taught me this unpopular reality—only those who have paid the price to love someone have ever really loved at all. It isn't something you can purchase on a shelf. It has to be experienced, and it has to hurt.

People with a disability bring the stark truth to a conversation—there is no room for pretense. They encourage those around to sacrifice and express a love that confronts selfishness, which is often at the root of all bad things. When I sacrifice to better the life of Sunshine, a harmonious chord resonates across the sky and humanity is somehow better. The pursuit of success while neglecting the less fortunate is toxic, and most people would agree it is a precarious path. Perfection doesn't make me a better person, sacrifice does.

So the question isn't about whether Sunshine would have been better off passing away in those early days, but rather, is the world a better place because of her? I of course already know the answer to that.[57]

There is no need to add commentary; Jay's reflection speaks profoundly. But if he were to write this post again, I would encourage him to add something about the character and choices of Sunshine herself. She also models virtue by the way she understands and responds to the ups, downs, and monotonies of her daily experience, and so also sacrifices to contribute to the flourishing of her family. Perfection does not make Sunshine a better person, but her character in and through hardship and inactivity does (and I reference boredom because quadriplegia has taught me something of the challenge that results from a reduced capacity to participate in everyday activities. Whether or not Sunshine experiences such boredom is speculation). In elevating Sunshine's independent practical reasoning—her moral agency—I am not pretending that her decisions are not also shaped by her abilities and disabilities, as well as her social environment. We miss the point if we think agency is the same thing as pure independence and complete freedom of the will. The argument throughout this chapter (and in our previous discussions of free will and theodicy) is that freedom and independence are never absolute, but, rather, are enabled and maximized by the type of support we are a part of, which ideally is competency-enhancing support. The development of each person's independent moral agency occurs in the context of our interdependency, which is also just as capable of inhibiting us. Sunshine flourishes as a person when her agency is enhanced to whatever extent possible: by technological developments (cochlear implants, a wheelchair, and hopefully at some point in the near future, a means of complex communication), the loving care of her family and friends, and the shape of her social world.

Of particular importance is the nature of the education she receives, which has to find ways of drawing out her unique capacity and potential, as well as shaping her environment so as to make space for her to flourish.[58] In Sunshine's case, this has meant dual schooling, part-time at a special school targeting the special needs of people with disabilities, and part-time at a public school where she takes her place in the "normal" structures of society. Helena has had to fight "the system" to get this arrangement in place, a far too common experience for mothers with disabled children. Helena's advocacy for her daughter brings me back to the argument of Kittay. I erred earlier in this chapter by seeming to dismiss her insight too quickly. If Kittay's emphasis on the value of persons as "some mother's child" complemented rather than replaced the value of independence, then it may be that our education systems would be more willing to consider the individual vulnerabilities and support needs of disabled children and their parents. One of Kittay's fundamental ideas is that mothers/parents provide support and need support, and that political justice needs to be directed not just at individuals, but at families and carers. Again, this highlights the centrality of our vulnerability and dependence to our personal identity, recognizing the fact that we flourish together, and so have an obligation to one another's well-being. And it is surely true that our society would be transformed if the values of motherly care came to inform the priorities of political justice. As feminism has reminded us, if (masculine) individual agency is oriented to competitiveness and war, maternal thinking takes its stance for peace and nonviolence.[59]

THE UNITY OF A NARRATIVE LINKING BIRTH TO LIFE TO DEATH

Independent practical reasoning is essential to the good life but does not constitute it. It is true that the person who lives authentically earns the satisfaction that goes with virtue, and all things being equal, gives herself every chance to do well in her endeavours, make good friends, and so on. But there is no certainty to flourishing, and luck plays its part. A person striving for authentic moral agency may have any number of things go seriously wrong, sometimes as a result of the biological hazards that are inherent to animal life, other times due to individual and social injustice, and very often because of the failure to live according to values. Once again, the principle that another's misfortune might have been our own reminds us of our responsibility to do what we can to moderate biological hardship, confront injustice, and move from inauthenticity to authenticity.

We tend to think of life as a series of events, and happiness as a thing that comes and goes, but an authentic life can only be conceived and evaluated as a whole. Our concept of self, which is a part of developing moral agency, "resides in the unity of a narrative which links birth to life to death."[60] In this way we judge our own and others' actions in particular events in the context of the broader narrative of life:

> A central thesis then begins to emerge: man is in his actions and practice, as well as in his fictions, essentially a storytelling animal. He is not essentially, but becomes through his history, a teller of stories that aspire to truth. But the key question for men is not about their own authorship; I can only answer the question "What am I to do?" if I can answer the prior question "Of what story or stories do I find myself a part?"[61]

Thus, the good life is not a single thing—it is not based on some exclusive vision of human nature—but it is one about which we can tell a meaningful story, in which a person has lived authentically as a moral agent, loved and been loved fully, made it through obstacles (including personal failures), experienced the full range of human emotions, and so forth. From this perspective, it is already apparent that, at eleven years old, Sunshine is living a good life.

MARTHA NUSSBAUM—THE CAPABILITIES APPROACH

Thus far I have been defending the importance of "independent practical reasoning," but I admit that the blandness of the label reflects something of the colorlessness of the construction of happiness that would result if we failed to recognize that human nature includes other vital capacities, and that play, creativity, aesthetic wonder, spirituality, and the like are also central to our agency and happiness.

Our final conversation partner in this chapter is Martha Nussbaum, whose long-standing concern has been for the social and political justice of marginalized people, including those subject to poverty, political oppression, gender and sexual marginalization, and so on. Her earliest writings explored the contribution of Aristotelian virtue ethics to political justice, and in collaboration with Amartya Sen, she has developed a philosophical conception of justice labeled the "capabilities approach."[62] Following Aristotle, her logic begins with a description of human beings as social and political animals, and thereafter she analyzes the different spheres of life in which humans are typically involved to draw out the capabilities she takes to be the minimum basis for a good life.[63] She thus resists the relativism common to many contemporary defenders of virtue ethics so as to find ways to conceive of universally valid political principles of justice.[64] Her list of capabilities, which builds on and modifies Aristotle's original construction, recognizes that there is much that is common in human flourishing, but is also framed in such a way as to value cultural and individual diversity and freedom. The list of capabilities is as follows:[65]

1. *Life*. Being able to live to the end of a human life of normal length; not dying prematurely, or before one's life is so reduced as to be not worth living.

2. *Bodily Health*. Being able to have good health, including reproductive health; to be adequately nourished; to have adequate shelter.

3. *Bodily Integrity*. Being able to move freely from place to place; to be secure against violent assault, including sexual assault and domestic violence; having opportunities for sexual satisfaction and for choice in matters of reproduction.

4. *Senses, Imagination, and Thought*. Being able to use the senses, to imagine, think, and reason—and to do these things in a "truly human" way, a way informed and cultivated by an adequate education. . . . Being able to use imagination and thought in connection with experiencing and producing works and events of one's own choice, religious, literary, musical, and so forth. Being able to use one's mind in ways protected by guarantees of freedom of expression with respect to both political and artistic speech,

and freedom of religious exercise. Being able to have pleasurable experiences and to avoid non-beneficial pain.

5. *Emotions*. Being able to have attachments to things and
people outside ourselves; to love those who love and care
for us, to grieve at their absence; in general, to love, to
grieve, to experience longing, gratitude, and justified anger.
Not having one's emotional development blighted by fear
and anxiety. (Supporting this capability means supporting
forms of human association that can be shown to be crucial
in their development.)

6. *Practical Reason*. Being able to form a conception of the
good and to engage in critical reflection about the planning
of one's life.

7. *Affiliation*.
   A. Being able to live with and toward others, to recognize
   and show concern for other human beings, to engage
   in various forms of social interaction; to be able to
   imagine the situation of another.
   B. Having the social bases of self-respect and nonhumil-
   iation; being able to be treated as a dignified being
   whose worth is equal to that of others. This entails
   provisions of non-discrimination on the basis of
   race, sex, sexual orientation, ethnicity, caste, religion,
   national origin.

8. *Other Species*. Being able to live with concern for and in
relation to animals, plants, and the world of nature.

9. *Play*. Being able to laugh, to play, to enjoy recreational
activities.

10. *Control over One's Environment*.
    A. *Political*. Being able to participate effectively in polit-
    ical choices that govern one's life; having the right of
    political participation, protections of free speech and
    association.
    B. *Material*. Being able to hold property (both land
    and movable goods), and having property rights on
    an equal basis with others; having the right to seek
    employment on an equal basis with others; having
    the freedom from unwarranted search and seizure. In
    work, being able to work as a human being, exercising
    practical reason and entering into meaningful rela-
    tionships of mutual recognition with other workers.

Nussbaum's outline of the capabilities is in continuity with MacIntyre, not only because both draw on the virtue tradition or because practical reason is on the list, but because moral agency lies at the heart of most of the capabilities. What MacIntyre means by independent practical reasoning is that our senses, imagination, and thought are cultivated by appropriate education, that we develop our emotional disposition, that we have self-respect and character shaped by virtues that enable us to live well toward others, and that we exercise control over our political and material environment. Nussbaum thus clarifies and fleshes out the virtue tradition's understanding of flourishing, but also expands it in important ways—particularly in emphasizing laughter and play, and insisting on the importance of our relationship with animals, plants, and the natural world.

In listing specific capabilities, Nussbaum is not limiting the good life to these categories, nor is she suggesting that they provide a guarantee of happiness. Rather, her point is that the capabilities, which are derived from an analysis of our human nature as intelligent social animals, are minimum ways of realizing a life of human dignity. Each category encompasses a range of possible outcomes, but since the concern is political, the capabilities approach holds that justice depends on achieving a threshold level of each capability, a minimum beneath which a good and dignified life is not available.[66] To take away any one of the capabilities from the social values that inform political policy is to undermine the capacity for people to flourish in one or more substantive spheres of life. Nussbaum clarifies what she means by a threshold in a later text, noting that the threshold is determined by adequacy rather than equality (e.g., it is necessary that all people have access to adequate accommodation, not equal accommodation).[67] Precisely what constitutes "adequate" will need to be thrashed out in the political process. And in some cases, an adequate threshold only occurs when equality is secured, such as ensuring equal access to voting rights, religious and civil liberty, and so forth. It might be up for debate whether adequacy in education services and health care demands equality (i.e., should the wealthy have access to better schools and hospitals?). A strong case can be made that we should work for the movement toward equality in schooling, since education is central to almost all other capacities. But equality does not mean every student should be educated the same way.

In fact, for people with disabilities to have access to an equal quality of education, schooling services have to be shaped to meet the unique needs of each person. Similarly, health care is of such import to the flourishing and dignity of life that movement toward equal access to services best realizes human dignity. Such, at least, is the view of citizens in countries such as Australia, which have long established universal health care systems.[68]

In applying the capabilities approach to disability, Nussbaum draws on the foundational ideas we have been addressing throughout this chapter, highlighting our vulnerability and acknowledging "that we are needy temporal animal beings who begin as babies and end, often, in other forms of dependency."[69] As with others, she emphasizes the importance of care, arguing that care (or caring) is not an extra capability, but that we need to think about both the cared for and the caregiver across the range of capabilities.[70]

It is readily apparent what the capabilities approach can contribute to the justice of people with disabilities. That bodily health and bodily integrity are listed first confirms our intuition that sterilization and growth attenuation therapy are abusive—a clear abrogation of the dignity of disabled people. The capabilities approach reminds us that, far from being asexual, disabled people deserve the opportunity for sexual satisfaction. It highlights the importance of moving people out of prison-like institutional housing and into environments where they can enjoy the love of family and friends. It cements the importance of providing education that meets the individual needs of people with diverse learning capacities and abilities.

One of the key questions in thinking about the capabilities in the context of disability is whether they are all important for all people, or whether an alternate list should be created. Nussbaum, whose entire argument is based on the universality of the capabilities, notes that to exclude any one of the capacities from values and policies of justice is inherently dangerous, especially given the persistent tendency of most societies throughout history to underestimate and denigrate the abilities of disabled people. But what does her insistence on the universality of the capabilities mean in terms of our understanding of disabled personhood?

Nussbaum considers this issue by contemplating the situation of Eva Kittay's daughter, Sesha. The question is whether Sesha has a different form of life altogether, whether she is something other than what we mean when we use the metaphor "human," or, alternatively, whether she is simply unable to have a flourishing human life?[71] Citing the example of the anencephalic child and a person in a permanent vegetative state, she wonders whether it is only sentiment that leads us to consider them human.[72] But she rejects this conclusion because these people are children of human parents (i.e., they are some mother's child).

But while we may conclude that the anencephalic child born without sentience cannot live a flourishing life, is the same true of Sesha? Nussbaum concludes that although not all the capabilities will be available to Sesha, her humanity resides in the fact that some of the most important capacities reside in her. We might well consider this matter in relation to Sunshine, since we need not rely on abstraction, having the gift of the firsthand perspective of her parents, Jay and Helena. It is a fact that some of the capabilities are likely to be beyond Sunshine's ability. Her bodily health and her control over her environment—her political participation, opportunity to work and hold property—are drastically compromised, and are likely to be below the minimum threshold. We remain hopeful but unsure of some of her other capacities, so that we do not yet know whether she will be able to cultivate literacy and develop mathematical, scientific, and musical knowledge and skills. Given the facts of Sunshine's disability, we can say that she is not able to flourish to the extent that we would wish, and we thus sympathize with her parents' grief at the realization that she does not have the same opportunities as her twin sister, Jazmine. We also understand their lament, their complaint to God that things have turned out this way. But, we also know that many of the listed capabilities are within Sunshine's reach, and in fact, that in some areas she excels to the extent that she can show us what it is to flourish in particular spheres of life. Sunshine teaches us, for example, that a life that seems from the outside to be so reduced as not to be worth living (see the first capability) is capable of being one of abundant joy, rich emotion, and deep love; one in which laughter rings out as a symbol of the wonder and lunacy of the universe.

When we consider Sunshine's life in the context of her family, we not only see that she is able to accomplish some of the absent capabilities through the support of carers and guardians (such as holding property), but that she makes a vital contribution to the capabilities of others. We have considered what Sunshine brings to the flourishing of family and friends earlier, so there is no need to flesh this out again. But taken all together, we can certainly conclude that within the severe constraints of her disability and against all expectations Sunshine is flourishing, and certainly helps others to do so.

MORAL SENTIMENT AND THE CONTRIBUTION OF FAITH

Nussbaum concludes *Frontiers of Justice* with an extended discussion of the need to cultivate moral sentiments so that society as a whole is motivated to shape its institutions and systems according to the capabilities approach. The magnitude of the problems of poverty, disabled alienation, and environmental destruction require communities to have deep sympathy and benevolence, and to sustain these sentiments over the length of time that it takes to bring substantive change.[73] We might label such sentiments as cultural virtues, and remember that cultural vices too often militate against benevolence.[74] One example is the tendency in capitalist nations to argue that the poor are the cause of their own poverty, that neediness is unmanly, and so forth.[75] These values prevent the establishment of social supports that are needed to protect people in poverty and those with disabilities—and of course, the two often go hand in hand. Nussbaum, though, sees reason to hope, as some of the pernicious sentiments that dominated in the recent past—such as racism and homophobia, as well as the stigmatization of disabled people—have been criticized and changed over time.

Nussbaum argues that our educational institutions should seek to cultivate three capacities that are essential to our humanity: (1) the capacity for critical self-examination and critical thinking about one's own culture and tradition; (2) the capacity to see oneself as a citizen of the world, whose own well-being is intimately bound to others; and (3) narrative imagination, which is the capacity to think about what it might be like to be in the shoes of another person.[76] Nussbaum also emphasizes the importance of narrative in framing and communicating the meanings of life, and in supporting the values of the capabilities approach.[77] We learn narrative imagination by immersion in stories; wherein we come to understand others and ourselves. Narrative imagination shapes our moral interaction, cultivating habits of sympathy, teaching virtue, confronting prejudice, and so forth.[78] It is through narrative that we come to understand what the good life is, and therein interpret our own journey. And the beauty of narrative is its capacity to speak to people at almost any stage of learning. Stories and their meanings are not the exclusive domain of the intellectual.

In terms of cultivating moral sentiments, it is noteworthy that religion has a central role to play. In essence, religions tell stories that shape a person's worldview, generally for better but sometimes for worse, depending on how those stories are told:

> Politicians have power, but religions have something stronger: they have influence. Politics moves the pieces on the chessboard. Religion changes lives. Peace can be agreed around the conference table; but unless it grows in ordinary hearts and minds, it does not last. It may not even begin.[79]

If this is so, then what the church believes about the humanity of people with disabilities matters, and it is to that we now turn.

THEOLOGICAL ANTHROPOLOGY AND FRIENDSHIP

While this chapter is principally about contemporary constructions of the virtue tradition and what they say to us about the good life and disability, at a deeper level it is an exploration of our understanding of human personhood. Theological anthropology is a central concern for theologians interacting with disability, and one of the most substantive and important reflections on the topic is Hans Reinders' *Receiving the Gift of Friendship: Profound Disability, Theological Anthropology, and Ethics*. Noteworthy for our purposes is that Reinders develops his theological conclusions with profound intellectual disability front and center, beginning by introducing his readers to Kelly, a young girl born as a micrencephalic. This is a condition that causes the brain not to develop properly, and in Kelly's case it caused severe intellectual impairment and drastically restricted her ability to understand and interact with others.[80] With this case study in mind, and in the light of prevailing assumptions that notions of selfhood and purposive agency are crucial to what it means to be human, Reinders asks a now familiar question: "Should we not say, then, that the language implying that Kelly is a human being must also be spoken metaphorically?" In answering, emphatically, "no," he then sets out to provide a theological rationale for that conclusion. In so doing, he reframes traditional Christian anthropology (and the insight he draws from disability is a perfect example of why it is unfortunate that disability is marginal to mainstream theological reflection).

Reinders' argument is largely a criticism of the logic developed in this chapter. Indeed, he writes from a Reformed theological tradition that rejects some of the basic assumptions that shape my project, in particular, that I utilize Roman Catholic sources affirming the importance of natural law, those arguing that we can and should draw theological conclusions from our understanding of the natural world. There is no need here to outline the vexed debate between those in various Christian traditions who have different perspectives on the relationship between revealed and natural theology, in some cases rejecting the latter altogether. Reinders' concern, shared by other theologians of disability, is best summed up in his own words:

> Culturally dominant conceptions of what it means to be human exclude human beings with profound intellectual disability because such conceptions are predicated on capacities for selfhood and purposive agency. These concepts reflect the long-standing orientation in the tradition of Western thought by which being human is distinguished according to the faculties of reason and will. Since this view apparently does not speak to the humanity of all human beings, there is a need for a fundamental rethinking of this tradition, in particular of its theological origins.[81]

An approach to theological anthropology shaped by Roman Catholicism has two aspects. The first, which identifies human life as beginning at conception irrespective of its stage of development, protects every person's right to life. In identifying a fetus as a person, by extension the full humanity of every person is affirmed, irrespective of their intellectual capacity. The second is teleological, and focuses on the qualities that allow human beings to pursue their ends. According to a traditionally Catholic approach to anthropology, a person is a rational soul with the powers of reason and will. The problem for Reinders is that this second theological affirmation seems to contradict the first: "all human beings are protected in order to actualize their potential for becoming what they are meant to be. But . . . how is this argument going to work out for profoundly disabled human beings?" If the latter constitutes the dignity of the human person, it casts doubt on the dignity of persons without that capacity, so that, for all intents and purposes, they are "subhuman." Reinders explains the issue with a potent analogy using an apple. The tradition argues that an apple does not need to be perfect to be an apple; a bad apple is still an apple on the basis of its origin. From the perspective of its final end a bad apple is not one that carries any value. "It does not count for much. It will be trashed—if someone bothered to pick it up at all."[82]

The apple analogy highlights the fundamental issue, which is that of value. Indeed, throughout our discussion of virtue I have identified the same problem, that constructions of virtue tend to create hierarchies of value, elevating one or another version of rational superiority in their construction of human nature. In this light, and with Kelly's humanity as his guiding principle, Reinders turns to trinitarian theology for an understanding of the human person that he believes is properly universal—that fully embraces Kelly. While trinitarian theology is complex, the essence of the argument is relatively straightforward. The trinitarian God is in very nature relational, and humanity created in the image of God is likewise relational: "theologically speaking, we are truly human because we are drawn into the communion with God the Father, Son, and the Holy Spirit."[83] Relationality thus constitutes the essence of human nature, an affirmation that embraces people with profound disabilities, because God loves them and draws them to himself, regardless of whether they understand it. From this perspective, modern individualism is a mark of the separation from God and others, and the incarnation, death, and resurrection of Jesus Christ are intended to restore our relationship with God and with one another. And the church, as the body of Christ, exists (or at least is meant to do so) as a foretaste of God's promise of fully restored relationships—of our becoming who we were created to be. With this theological affirmation in place, Reinders goes on to develop a theological ethic that prioritizes friendship with God and one another.[84]

Relational anthropology holds that every person is a child of the trinitarian God, and so mirrors the assertion that every person is some mother's child. A noteworthy difference between the two proposals is that the latter chooses a truly universal relationship (mother and child), whereas reference to relationship with the God of the Christian Trinity potentially excludes all non-Christians—or at least it is likely to give that impression to people of other religious faiths or none. That Christians might under-stand trinitarian theology as being inclusive of all people, irrespective of faith, does not solve the problem of communicating this idea to others. Indeed, one of the key advantages of the Roman Catholic affirmation of natural law reasoning is the deliberate effort to utilize explanations and language available beyond the confines of Christian faith.

In any event, I have no substantive criticism of relational anthropology. I have argued throughout this book that friendship is central to the good life. It is important to note that there is more to Christian anthropology than relationality. The assertion that humanity is made in the divine image is central to Christian (and Jewish) belief. The *imago dei* is traditionally associated with rationality and morality; the image of God references our rational capacity, and the likeness of God (impacted by the fall) our moral nature. Early Protestant theologians preferred a relational understanding of the image—as outlined above. But other versions are also theologically important. There is a strong consensus among biblical scholars that the reference to the image of God in Genesis 1:26-28 is functional, describing humanity as God's delegated representatives, who exercise "dominion" (delegated responsibility) by caring for the earth and each other.[85] But function is another way of talking about capacity, and requires the exercise of reason and will. In the Christian scriptures, the *imago dei* also has a teleological meaning. Christ is God's image, and we are being transformed into his likeness (Rom 8:29, 2 Cor 3:18), a transformation that is as much about our character as anything else. It is brought about by being filled with the Spirit, and is evident in the fruits of the Spirit—love, joy, peace, patience, kindness, goodness, faithfulness, gentleness, and self-control—which are virtues. There are, therefore, multiple ways of understanding the image of God. Since the alternative constructions are complementary rather than contradictory, theological anthropology should not be reduced to the single category of relationality—a conclusion that coheres well with our earlier consideration that human nature should/must include a list of different and diverse capabilities.[86]

My primary concern is that rejecting reason and will from concep-tions of human nature sets aside the individual moral agency that both the social model of disability and the virtue tradition claim is central to flourishing. In terms of disability, the affirmation of people's rights to speak for themselves, to flourish in their own way, and to make decisions about their own future is so important that it cannot be dispensed with, even for Kelly. But what I have tried to show in this chapter is that people with profound intellectual disabilities are not excluded by affirmation of reason and will. On the contrary, they are diminished if we deny their agency, even if it needs substantive support. In fact, Reinders' insight that relationship with God determines a person's humanity and value is best understood if individual moral agency is part of the equation. A notion of personhood determined only by the love of one of the parties (in Reinders' case, God; in Kittay's, a mother) effectively eliminates the other party altogether.[87] Thus, relational anthropology is strengthened by retaining rather than rejecting the significance of individual reason and will.

The account I have given of reason should also negate any assertion that cognitive capacity establishes a hierarchy of value. If there is a hierarchy, it is one of morality (the transcendental precepts—be attentive, be intelligent, be reasonable, and be responsible—elevate goodness above all else), and this may be to the advantage of people like Kelly—it certainly seemed to be so for Sunshine. That is to say, Sunshine's goodness would certainly outrank my own, except that from the perspective of Christian theology we are all equally bound by sin as victims and perpetrators, and all equally recipients of divine grace. There is no such thing as a moral hierarchy.

One might respond that the nature of Kelly's cognitive impairment exceeds that of Sunshine's; that Kelly has no capacity to understand or respond to others. My tentative reply is that we cannot know what a person's reasoning capacities are if they are unable to communicate in ways that we recognize (and it is normally our inability to understand what a person is "saying" that is the problem). But if Kelly's impairment is such that she can have no interaction with the world—similar to an anencephalic, or a brain-dead and unconscious person—then does it reduce her humanity and the need for us to treat her with loving-kindness if we also admit that her condition is unfortunate, and hope for a heavenly future when she might be able to understand and respond to God and to her friends? Earlier, I noted that it is not wrong that Jay and Helena lament the fact that oxygen deprivation robbed one of their daughters of potential future opportunities. This does not mean they think she is any less human, any less lovable, or that they have not come to appreciate that she is a precious gift, in spite of and sometimes because of the complications of her disability. They have done their best to help both of their daughters to flourish, each in her own way, and look forward to a future when Sunshine is able to say and do all of the things that were in her spirit all along (whether by medical and technological breakthrough this side of heaven or divine grace postresurrection).

THE GIFT OF FRIENDSHIP

Beyond theological anthropology, Reinders' principal purpose is to advocate for the value of friendship with profoundly disabled people. Because God in his triune nature is "friendly," and chooses to befriend us, so the fact that we are made in the divine image empowers us to be friends with others, especially those subject to isolation and rejection. Because creation is meaningful and purposeful, personal existence comes with a mission; a fact that is as true for profoundly disabled people as it is for us. Drawing on the insight and experience of John Vanier and the L'Arche communities, Reinders concludes that the mission of profoundly disabled people is to teach us that, irrespective of our capacities and strengths as "temporarily able-bodied," we are recipients of the gratuitous grace and charity of God. In this way, profoundly disabled people teach us to see ourselves differently; they help us discover a deeper, truer identity as people that are graced, loved, and valuable. This mission is of great import in societies such as our own, where self-worth is judged against shallow mass media ideals of the perfect body and mind, completely abstracted from the beautiful messiness of real life.

Emphasizing the importance of friendship with the profoundly disabled extends to disability as a whole. The virtue tradition insists that friendship is central to flourishing, and this is doubly true for disabled people who often need help to negotiate day-to-day life, and for whom friendship serves both practical and psychosocial needs—as it does with everyone. But this need for friendship is offset by the fact that disabled people commonly experience isolation, with studies finding that they tend to have fewer friends, report high levels of loneliness, and spend more time at home and alone than do the nondisabled.[88] Indeed, exclusion and marginalization are of the essence of what disablement means.

It is true that impairments can complicate relationships. A person with an SCI (who uses a wheelchair) can be prevented from accessing some communal spaces, and comorbid conditions as seemingly insignificant as increased tiredness can keep people away from nighttime social gatherings. Cerebral palsy can complicate oral communication, and, likewise, if no interpreter is present, deaf people can be isolated in a crowd. People with long-term mental illnesses are not only subject to people's fears and judgment, but the impact of psychosis on mood and behavior can exacerbate the difficulties.[89] People with autism spectrum disorders can have trouble interpreting social cues, and can be irritated by visual and auditory stimuli that are common in public places.[90] Intellectual disability, likewise, can cause people to interact awkwardly and inappropriately, and so diminish a person's social competence.[91] In each case, the issue is not that disabled people are unfriendly, but that their relational capacities and needs differ from the norm. The label "misfit" has been used to describe the incongruous relationships that result from a person's inability to fit within a particular social context—they are "a square peg in a round hole."[92] Building upon feminist theories of embodiment, the concept of "misfitting" highlights that the social world we inhabit is designed to "fit" majority bodies, but in so doing, it creates a misfit for certain minority bodies and minds. It emphasizes that the social problem experienced by disabled people is not the fault of their impairment, but of a social environment that needs reshaping.[93]

While disabled people are subject to the isolation that comes from misfitting, they should not be thought of as powerless. Misfitting has the potential for generative power: misfits can be agents of social transformation. Precisely because such individuals are misfits, their unique perspectives and diverse capacities and talents can stimulate resourcefulness and adaptability.[94] This logic applies with respect to large-scale social transformation—and the impact of disability advocacy and creativity on the shape of our present society is undeniable—as well as to the intimate context of personal friendships.

Meaningful, loving friendship, Aquinas tells us, entails two interconnected desires: first, the desire for the good of the beloved, and second, the desire for friendship or union with the beloved.[95] When it comes to disability, we tend to think of these goods paternalistically, as though we are doing the disabled a favor when we befriend them: that they need the goods that friendship with us can bring to them, and that the joy of intimacy is to their benefit. And so it is. But as Reinders makes clear, the gift of friendship goes both ways, and the benefits we receive are more than just lessons about grace and identity. When we have disabled friends, we earn the same goods and intimate joys of any relationship, but we can also be recipients of the good of misfitting. This is not to instrumentalize friendship—as Aristotle is guilty of doing—but to recognize that friendship is good. Disabled intimacy unmasks the tedium of the status quo and opens our eyes to the beauty of interdependency, the emotional richness that attends to vulnerability, the laughter that comes from life's absurdities, the creativity that is needed to accomplish everyday activities, and the meaning that consists in being needed and loved and in needing and loving.

Such at least is the ideal, but in the everyday world, loneliness is far too common among the disabled and nondisabled alike. There is no easy fix to "the friendship gap"—the gulf between the disabled need for friendship and present levels of loneliness.[96] Political measures, such as antidiscrimination laws, can only do so much. But it is here that the Christian church, along with other religious traditions, might make a substantive contribution. Government policy can lay the groundwork for social inclusion, but as noted earlier, religion is capable of changing hearts and minds. Christian theology can be more than mere abstraction if it teaches us to recognize the image of God in all people, and to respond to the gracious gift of divine friendship by making friends with those suffering from isolation and exclusion.

7

Disability, Sexuality, and Intimacy
Happiness under the Covers

If intimate friendships are central to the good life, then so too is sexual intimacy. The joy of sex is magnified by its contribution to loving relationships, marriage, parenting, and the whole range of meanings, values, and protections that attend to family life. The meaning of our sex lives is especially linked to ideas about beauty, bodies, and constructions of gender, and is, therefore, vital to the outworking of personal and social identity. Far from being a purely private affair, sexuality is politically significant.

That sexuality is central to flourishing is set against the fact that, for a variety of reasons, people with disabilities are often assumed to be asexual. In fact, against nondisabled expectations, many people with disabilities are having sex, although navigating their sexuality often requires them to deal with prejudice and presumption, and the barriers against developing meaningful long-term sexual relationships can be substantive.[1] In response, disability advocates have drawn on the insights of feminist and queer studies to deconstruct traditional sexual assumptions and norms, with the express purpose of sexualizing disabled people. The challenge of this deconstruction is that it has tended to reject traditional and religious norms, and so stands in opposition to Christian faith. In this context, the question that arises is whether faith, along with the tradition of virtue ethics, has anything to offer that might facilitate rather than suppress the sexual and sensual flourishing of people with disabilities. What is envisaged is a reimagining of a spirituality of sex from a disabled perspective, one that embraces the queer shapes of disabled bodies, redraws gender expectations, and opens a theological ethics of sexual play that is capable of making sex transcendently fruitful. That, at least, is my fantasy.

THE SEXUAL EXPERIENCES OF PEOPLE WITH A PHYSICAL DISABILITY—"CAN YOU HAVE SEX?"

To construct a theological ethics of sexual flourishing that embraces disabled bodies (and, therein, the diversity of all our bodies) requires, first, that we confront the assumptions and discriminatory attitudes that have thus far prevented this kind of discourse from occurring. There are multiple dimensions to sexual discrimination, the least of which often looms largest in people's minds; the biomechanical problems that result from the impact of disability upon a person's capacity for intercourse. There is an overriding curiosity about the sex life of disabled people, apparent in the all-too-often-asked question, "Can you have sex?" It is a curiosity that arises from the assumption that the answer is, "No."[2]

In fact, physical disability does not always affect the mechanics of sex, but often it does. This is perhaps nowhere more obvious than in injuries similar to my own, as spinal cord injury has depressingly negative effects on sexual capacity. The loss of sexual potency is almost always devastating, at least initially. As one young man said to me a few months after his injury, "I'm nineteen, and my sex life is screwed. It is so fucking unfair."[3]

In fact, the impact of spinal cord injury on sexual function is both better and worse than is usually imagined. For men, the injury affects the capacity to achieve erection and orgasm, and also eliminates or distorts sensation, thus undermining the physical pleasures of sex. Even so, the experience of men varies depending upon the level and extent of the injury, so much so that one cannot assume what the sexual function of any one person might be. Studies suggest that while the majority of men cannot achieve a psychogenic erection (i.e., imaginative and visual stimulation), the majority can have a reflexive erection (i.e., an automatic response to touch), especially when supported by chemical aids such as Viagra and Cialis. Likewise, around 40 percent of men with the injury can orgasm.[4] It is noteworthy that the overwhelming focus of the literature on spinal cord injury and male sexuality is on the penis; a fact that is true of online peer discussion of sexual function.[5] This is perhaps unsurprising given the phallocentric focus of a hyper-sexualized modern world, as is readily apparent in the contemporary proliferation of online pornography.[6] And we should not understate the grief that comes with the loss of genital sensation and function. Intercourse and orgasm are immensely pleasurable, and the sting of their loss never fades. Even so, SCI raises the question, "Might there be more to male sexuality than the potency of the penis?"

The sexual challenges confronting men with a spinal cord injury also arise from the impact of the injury on a person's broader motor function. At its best, the physicality of sex is an embodied dance, an intertwining play of hands, arms, legs, mouths, and genitals that results in a mutually active coming together of bodies. But SCI renders people more or less inert, and the higher the level of injury, the more passive a person becomes—at least at first glance. Orgasm may well be less of a loss to the mutuality of sex than is the forfeiture of function in arms and hands. Taken altogether, spinal cord injury does not merely impact on sexual function and pleasure, it problematizes sexual self-understanding and—as we shall see later—confronts our assumptions of masculine strength and virility.

If men are confronted with a seeming loss of potency, women with a spinal cord injury are considered doubly passive, as both female and disabled. In terms of biomechanics, women experience much of the same loss as men. Again, depending upon the level and extent of injury, studies have found that many women cannot experience psycho-genic stimulation, and less than half are able to achieve orgasm (which means, on the other hand, that almost half can). For many, interest in sexuality declines following the injury, as does the frequency of inter-course and sexual satisfaction.[7] Even so, female sexuality seems largely forgotten in the educative literature of SCI, and when women are the focus of attention, the information provided usually concentrates on pregnancy and pregnancy prevention.[8] This is sometimes considered to be the result of the fact that men outnumber women with SCI by a ratio of more than 2 to 1, but, in fact, it reflects gendered assumptions about sexuality.[9] "Women's sexual roles have been understood to be passive, and women's sexual functioning has been evaluated in terms of their ability to satisfy their partners, rather than in terms of their own pleasure."[10] At its worst, the result is that women with an SCI (as with other disabilities) are more likely than women without a disability to be subject to abuse, such as unwanted sexual touching during caregiving.[11] More broadly, the sexual pleasure of disabled women is ignored.

Men and women alike (people with SCI as well as many other disabilities) may also have to deal with the intrusions of third-party care; of needing help to get into and out of bed, go to the toilet, shower, and so on. Many of these functions are intensely intimate, but in a unidirectional way. It is the disabled person who is laid bare, whose privacy is invaded, and who has to deal with the awkwardness of third-party exposure. Personal care might even be needed in preparation for and performance of sexual activity, a fact that too readily becomes prohibitive if a carer does not believe that sexual needs are their responsibility, or the disabled person feels unable to ask for sexual help.[12]

But the sexual story of people with a physical disability is not all bad news. In one of the rarer and more interesting studies of the sexuality of women with SCI, it was observed that a process of sexual adjustment occurs following an injury.[13] Initially, women tend to set sexuality aside, focusing on other priorities, and soon thereafter, sexual experimentation proves disappointing. Unsurprisingly, women feel cheated out of sexual experiences. Over time, however—usually after many years—some women with an SCI begin to rediscover sexual pleasure and intimacy, and so experience sexual reintegration. This creative reintegration involves the regaining of control over sexual experiences, a move away from passivity to an insistence on mutual pleasure, and a broadening of sexual enjoyment beyond genital sex. As one woman observed, "It took me a long time to realize that there are other ways, that you don't have to have intercourse to have sexual feelings and get sexual arousal and be able to enjoy it."[14]

Studies of men reveal the potential for the emergence of a similar creative reawakening. Indeed, while men (and women) continue to lament the loss of sensation and orgasm, many also believe that they have learned to become better lovers. This is because SCI orients a person to focus on their partner's pleasure—to enjoy the thrill of giving sexual delight. This giving is achieved inventively; not merely by developing an expertise in oral sex, but also by learning to be creative with the disabled body. More significantly, many people gain fresh insight into the sexual potency of loving speech and actions, recognizing that foreplay is more than just the lead up to sex.

But all of this creative possibility is subject to the overriding assumption that people in a wheelchair, and more broadly anyone with a disability, cannot have sex. In her deeply moving and insightful article "Sex-Ability," Rania Abi Rafeh, who lives with diplegic cerebral palsy, describes the rejection she faced after joining the dating website OkCupid. Initially, mention of her disability resulted in numerous profile views, but no requests for dates. Deciding to remove her up-front reference to cerebral palsy, she received a number of messages from interested parties, and ended up finding someone that seemed worthy of a first date. She recalls:

> Before our date, we had chatted online and immediately hit it off, sharing our mutual love for animals, comic books, and TED Talks. As our relationship grew via text, he seemed genuine and sweet. By the time I divulged my disability to him, I felt I'd given my humor, wit, and kindness enough time to define me. I made a joke about the upside about my cerebral palsy, claiming that I was a pro at dancing the sprinkler, which he laughed at and joined in by admitting that I was probably a better dancer than he, a "white guy with two left feet."
>
> My sense of humor was the deciding factor: He wanted to meet me in person. On the day of our date, my nerves got the best of my mobility, making me wobble and stumble more than usual. I asked to hold his hand since my trembling legs couldn't keep me balanced. He obliged, but our walk felt stilted. I was an old woman he was helping across the street.
>
> "This is my first date," I told him. I still have the urge to bury my face in my hands when I think back on that moment. I must have seemed inexperienced, naïve, and desperate. But this was not a confession so much as an affirmation. By revealing my lack of dating experience, I confirmed some widespread stereotypes about disabled people—that we are sexually incompetent, asexual, or are too infantile for a mature relationship.
>
> He thought he was sparing my feelings by using my disability as a reason to reject me. But it was my nervousness about the date that had made me act the way I did. Because of it, he didn't see the real me, and it wasn't the real me he rejected. In his eyes, I wasn't a failed date, or even an autonomous human woman. I was an object of pity.[15]

Her narrative goes on to tell of other instances of prejudice and pity, but also of the joy of meeting someone who, "unlike the others, . . . chose not to see my physical particularities as unattractive, but as what made me special." Most of her experiences on OkCupid, though, were a sad reminder of sexual prejudice and stereotypes about disabled people. As another participant in a study of disabled sexuality observed, " 'My impairment itself doesn't restrict my sexual activity, what restricts my sex life now is other people's perceptions about my impairment, very definitely!' "[16] Despite the overwhelming evidence of the creative sexual potential of people with disabilities, the perception that severe disability destroys sexual function persists, and the result is that disabled people are "actively constructed as nonsexual."[17]

The problem is exacerbated for people with an intellectual disability, because sexual prejudice is mixed in with an abusive paternalism that has especially targeted disabled women. Once again, women are especially vulnerable, and are treated as if they have no control over their sexual and reproductive choices. As recently as 2014, the World Health Organization has found that women "may be forcibly sterilized or forced to terminate wanted pregnancies, based on the paternalistic justification that it is 'for their own good.' "[18] Intellectually disabled men, likewise, have been subject to chemical sterilization and even castration. And the problem is not pregnancy alone, but the nondisabled assumption that adults with intellectual disabilities are "perpetual children"—as though IQ were the equivalent of mental age—and so without the emotional resources for healthy sexuality.[19] The barriers are multifaceted:

> People with intellectual disability may find sexual expression inaccessible because of service barriers including institutionalised living, lack of privacy, lack of knowledge about what sexuality is and opportunities to express themselves. Service responses to sexual behaviors in men with intellectual disability have ranged from the instigation of aversion therapies such as lemon juice on the penis to chemical or surgical suppression of sexual drive. Care providers can block people with intellectual disability access to sex education and can unwittingly give sexual misinformation. There is a general fear that if we open the door to talking about sexuality, then people with intellectual disability will be abused or become sex offenders. Even with people

with autism, we make false assumptions that they will not be able to connect with others in deep and profound relationships.[20]

I focused on intellectual disability and agency in a previous chapter (also touching on disabled parenting), so I will not revisit those arguments here. Suffice it to say that with appropriate education and support, people with an intellectual disability are as capable as any of us of enjoying their sexual capacities and building intimate and fruitful relationships. Again, the issue is not capacity but perception and prejudice.

Taken altogether, the negative effects of this constructed asexuality upon the day-to-day sex lives of disabled people are obvious, and are exacerbated by the fact that disabled people themselves can internalize these negative attitudes.[21] This internalization is further entrenched for disabled people who are part of conservative communities—such as churches—since it may be that the options available for sexual expression will transgress normative sexual boundaries.[22]

SEXUALITY, PERSONAL IDENTITY, AND GENDER

Socially constructed asexuality does not just present a barrier to sexual experience, it also impacts upon personal identity and gender. Perhaps the most famous and sensual story of disabled sex is told in the 2012 film *The Sessions*, starring John Hawkes as polio survivor Mark O'Brien (as usual, the disabled person is played by a nondisabled actor) and Helen Hunt as sex therapist Cheryl. Contracting polio at age six, O'Brien was left almost completely paralyzed and, suffering from greatly reduced lung capacity, was forced to spend the bulk of his life lying flat in an unwieldy iron lung. The film is based on O'Brien's magazine article "On Seeing a Sex Surrogate" (1990),[23] and focuses on his efforts to lose his virginity. In the context of this chapter, it is noteworthy that the lead-up to "the sessions" with a sex therapist sees O'Brien conversing with his priest to ascertain what God might think of his sexual desires and out-of-wedlock plans. The open-minded priest responds by telling O'Brien, "In my heart, I feel God will give you a free pass on this one. Go for it."

O'Brien's autobiography, released concurrently with the film, is entitled *How I Became a Human Being: A Disabled Man's Quest for Independence* (2012). The title comes from a group therapy session that aired a scene from a documentary showing five able-bodied men laughing about how they once carried a crippled friend up a flight of stairs to a "whorehouse" [*sic*]. O'Brien recollects:

> I found it embarrassing, and I suspect that it wasn't just my shyness, but there was something wrong with the film. After the movie, a doctor talked about disability and sexuality. I forget most of what he said, but I will always remember his closing line: "You may think you'll never have sex again, but remember . . . some people do become people again."[24]

The connection here between sexuality and personhood (or rather, between forced asexuality and nonpersonhood) is stark. Our intuition is angrily to dismiss the doctor's thoughtlessness, but we should not move too quickly past the importance of sexuality for personal identity. In the years leading up to his encounters with Cheryl, O'Brien's sexual frustration colored his self-understanding:

> Even though I was in my 30s, I still felt embarrassed by my sexuality. It seemed utterly without purpose in my life, except to mortify me when I became aroused during bed baths. I would not talk to my attendants about the orgasms I had then, or about the profound shame I felt. I imagined they, too, hated me for being so excited. I wanted to be loved. I wanted to be held, caressed, and valued. But my self hatred and fear were too intense. I doubted I deserved to be loved. My frustrated sexual feelings seemed to be just another curse inflicted upon me by a cruel God.[25]

While the film *The Sessions* concentrates on O'Brien's sexual encounters, and in so doing capitulates to the penis-centric priority of contemporary society, the message of the book ties his humanity to his emerging independence, and locates his sexual development in the context of his more vital longing for intimacy. Indeed, unlike in the film, in both the magazine and the book O'Brien is relatively ambivalent about the physical experience of sex, instead prioritizing the friendship that he developed with Cheryl and other companions and girlfriends over the course of his life. Reflecting on the sessions, he notes:

> I began this essay in 1986, then set it aside until last year. In re-reading what I originally wrote, and my old journal entries from the time, I've been struck by how optimistic I was, imagining that my experience with Cheryl had changed my life.

But my life hasn't changed. I continue to be isolated, partly because of my polio, which forces me to spend five or six days a week in an iron lung, and partly because of my personality. I am low-key, withdrawn, and cerebral.

I wonder whether seeing Cheryl was worth it, not in terms of the money but in hopes raised and never fulfilled. I blame neither Cheryl nor myself for this feeling of letdown. Our culture values youth, health, and good looks, along with instant solutions. . . .

One thing I did learn was that intercourse is not an expression of male aggression, but a gentle, mutually playful experience. But has that knowledge come too late?

Where do I go from here? People have suggested several steps I could take. I could hire prostitutes, advertise in the personals, or sign up for a dating service. None of these appeal to me. Hiring a prostitute implies that I cannot be loved body and soul, just body or soul. I would be treated as a body in need of some impersonal, professional service—which is what I've always gotten, though in a different form, from nurses and attendants. Sex for the sake of sex alone has little appeal to me because it seems like a ceremony whose meaning has been forgotten.

Not everyone would agree with O'Brien's conclusion about prostitution, and charitable organizations such as Touching Base exist "to assist people with disabilities and sex workers to connect with each other, focusing on access, discrimination, human rights, legal issues and the attitudinal barriers that these two marginalised communities can face."[26] The motivation of such organizations reflects that which drove O'Brien to consult with a sex therapist; that he was disabled *and* sexual, and longed to experience the pleasures and intimacies that are an important part of "normal" human life. Even so, O'Brien reminds us that his personhood, his humanity, emerges from intimacy rather than merely from the pleasure of orgasm.

Personal identity is particularly framed by the ways in which individuals embody (and potentially reject) social constructions of gender. One of the challenges of disability is that it can make it difficult for people to embody gender in "normal" ways. Regarding masculinity, for example, even the simple act of dating can be difficult, as disabled men may struggle to meet gender role expectations, such as opening doors, hugging, initiating a kiss, and so forth.[27] More broadly, masculinity is normally bound up with notions of independence, strength, and power, but disability is conceived of as dependency, vulnerability, and impotence. This gender contradiction affects men's identities in general, and their sexual experience in particular, with the effect that they are too often rendered sexually passive.

Responses to this gender contradiction vary. Some communities of disabled men react by emphasizing normative gender assumptions, as occurs in some disabled sports. The excellent film *Murderball* (2005), which is a documentary exploring the rivalry between American and Canadian wheelchair rugby players, provides a powerful insight into the ambiguity of disabled masculinity. Wheelchair rugby is a thoroughly masculinized activity, involving pushing, crashing, falling over, and getting up. It requires aggression, violence, bravery, skill, and team bonding.[28] Just in participating, players make the statement that disability has not diminished their manly power. The sport's genius is in providing an even playing field for different types and levels of disability, and giving those with higher levels of injury a vital contribution. The documentary, though, is not so much about sport as it is about the ways in which disabled men express their masculinity through sport. And because sexual potency and masculinity are inevitably tied together, in *Murderball* sexual bravado is a central theme. On the one hand, the film describes men who are sexually active and potent lovers who are more focused on female pleasure than orgasm. At the same time, these athletes enact a hypermasculinity; "a patriarchal, heteronormative, hegemonic masculinity, with bombastic male bravado in regard to sexual conquest, homophobia, and so forth."[29] But while hypermasculinity is one way of dealing with stereotypes, another is to embrace the liberty that comes with gender contradiction. More on that later.

In respect to femininity, women may face the reverse difficulty, where sexist stereotypes are reinforced by disability prejudice, so that disabled women are presumed to be doubly dependent, vulnerable, and frail.[30] Sexism and disableism/ableism together create the danger of degendering: of disabled women being treated as neither masculine nor feminine, incapable even of the traditional women's roles as wife and mother.[31] Again, whether this degendering is considered discriminatory or liberating is a matter of perspective. But as much as embracing degendering might be a strategic response to sexual and gender discrimination, the fact remains that stereotypical assumptions about the gender capacities of people with a disability are a barrier to flourishing. Describing her experience of gender exclusion at a special high school, Riva Lehrer—an artist with spina bifida whose work includes spectacular self-portraits—says:

> Outside of "special" school, I saw the normal girls being prepared for womanhood. Early gifts of kitchen toys and playtime make up led to prom frocks and high heels. Women's studies has taught us to see the damage caused by rigid gendering. But there is a different kind of confusion and hurt caused by its absence, when it's clear that you're not being included because you've been disqualified. Disabled women must continually claim their gender in the face of active erasure. Equally, disabled boys are often deprived of routes to masculinity. Parents of disabled children get inculcated with the message that letting us enter the sexual marketplace will only cause us pain and rejection.[32]

THE BODY BEAUTIFUL

Sexuality, personal identity, and gender are intimately linked to perceptions of the body. It is not only disabled people who are confronted with the impossibility of cultural ideals of the body beautiful; everyone—including those popularly thought to be beautiful—negotiates the sharp distinction between photoshopped constructions of beauty and the reality of bodies that are inevitably "flawed." But disability makes the issue acute.

While disabled bodies come in all shapes and sizes, impairment often results in a person being perceived as sexually undesirable, even grotesque. This is readily apparent in the language associated with impaired bodies; mutilated, deformed, crippled, and so forth. The monstrous visualization of disability is most clearly on display in the history of the freak show, at which audiences stared at freaks to show the "normate" population—where normate describes the constructed bodily identity of those in power—"what they imagine themselves not to be"; to establish normal beauty over and against disabled freakishness.[33] And while freak shows today are rare, disabled people are still stared at. Once again, there is resonance between the female and disabled experience. Just as for women the male gaze can be a mechanism of domination and violence, the stare constructs the disabled person as inferior and undesirable:

If the male gaze makes the normative female a sexual spectacle, then the stare sculpts the disabled subject into a grotesque spectacle. The stare is the gaze intensified, framing her body as an icon of deviance. . . . The stare is the gesture that creates disability as an oppressive social relationship. And as every person with a visible disability knows intimately, managing, deflecting, resisting, or renouncing that stare is part of the daily business of life. . . . In a society in which appearance is the primary index of value for women (and increasingly for men), beautification practices normalize the female body and disabilities abnormalize it. Feminization prompts the gaze; disability prompts the stare. Feminization increases a woman's cultural capital; disability reduces it.[34]

The judgment that one body is beautiful or perfect and another grotesque or ugly is politically significant, since social stigma exclude the latter from status and power. This exclusion is also sexually significant or, more to the point, sexuality itself is political, since the prejudices constraining an individual's sexual citizenship—their right to take part in the sexual life of the community—are socially constructed.[35]

Unsurprisingly, disabled people are not immune from aesthetic hierarchies, sometimes preferring to date able-bodied people, or those that look less disabled.[36] Nobody is immune from internalizing normate notions of beauty and, consequently, many people struggle with their self-image. Nancy Mairs, who lived with mental illness and multiple sclerosis and wrote profoundly about her experiences, said of herself:

My shoulders droop and tiny pelvis thrusts forward as I try to balance myself upright, throwing my frame into a bony S. As a result of contractures, one shoulder is higher than the other and I carry one arm bent in front of me, the fingers curled into a claw. My left arm and leg have wasted into pipe-stems, and I try always to keep them covered. When I think about how my body must look to others, especially to men, to whom I have been trained to display myself, I feel ludicrous, even loathsome.[37]

And if disability is not considered loathsome, then it is too readily fetishized. Devotees of amputees, wheelchair users, the blind, and so forth find disability attractive (yes, disability is a "thing"). But devotee exceptionalism—the avowal that "we desire what repulses everyone else"—simply recreates the issue from the opposite direction. It takes disgust as its starting point, and then fetishizes impairment, reducing a person to their disability, "in which the absence of a limb is cast as the sum total of identity, existence, and worth."[38] Alison Kafer, struggling both with her self-image as an amputee and the desires of devotees, rejects the devotee logic (i.e., "I'm the only one not disgusted by you, so you should welcome my attention, whatever its form"), but is stimulated by the idea of disabled bodies being desirable. She asks:

> Can we desire disability, disabled bodies, without falling into the exceptionalist logic of desire and disgust that pervades devotee-ism? How can we eroticize extraordinary bodies without fetishizing impairment, without reducing human beings to spare parts and effacing the lived experience of disability?[39]

To eroticize and sexually empower disabled people, there is value in using the resources of critical and constructive methods that have served well other disempowered identities.

FEMINISM AND QUEER STUDIES

In response to the various factors that have led to the presumption of asexuality, disability scholars have drawn on the insights and methods of feminist and queer studies. The feminist insistence that the personal is political drives the logic of this chapter. Indeed, the categorizing of particular experiences as private is "a profoundly political act, often with insidious effects," since that which is deemed private is unseen and unheard of, and so cannot be changed.[40] The private/public split is also established on gender lines (female roles tend to be understood as private, and masculine roles as public), and so acts as a source of gender and sexual oppression. Thus, just as feminism begins by unmasking the female experience of patriarchy by narrating women's experiences, so have disability scholars sought to unmask experiences of sexual oppression.

There is some irony here, and the need for sensitivity, since the politics of sexuality requires the defeat of the private/public split, but one of the common experiences of people with disabilities is that they have very little sexual privacy, especially under the medical model.[41] To speak publicly about disabled sexuality is not to make a spectacle of individual sex lives, nor to satiate the curiosity of the normate population about disabled sexual function but, rather, to insist that the secrecy that has established and reinforced disabled asexuality must end. And to take a political view is to realize the importance of activism and to invite a "collective reimagining" of the sexuality of disabled people—or more to the point, of sexuality itself.[42]

Feminist theory challenges assumptions about the naturalness of gender constructions, in particular, the essentialist expectations about the female body and femininity. It achieves this by way of deconstruction, by utilizing a hermeneutic of suspicion that explores oppressive values inscribed in cultural texts, as well as a hermeneutics of creative reimagination that highlights liberating visions.[43] Likewise, in adapting the political insight of feminist theory, disability scholars unmask the various ways in which assumptions about disability and disabled bodies lead to oppression: in the context of this chapter, to an assumed asexuality that is too often an impenetrable barrier to the sexual flourishing of disabled people.

While feminist theory tends to deconstruct notions of femininity and gender, as noted earlier, the problem for people with disabilities is that they are excluded from embodying "normal" gender identities. It is precisely this exclusion, and the abnormal nature of disabled gender and sexual practices, that lends itself to the insights of queer theory. In the earlier overview of the sexual experiences of disabled people, I did not attend to the experiences of lesbian, gay, bisexual, and transgender people, even though they face the same sorts of challenges, with the double disadvantage of being excluded due to both their sexuality and disability. Gays and lesbians with disabilities are just as likely as any disabled person to be considered asexual, and so to suffer exclusion and rejection. In fact, the gay community is not always welcoming of its disabled members, and often has a preoccupation with looks and youthfulness (a "body fascism"), as well as an appetite for sex that it is assumed cannot be satisfied by disabled men.[44]

But beyond the day-to-day experiences of disabled gays and lesbians, queer theory is an embrace of abnormality, unnatural sexual desires, fluidity, ever-changing horizons, and paradoxical notions of identity and gender. Disability theorists who draw on queer theory argue that because "disabled sexuality is somehow both lack (innocence, incapacity, dysfunction) and excess (kinkiness, weirdness, perversion)," it is also queer.[45] From this perspective, the political solution to society's negation of disabled sexuality and gender is to embrace its "queer negativity," and in so doing, to shake up conceptions of what is normal regarding gender identity and sexual practice. It affirms that the way to overcome the stigmatism resulting from failure to comply with heteronormative mandates is to take ownership of the stigma, and so reject the premise that there is a "normal" gender and sexual practice. As Riva Lehrer notes of her identity as a disabled bisexual woman:

> The other glorious aspect of being bi was that I felt liberated from the unattainable standards of the female body. I was not meant to interlock with a single gender but could be part of a misty continuum. The word "queer" captures—better than any other term—the way I feel about my body.[46]

Queer theory is also relevant for heterosexual people with disabilities, since they are not treated as straight by the normate community. A parallel logic is found in "crip" activism. Like the label queer, the use of the term crippled or crip makes people wince, deliberately:

> This desire to make people wince suggests an urge to shake things up, to jolt people out of their everyday understandings of bodies and minds, of normalcy and deviance. It recognizes the common response of nondisabled people to disabled people, of the normative to the deviant—furtive yet relentless staring, aggressive questioning, and/or a turning away from difference, a refusal to see, . . . and turns it back on itself. . . . "Queer," "crip" and "cripple" are words to help forge a politics.[47]

Queer theory is appropriated by disability theorists to critique and disrupt the binary ways of thinking that are characteristic of Western conceptions of the world: male/female, active/passive, animal/human, and disabled/nondisabled.[48] Binary thinking defines one person or group against another, and fails to account for both difference and commonality. From a queer theory perspective, the boundaries that constitute disability and sexuality are disrupted. Disability itself is an open category, not only because every person might become disabled at any point in time, nor because the boundaries of disability are fuzzy (at what point does an impairment get categorized as a disability?), but because disability encompasses enormous variety (as does sexuality), which cannot be contained by stereotypes or by binary ways of thinking.[49]

The strategy employed by disability theorists drawing on feminist, queer, and crip studies is to celebrate all that is normally judged to be negative about disabled sexuality. It is to reject a phallocentric and orgasm-focused sexuality that is restricted to the missionary position, and instead value creative whole-of-body sexual experiences, including that which may be thought of as weird and perverted (e.g., sexual relationships that include personal assistants). It is to renounce masculinity as solely defined by strength and control, and femininity as passive submission, and so redefine gender and identity in fluid and open ways. It is also to insist that disabled people are sexual (that they are persons, as O'Brien reminds us), and so have the right to full sexual citizenship.

One practical result of the sexual politics of disability has been activism that has sought to provide people with disabilities with legal access to the services of sex workers. While there is a danger that advocating for the use of sex workers reinforces the idea that disabled people are unable to form "normal" sexual relationships, the intent is to facilitate sexual pleasure for people who, for a variety of reasons related to their disability, have been denied access.[50] It is noteworthy that facilitating access to commercial sex brings together two otherwise marginalized groups of people—those with a disability and sex workers—and that the intimate encounters that follow have been found to be enjoyable to both.[51] What sometimes develops is more than just intermittent paid-for sex, but longer term relationships that are friendly, intimate, and mutually enriching.[52]

The great strength of these related political theories is that they resist totalizing and closed constructions of identity, gender, and behavior that inevitably alienate people considered abnormal. This critical stance has a prophetic dimension that should resonate with Christian faith, which at its best is oriented to empower outcasts of every variety: those who are poor, powerless, marginalized, broken and so forth. It is possible to narrate the history of the church as a process of becoming the power it once resisted, and itself marginalizing outsiders, especially those it considered to be sexually deviant. It is thus understandable that feminist theory and queer theory have taken aim at the church, and it should come as no surprise if crip theory does the same. The potential weakness of these theories is that they deconstruct traditional notions of identity without establishing a basis for reconstruction. The suggestion that there is no such thing as femininity or masculinity is rejected by disabled people themselves, who insist that their disability should not undermine their status as women and men (which is not to deny alternate gender identities). Similarly, these theories have no real way of identifying good or bad sexual behavior, other than consent, which of course is the key point; constructions of "good" and "bad" are too often means of control and exclusion. But to eliminate transcendent notions of truth, goodness, and beauty is to eliminate God and to capitulate to nihilism.

BEAUTY AND DISABLED ART

In respect to beauty, new forms of art that repudiate perfectionist constructions of beauty, and instead look with fresh eyes at the aesthetic wonder of uniquely shaped, sensual, disabled bodies have a final development that has occurred in parallel with the emergence of feminist, queer, and crip theory. Of particular significance is the work of Frida Kahlo, whose art is replete with self-portraits that highlight her pain and disability, doing so beautifully. As one disabled critic noted of Kahlo's self-portraits:

> Frida, who lifts her skirt to reveal the gaping, cunt-like wound on her leg, who rips her body open to reveal her back, a broken column, her back corset with its white canvas straps framing her beautiful breasts, her body stuck with nails: but she can't be Disabled, she's Sexual.[53]

In her day, Kahlo's artwork was deliberately shocking (as is the above description). Kahlo's work is ahead of its time "in her unashamed, graphic, and performative bodily displays of disability," portraying her history of suffering, but also her beauty and sensuality.[54] Kahlo has inspired a subsequent generation of disabled artists, who invite the world to stare at their strange bodies, and in so doing, transform the gaze/stare into a spectacle of wonder:

> Many disabled artists choose to parade their abnormalities and display their spectacular bodies to shake notions of normality to the core. They solicit and reverse the gaze/stare and optimize their status as a spectacle. The spectacle, in the language of theater, refers to visual attributes and qualities that elicit wonder . . . Their agency lies in the power of self-representation and strategic, performative (in)visibility. These performative acts are shocking, often playfully so, confrontational, and revisionist.[55]

In this way, disabled artists remind us of the absurdity of the contemporary photoshopped construction of the body beautiful, and instead invite us to see the wonder of the human body in all its diversity and deformity. This is not to say that disabled bodies are always beautiful, at least in the traditional sense. For example, Riva Lehrer (whose self-portraits I mentioned earlier) labels herself as "Golem Girl," and describes being called "ugly chick" and told that "if I looked like you, I'd kill myself." Even so, she talks about an evolving relationship with her body, noting that by "looking at others and looking at myself—I have evolved and deepened my sense of connection to other human beings."[56]

One art critic describes this emergence: "'disability aesthetics' [is] a sea change affecting the history of art, which increasingly provokes a preference for disabled bodies over non-disabled ones."[57] This artistic sensibility, which appreciates the uniqueness of disabled bodies, stands in stark contrast with contemporary conceptions of flawless beauty, and the fact that disabled people are almost "everywhere stigmatised and disdained as inferior and ugly."[58] Yet if art serves a prophetic function, it has the potential to change cultural conceptions of beauty. And there is reason for hope. Contemporary advertisements, while always prone to shallow visions of beauty, are increasingly likely to display bodies that might once have been kept out of view; older, fatter, queerer, and occasionally even disabled.[59]

CRIP THEOLOGY

The content and argument of the chapter thus far seem a long way from both the virtue tradition and Christian sexual ethics. It is humbling, though, to realize that most of the work that has been done on the topic has little if anything to do with faith or virtue. More to the point, Christian sexual ethics is often seen as part of the problem that needs to be overcome, as one of the primary causes of narrowly conceived views of sexuality and gender that deny sexual citizenship to disabled people. As one disabled scholar observed:

> For those of us within disability studies, religion is not only an aca-
> demic and political dead-end, but also a personal one. Many of us and
> our loved ones have experienced discrimination within faith tradi-
> tions. Perhaps, rather than engage these traditions, it might be easier
> to leave them behind?[60]

Certainly, when it comes to sexuality, it is unsurprising that some crip scholars feel this way, since the church has rarely addressed the question of disabled sexuality, at least not positively. How then to proceed? One important approach would be to integrate the critical methods of theology with feminist/queer/crip insights for the purpose of deconstructing the sexual oppression of disabled people that is explicit and implicit in the Christian scriptures and tradition. Nancy Eiesland, Amos Yong, and others have applied their critical skills to the deconstruction (and reconstruction) of the scriptural treatment of disability in general, and there is no need for me to repeat their work here.[61] The biblical narrative is shot through with sexual encounters, injunctions, prohibitions, and imagery, but often lacks an explicit or helpful sexual ethic for contemporary discourse about the goods of sexual life. And when texts such as Song of Songs do celebrate sex and sensuality, it is with images of perfect male and female bodies, and stereotypical sexual roles: the powerful man—with his golden hair, arms like rods, body like polished ivory, legs like pillars of marble (5:10-16)—pursues his beautifully flawless lover—with her eyes like doves, lips like a scarlet ribbon, breasts like two fawns (4:1-15). There is nothing wrong with youthful beauty, and here at least is a celebration of bodies and passionate sensuality. This celebration is at least an advance on Christianity's perennial temptation toward a dualism that prioritizes the spiritual over and against the physical.[62] But it is a long way from modeling a sexuality that includes and empowers disabled people.

In respect to sexuality and theology more broadly, scholars such as Marcella Althaus-Reid and Lisa Isherwood have understood themselves as sexual theologians, and sought to develop queer theology, which takes up the struggle of queer theory against heterosexual ways of knowing, and reflects critically on the sexual constructions and ideologies of theology.

> Queer theology takes seriously the queer project of deconstructing heterosexual epistemology and presuppositions in theology, but also unveiling the different, the suppressed face of God amidst it. It is not only that theology has been traditionally obsessed with ordering sexuality but much of theology has developed forms of sexual orderings into doctrinal reflections or readings of the scriptures. As a subversive force, queer theology focuses on theological closets, in what has not been said or has been hidden. It is a theology which denounces the domestic sexual violence of theology on its dissidents.[63]

Whatever the potential critical contribution of queer theology, the notion of "a lesbigay Christ" and "queer God" is self-consciously at the margins of Christian faith—or, rather, deliberately beyond those margins.[64] My purpose in this chapter is not to take a stand for (or against) queer studies or its subsidiary queer theology. But because Christian theology has done so little work in this field, neither do I have the right to ignore the liberative efforts of the disability scholars who have led the way in understanding the sexual oppression of people with disabilities and, thereafter, advocated for change.

Although theology has thus far operated primarily as the implicit undercurrent of this chapter, the story that it tells and the critique that it makes can be understood as part of the work of a "crip theologian." The critical suspicion of crip theology would go further, identifying the various ways in which Christian beliefs and practices—which might be summarized as "sexual experience is for marrieds only"—effectively sustain and entrench the asexuality of disabled people. But that point has already been made, and the real question is whether there are resources in Christian faith for more open ways of thinking and, more importantly, for contributing something positive to the conversation.

One place to begin this constructive approach is with a disability aesthetic informed by reverence for the broken body of Jesus. The tendency in modern art to prefer disabled bodies over sterile nondisabled bodies can be connected to the line of descent in religious art that depicts Christ's suffering and defiled body.[65] The Christian faith, it seems, finds at its very center a solid basis that enables us to see splendor in and through the twisted bodily distortions of Christ's pain. When gazing/staring at the broken body of Jesus, we see not only the agape (self-giving love) of God, but are motivated by eros (passion) for the embrace of the Christ.

Of course, the body of Jesus has been pressed into the service of an asexual vision as well, as a celibate role model for celibate priests. But his story can be read differently. If we look with the eyes of the crip, we see Jesus as a man who lives on the margins, a political outcast from Rome and mainstream Judaism. He was considered by the religious leaders of his day to be, not merely unorthodox, but indecent. As they do with crips, people have wondered about his sex life: could he do it, did he want to do it, did he do it? In the scriptures and Christian tradition we learn that he was not "sexual," by which it is meant that he had no phallocentric heterosexual love affair. But we also learn that he was passionate and sensual, and overflowed with love. He had an ardent love for men, who loved him in return; imagine the intimacy at the Last Supper of the beloved disciple leaning on his breast, or the subsequent kiss of the betrayer Judas. Wherever Jesus goes he is surrounded by women, many of whom are considered deviant, and he embraces them passionately, earning the disapprobation of religious leaders as a result.[66] In all of his actions and relationships, he refuses to conform to the masculinity of his day, and lives in such a way that women and men want to be like him. No binary complementarian logic can account for his strength in weakness, his feminine masculinity, and his embodied spirituality. He faces up to the brokenness of the cross, where he is naked, distorted, and yet beautiful. And even in his resurrection he carries wounds on his hands and feet; a permanently scarred body—a disability aesthetic—becomes the symbol of divine redemption.[67]

The New Testament exemplifies Christ as the image of God (Col 1:15), drawing on the metaphor of Genesis 1:26-28. The focus of Genesis is not on the difference between the sexes, but on the common sharing in the divine image. Likewise, the humanity of Christ speaks to men and women alike—and to queers and crips. This is not to do away with masculinity and femininity altogether, but to recognize both the masculine and feminine in God (and to this end, feminist theologians have highlighted feminine characteristics of the divine as one of the key strategies for empowering women). Just as in God, masculine and feminine are not binary categories, so it is with Jesus and with women and men. We might thus distinguish between shallow and deep constructions of masculinity, where the former is the binary and socially constructed proud, aggressive, independent, sexist male, and the latter is achieved by the journey of integrating the so-called feminine and masculine within oneself.[68] This usually occurs through meaningful relationships between men and women, where a man develops empathy, tenderness, intuition, nurture, vulnerability, and so forth—all character traits modeled by Jesus, and symbolized as feminine and characteristic of women. In taking such a journey, a man is not rendered genderless, but more deeply masculine. A similar passage is possible for women, whose socialized femininity (modeled on the pretty and passive princess) is enriched by integrating the so-called masculine traits of independence, strength, decisiveness, and the like into a deeply rich and potent feminine identity.[69] This way of thinking of both masculinity and femininity makes particular sense in the context of disability, as men are forced to wrestle with their dependence, vulnerability, and weakness, but are not any less masculine as a result—in fact, there is the potential for the development of a truer and deeper masculinity. Likewise, disabled women are not doubly passive, but in their struggle to achieve independence (or, better, interdependence) they reveal themselves to be potently female.

More than just a symbol of gender integration, Jesus' life, brokenness, death, and resurrection are redemptive for people with disabilities, not least because the example of Jesus offers a way of coming to terms with one's own unique glory and brokenness. A disability aesthetic learned by gazing at Jesus (or at Frida Kahlo, whose work often incorporates Christian imagery) does not assume that disability is always beautiful (even though it may be).[70] If the image of God in which we all partake is exemplified in Christ, then that image is not one of perfect beauty, but is symbolized through wondrous, earthy fragility. A disability aesthetic sees the value of strangeness, difference, deformity, fragility, aging, and so forth. It is not opposed to beautiful bodies but has much broader tastes, and in that way, is self-accepting and also embraces the uniqueness of others.

Kafer's earlier question remains: "Can we desire disability, disabled bodies . . . can we eroticize extraordinary bodies without fetishizing impairment, without reducing human beings to spare parts and effacing the lived experience of disability?" A disability aesthetic might begin by recognizing the desirability of disabled bodies, including the broken body of Jesus, but it is not about disability per se, and it is not only for disabled people. Rather, it is about learning to see beyond the constraints of the body beautiful, to recognize that every person is extraordinary and, in their own unique way, sexy. Each person's unique desirability arises, at least in part, because we share a common humanity, and because no one is the same, and no one is required to conform to the same old boring, shallow, and socially constructed feminine or masculine straitjackets. What is true of us as individuals should also be true of the body of Christ, which is also a disabled community of love and radical diversity. And if the argument seems to be taking us away from (or beyond) sex, perhaps that is as it should be.

EMBODIED SPIRITUALITY AND VIRTUE

For all of scholarship's vital contributions to the sexuality of disabled people, the potential weakness of the various approaches to the sexual politics of disability is that they seem to reduce sex to an individual's bodily pleasure. In a recent reflection on his earlier writing on sexuality, Tom Shakespeare observed:

> Back in 1996, when my colleagues and I wrote *The Sexual Politics of Disability*, I think we made an error. By making sexuality our primary concern, we failed to understand that intimacy is perhaps an even greater priority for disabled people. Sexuality is an important form of intimacy, and modern western societies are fascinated with sexual acts and sexualised bodies. But friendship and acceptance are more fundamental than sex.[71]

I disagree that making sexuality a primary concern was an error; as I have already argued, sex is central to human life. If Shakespeare and his colleagues did err, it was in the failure to look for a deeper understanding of the nature of sexuality, one that incorporates intimacy and friendship, among other things.

While Christian sexual ethics are sometimes reduced to narrow absolutes, at its best Christian tradition can invest sexual relationships with meaning that goes beyond *mere* pleasure. There are multiple sources within the tradition to access this meaning, but the virtue tradition offers a valuable place to begin.

Admittedly, drawing on the virtue tradition at the same time as engaging with feminist, queer, and crip theory is counterintuitive. Ever since Friedrich Nietzsche, the critical tradition of philosophy has understood virtue to be the enemy of sexual liberty, nothing more than the religious will to power, control, and repression. There is no getting around the fact that Aquinas' designation of sexual sin is appalling (or at least verges on nonsensical to the modern world); among other things, he elevates virginity over marriage (unsurprising for a celibate priest), and treats homosexuality and masturbation as unnatural sexual acts that are worse than adultery and rape.[72] But the virtue tradition need not be set against sexual flourishing. As we have seen in earlier chapters, virtue theory is at its best when it explores the meanings and goals of the good life, and identifies the importance of virtue for achieving those goals.

When those in power frame the conception of the good life and the identification of virtue for (and against) those on the margins, it is inevitably oppressive insofar as it excludes those at the margins from the conversation altogether. In the absence of real participation *of* disabled people in deliberations about virtue and flourishing, religious bodies falsely arrogate to themselves the right to speak *to* and *for* disabled people—particularly when it comes to those virtues that shape sexual flourishing. Neither is the constitution of the good life entirely subjective. Rather, what it is to flourish as a human has both objective and subjective dimensions, and so is best worked out in conversation. Disabled people can thus draw on the insights of the virtue tradition and positive psychology when reflecting on what a good sex life might look like for them, but their unique experience and desires are equally significant. If we do not prioritize the voices of disabled people, then the church has nothing to contribute to their sexual flourishing.

It is important to note that while the good of sex transcends pleasure, it also includes it. Human life is richer for the joys of sexual touch and orgasm. This should be obvious but has not always been so, especially in the church. In fact, the intensity of sexual pleasure contributes to the various other goods that flow from sex. A healthy sex life, for example, contributes to the happiness and stability of a marriage, and so indirectly advances the well-being of children. While there is a hierarchy of goods, which means that a person might be prepared to sacrifice some pleasures for more important goods (hence, most people choose fidelity to their long-term partner over the short-term pleasures that might be available in an affair), this does not render the thrill of sex as meaningless. As I noted in the previous chapter, play is central to human nature, and sexual play is thus a good in and of itself.[73] Hence, a disabled person's desire to experience sexual pleasure is important, and should not be too readily dismissed or traded away. For example, before religious authorities issue a judgment on whether a disabled person might (virtuously) employ a sex worker, it should engage much more deeply than it has in articulating the virtues and goods of human sexual flourishing as such. What these goods are, and their relative relation to one another, has been greatly neglected.

The virtue tradition suggests that meaning sublates (transcends but includes) pleasure. That is to say, meaningful sex is better than purely pleasurable sex (and both together is better again). But what is the meaning of sex? In general terms, it is "to help us to flourish," and thus the virtue tradition can help to frame a sexual ethic that celebrates sexuality, is open to diverse application, and draws on notions of virtue to facilitate flourishing rather than to insist on narrow regulations.[74] Humans are self-transcendent in their pursuit of truth, goodness, and beauty, and in their relationships with others, and sexuality is one way we express that transcendence.[75] Because we live in a world that is revelatory of the sacred, graced by God, self-transcendence is spiritual, and so is sex (or at least it can be). In reaching beyond ourselves we are always discovering something of the divine. Thus, we are embodied spirits, inspirited bodies, self-transcendent through our freedom to choose to enter into relationship with each other:

> When we open to relationship through knowledge and love, we transcend what we already are. To step into relation with another is to step out of a center that holds only ourselves. We open ourselves radically, whether minimally or maximally, to come into union by knowing and loving and sometimes also by being known and being loved. Our center is now both beyond ourselves and within ourselves.[76]

As noted previously, Aquinas talks about love as having two key desires: a desire for union with the beloved, and a desire for the flourishing of the beloved. In placing sexuality within the broader context of self-transcendence and, ultimately, love, I am not suggesting that sexuality—with all of its diverse pleasures and experiences—is only about the loving commitment of marriage. But it is oriented toward love and intimacy. Further, this orientation should shape sexual ethics. Taking the logic of the virtue tradition, this means that sexual activity will be at its best when our behavior is virtuous; "without any degree of virtue, it is hard to imagine sex that is good; without growing maturity in virtue, it is difficult to imagine sex that is great."[77]

It is beyond the scope of this chapter to list the virtues—the habits of character—that are vital for good sex. From a Christian perspective, virtues are considered fruits of the Spirit, and it is readily apparent how love, joy, peace, patience, kindness, goodness, faithfulness, gentleness, and self-control (Gal 5:22) can contribute to relationships at any stage of the sexual journey. In Aquinas, the focus of sexual ethics is the contrast between the virtue of chastity and the vice of lust, and comes under the

rubric of temperance. Aquinas understands "venereal acts" (his delightful label) as being good and chaste when they are directed toward their
natural purpose, which is the generation of offspring. Lust, which is disor-
dered sexual desire, is any unruly passion to engage in sexual activities
that does not have procreation as its goal.[78] From Aquinas' perspective,
sex outside of marriage is wrong not only because it generally does not
have procreation as its goal, but because it has the potential to do harm
to any resulting offspring (in his view, women do not have the intellectual and moral capacity to raise children on their own.)[79] Further,
masturbation, homosexuality, and the use of contraception are sinful
because they are "unnatural"—they cannot contribute to the purpose of
procreation. It is noteworthy that the Catholic Church continues to hold
to Aquinas' conclusions (at least formally), but much of the Protestant
church has moved away from some of these earlier strictures, particularly
with respect to masturbation and contraception. The problem is that
Protestantism's reasons for taking these new positions are not always
clear. Why has much of the church adjusted its attitudes toward some
sexual acts and not others? Why has it come to accept that contraception
is allowable in marriage, but that intercourse outside of marriage (whether
heterosexual or homosexual) is not? Clearly, there is now widespread
appreciation that sexual pleasure itself can be a natural good, one that,
as already noted, contributes to other goods, such as friendship, intimacy,
and so on. Just as clearly—and too often forgotten—sex can be physically
and psychologically abusive, controlling, destructive, and violent, and
both individually and socially harmful. Given both these potentials, is
it possible to reconstruct chastity and lust for the sake of developing a
contemporary sexual ethic with a broader definition of what is natural
and good, while also taking seriously the reality of sexual sin?[80]

To that end, the cardinal virtue of justice can serve to outline
norms for "just sex."[81] As a virtue, justice is the habit of rendering to
each person her or his due, and is thus concerned with fairness and
equality.[82] It is a virtue that begins with personal relationships and
comes to frame the social world, and that moves from a minimalist
conception of fairness to the affirmation that all persons have the right
to flourish. In that light, at least seven principles of sexual justice can be
identified. In ascending order, sexual relationships involve (1) no unjust
harm, (2) free consent, (3) mutuality of participation and pleasure,

(4) equality of power, (5) commitment, (6) fruitfulness, and (7) social justice.[83] It is readily apparent how the Christian ideal of marriage might benefit from such principles, and function as the ultimate context for sexual flourishing. The chaste wife or husband understands that the marriage vow does much more than simply provide a license to allow them to have sex (the reason some young people marry too quickly), but orients lovers toward each other's empowerment, sexual fulfillment, and joy. But does the elevation of this ideal mean that marriage is the only acceptable framework for sexual pleasure?[84]

One question arising from this chapter is how we might apply such principles to situations such as Mark O'Brien's use of a sex therapist, or a disabled person's desire to contact Touching Base to hire a sex worker. As I have already said, sexual virtue is not something to be decided by external authorities (whether churches, parents, or carers), but by individuals as they enter into relationship with one another. But we might envisage wise discussion about disabled sexuality starting with the issue of social justice, remembering that many people with disabilities are subject to the injustice of being treated as asexual, and so excluded from sexual citizenship. In such situations, disabled people may be harmed by their exclusion (by missing out on important human experiences), given no free choice, no opportunity for mutual pleasure, rendered powerless, and unable to experience the fruits of sexual pleasure. Our dialogue partner from earlier chapters, Martha Nussbaum, also argues that a sex worker involved in such a relationship need not be understood as a victim of injustice, since sex work parallels many other types of employment that involve taking money for bodily services.[85] From that perspective, it is possible for a sex worker to be done no harm, give free consent, experience mutual pleasure, and so forth.[86] In fact, sex workers report to earning great satisfaction in helping disabled people explore their sexuality.[87] Of course, this position is not without controversy, and for good reason some feminists and most Christians are likely to take a different view.[88] Crip activists are also critical of campaigns that promote sex work for persons with disabilities, since they tend to reinforce the assumption that disabled people cannot get sex any other way.[89] Certainly, my intent is not to endorse prostitution, but to recognize that difficult conversations about sexuality must be had, and must be led by the disabled people whose sexual personhood is at stake.

While I have taken up several instances where the virtue tradition might contribute to important deliberations, there are certainly others. To take another example, while the marriage relationship allows for the fullest expression of sexual flourishing, might premarriage experimentation be of value for people dealing with biomechanical sexual complexity? If marriage is a lifelong commitment, prior sexual experiences not only enable people to enter marriage with their eyes open, but may help them to be confident that, with a modicum of creativity, sexual flourishing is possible. In my own work with people with an SCI, I have encountered people with the injury who have never married, and sexual incapacity was one of the reasons given. But that rationale, which shapes the whole of life, may have been changed by wider sexual encounters.

More substantially, if our pursuit of sexual citizenship ends at helping disabled people to access sex workers or have sex outside of marriage, then we have not achieved very much, and may have done more harm than good. Farley argues that in the long run "sexual desire without interpersonal love leads to disappointment and growing disillusionment. The other side of this conclusion is that sexuality is an expression of something beyond itself. Its power is a power for union, and its desire is a desire for intimacy."[90] Union and intimacy can and should be achieved in nonsexual relationships with family and friends, and churches should be communities where disabled people experience love. But if nonsexual relationships are all we achieve for disabled people, then we also have not achieved enough. Like the rest of us, most people with disabilities seek long-term committed relationships (marriage) and the joys and struggles of parenting, none of which are easy to accomplish if they are continually treated as asexual. The Christian community is not a dating service, and we cannot pretend that we have the solution to a disabled person's sexual struggles. But we can contribute to social environments that treat the disabled as "people," and that expect them to participate in the full gamut of a normal social life, including the expectation that they will flourish sexually.

8

Disability, Limitation, and the Positivity Myth
Sara Chesterman's Story

Virtue ethics, as with the principles of positive psychology, is ever in danger of simplification. It is a short step from asserting that the good life is achieved by attending to meaning and purpose and exercising virtues, to the positivity myth: the prevailing cultural ideology that insists that right thinking and acting automatically lead to success. This is the stuff of self-help gurus and faith and prosperity charlatans, and it assumes—wrongly—that life can be controlled. In the penultimate chapter of this book, I intend to explore virtues that relate to letting go of control. To provide that chapter a contextual narrative, what follows is another short but profoundly insightful story from the "quadriplegia and the good life" study.[1]

At twenty-four years of age, Sara Chesterman was an intelligent, outgoing, and independent young woman, studying in her third year of architecture at the University of New South Wales, and working hard developing her skills as a dancer. While holidaying in Byron Bay in January 1996, she was on someone's shoulders in the surf when she came off and landed badly in shallow water. Immediately unable to move, Sara knew she was in serious trouble. After being rescued by the surf lifesavers, she was transferred by helicopter to Princess Alexandra Hospital in Brisbane, where she learned she had broken her neck and was diagnosed as C6/7 complete quadriplegia.

She spent three months in hospital in Brisbane (and a further seven months in Sydney); despite being a long way from her home, and dealing with the normal hardship of early injury rehabilitation, she was strengthened by constant support from her family and friends. While she knew from very early on that her injury was permanent, she says,

> I always felt like I would be okay. I had bad days, but I knew I would pull through. It was when I thought about other people worrying about me that I got most upset. I remember my dad saying to me on the phone one day, "Every time you speak to me Sara, you make me feel better."

It is often forgotten that encouragement is a "two-way street." As Sara makes clear, family and friends received as much support from her as she did from them. Her friends gave her perspective and helped her to laugh, even in the darkest times (and the contribution of laughter to resilience, especially the ability to laugh at the absurdity of living with disability, should not be underestimated):

> I don't think I was all that strong, but I was surrounded by people. Like my friend who is an actor and dancer—a 6′4″ English guy with Nigerian heritage. A huge man. He came to visit me the day after my accident. He walked into the Brisbane hospital wearing electric blue hotpants, shaved purple hair, beads from his elbow down to his wrist, thigh high leather boots, and a net singlet. This is in conservative Brisbane where men just don't dress like this. He looked like he had just walked off Oxford Street in Sydney. He made me laugh. And he said to me: "Sara, you know what, I'm going to make a theatre piece and we're going to do Metamorphosis, and you're going to be the cockroach." It wasn't till ten years later when I re-read Kafka's *Metamorphosis*, and I went, yes, I am the cockroach, and I knew what he was talking about. My friend had not had an easy life; he grew up in a tough environment. And now he had a CV including working with the Royal Shakespeare Company and travelling the world with theatre companies. So if people like that surround you, they often won't deny reality. I find that strengthening.
>
> A year after the accident, my dance teacher got me to come down to a dance workshop at the Sydney dance company studios—and she got me dancing in the wheelchair. I have been surrounded by people who were going to accept me for who I was and integrate me.

The idea of metamorphosis is a noteworthy metaphor for Sara's self-understanding, and the way she tells her story has echoes of Kafka's famous novel. She describes a series of transitions in her life that were often difficult and painful, in which she was trapped with very little control but eventually managed to find ways to maintain and remold her sense of self, and so emerge to a new reality, with fresh strategies and skills for coping with the challenges of her disability.

In the initial stage, after ten months of rehabilitation, she left the hospital to live with her aunt for six months and then to a newly purchased and renovated home in Bondi, determined to continue to be the independent, busy, and accomplished person that she was before the accident. She returned to university, changing her program from architecture to fine art. She loved it, and was clearly talented, eventually earning her honors degree. Pushing a manual chair at the time (she has since transitioned to a power chair), she initially drove herself to classes, with help getting in and out of the car at either end. Although living with flatmates, she also did much of her own cooking and functioned as independently as she could. She was also invited to teach classes at university, a task she initially took to with some relish. To all outside appearances, she was coping exceptionally well, but eventually she fell apart. Recalling these events, she notes:

> I call it super cripple complex. I was being a super cripple. I was achieving everything but not really for myself. It was my way of trying to make everything okay for my parents and, I thought, for myself. . . . Really, though, it was a pattern within our family. We were always very busy—busy and achieving. That was the way I'd grown up—happiness in our family was to be busy and successful.
>
> And I was happy. I got a lot of joy from my art, and interacting with people, but I was also in complete denial of the impact it was having on my body. My body was weak, I was in a manual chair, and it was crazy what I was doing. I was teaching classes of 80 students with no experience in teaching, little support, in a manual wheelchair, a quadriplegic, for hours, and then coming home and doing my degree and cooking and on and on. I'm a high achiever. If I'm going to do something, I do it fully. And I try to do it really, really well. I'm competitive.

It took some time, but ultimately she discovered that her body could not keep up. The result:

> I completely collapsed. I could no longer push my manual chair or drive. So I couldn't get out of the house. I was just too weak to push the chair or do anything, even picking up a bottle of water to take a drink was too painful. . . . This occurred because I was trying to live

in denial of my situation. I was finding happiness through doing—through being busy.

Sarah spent six months in severe pain, physical and psychological, and her gradual healing owes much to the love and care of her partner Ben. Their relationship began at the height of her busyness; as flatmates who fell in love. Her stress, and other factors, led to a separation, but a few months after her collapse, when she was "really alone and helpless," in desperation Sara phoned Ben, and he moved back to her home and supported and loved her as she returned to better health.

Over time the couple had to work through the difficulty of differentiating Sara's need for disability care from her relationship with Ben. Vital to the task were changes in the NSW Government's funding of attendant care that enabled Sara to take control of her carer support. Indeed, Sara is now a passionate and public advocate of self-directed care, and her experience testifies to one of the central claims of this book, which is that independence is not the absence of care, but the ability to shape and direct the nature of that care. Support services (from individuals, communities, and governments) should not be understood as providing care to incompetent dependents, but as enhancing a person's agency. In Sara's case, one of the immediate impacts was that Sara's relationship with Ben could start to move beyond that between a carer and dependent, and become one between mutually supportive lovers: "We love hanging out with each other. You see a lot of couples who don't seem to enjoy each other's company, but we do, and that's very clear."

Notwithstanding her emergence from the state of collapse, Sara has since lived with continuous pain, recurrent health difficulties, tiredness, and so forth; recovery from a spinal cord injury is rarely a completed task, and life is inevitably constrained, complicated, and difficult. The collapse, though, started Sara on a journey of searching for a stillness of body and mind that, in her busyness and striving, she had not previously experienced. Meditation, spiritual practices, dance, art, massage, acupuncture: Sarah describes a number of practices that together serve a common purpose, helping her to be at peace with her body and to flow with its ups and downs:

> Anyway, I was talking about dance and meditation. I was determined when I broke up with Ben not to close down, and to keep my heart open, and for me, that was a physical sensation that then manifested

as love. And so I'd do this dance where I would just cry and cry and cry, but my determination was to keep my heart open despite the pain, I knew that Ben and I [had] a very strong connection beyond the disability. I was also painting. So I meditated for an hour and then I would use the paint—to paint the sensation in my body and then I'd put a mark on the page. I'd then look at that mark, and I'd make the feeling of that mark come into my body, and then I'd try and relate that to the sensation in my body. And then I'd make the next mark, mapping it next to the first mark and then repeat the process. This was a melting together of meditation techniques, Aikido practice, BMC (Body Mind Centring) dance and painting—a slow dance with the page as my partner. I'd do this process for three hours, and I'd come out of it in less pain than when I went in. I had discovered a way of doing something without further contributing to my pain.

Here, Sara is utilizing a variety of spiritual and meditative practices to help her be at peace with her body's pain and loss. Rather than accede to the dictates of the positivity myth and fight to overcome the constraints of her disability—an approach she has discovered does not work—Sara has found ways to let go of the need for control. Her insight is profound:

One thing that has really helped me is going to Aikido (a Japanese martial art). My teacher is Sensei Ken McLean. He teaches Ki (chi when translated into Chinese) cultivation classes and what you're working with is your own Ki, or energy; feeling a connection to something greater than yourself—the universe of energy. You also learn how to interact with other people, and how to notice other people's energy and to work with your own energy . . . it's very hard to explain. I'm in a manual chair, so, of course, I can't move much. But I've done a lot of dancing before, where I was the only person in the wheelchair, so it wasn't new for me to interpret the movement and do it from the chair. Aikido is amazingly physical, and it's beautiful to watch. The Ki cultivation classes are more static—sitting meditation, slow-moving meditation, deep breathing—ways of cultivating Ki. These classes have been incredibly useful, helping me to stay present and centred in everyday life.

Interviewer: And that contributes to your well-being, to your happiness? In what way?

Absolutely. For example, when I'm trying to get somewhere fast, and [with] a carer who is new, or not doing things quite like I want them done, I struggle, thinking, "I could do it so much better." (Remember

I am "super cripple"). And then I remember my Aikido, and it helps me not to push, but to stay present and centred. It's amazing. You know what it's like. You're watching someone do something; it's frustrating, and it's making you physically tense. But then I realize, okay I'm in a rush, but I'm going to remain centred. When I stay in my centre and practise directing my Ki, then I use my body and mind more effectively to achieve what I am trying to achieve. For example, when I am rushing and interacting with my carer, if I remember to use the Ki principles I have learned in class, then I find that my body relaxes, my racing thoughts subside a bit, my voice relaxes, and often my carer relaxes as well. And even though things may not get done that much faster, it doesn't matter, because everyone is that much happier and I am not putting my body through unnecessary stress and continuing the pain cycle.

In 2008 Sara suffered a health scare related to long-term use of a prescription medicine; she experienced repeated episodes of dysreflexia and lost 12 kg (roughly 26 lbs). But in the process of recovering, she was surprised to discover she was pregnant. For obvious reasons, pregnancy was a challenge, and she spent her final two months under supervision in hospital. But in giving birth, she discovered some of the advantages of having a spinal cord injury:

I had to have the epidural to control the dysreflexia. But I was having a great time. I really was. I already knew the sensation of not being able to feel or move my legs, and as I had spent so long in the hospital, I felt I was well prepared to negotiate with staff during the birth. So, the whole process was a lot less scary than it could have been.

In motherhood Sara has flourished, notwithstanding the challenge of negotiating the need to provide care while being be cared for:

I've absolutely loved it, and it's something that feels like it comes to me naturally. You know my mother always called me "Mother Sara" when I was little because I just loved little kids. . . . And Ben is similar; he's one of those kid-magnets. I have been very thankful for the meditation and Aikido. The biggest challenge has been negotiating with other people to help me—having to have an intermediary (the carers and Ben) to do a lot of the physical stuff. The key has been maintaining a strong relationship and bond with Jake, despite the many hands and personalities that came in to support the physical care of him.

WHAT DO WE LEARN FROM SARA'S STORY?

The measures of resilience and psychological health used to survey people that have experienced spinal cord injury are "subjective well-being," "life satisfaction," and the like, but these subjective assessments simply cannot capture the extent to which resilience is a journey that very often has little to do with subjective happiness—however measured—but is more to do with acceptance, letting go of the past, letting go of control, and then taking it back where you can. Sara uses Kafka's metaphor of metamorphosis to speak of the personal trans-formations that were forced upon her, and through which she adapted and changed—and continues to do so.

It is also the case that much of the literature focuses on the need for a person to gain "a locus of control." And it's certainly the case that Sara benefited from being given agency over her attendant care services. At the same time, Sara's story is a reminder that life's journey cannot be controlled; that sometimes, all one can do is let go and flow with its ups and downs. In Sara's case, there was the need to bring her mind and body into harmony; to learn the rhythm of her body and accept its pains and limitations. For her, spiritual practices have been central to this learning—dance, art, meditation, Aikido, massage, and so on—a merging of practices that she has used to find peace.

Happiness is not simply a product of an individual psychological capacity. In fact, Sara's belief in her own capacity was originally part of the problem; she tried too hard to be independent and accomplished. After the resulting collapse, she started to rely on others. The love and care of family and friends—as has been identified in almost every study of resilience and spinal cord injury—is vital. But her story also hints at the insights of the social model of disability. Sara's relationship with her partner benefited substantially from changes to governmental policy that tied the provision of care services to the agency of the person with a disability. Without such policy changes, it's entirely possible that Sara would not be as well-rounded as she is today. Sara's story thus makes it clear that the social model of disability and the virtue tradition go hand in hand in the construction of the good life for the kind of creatures we are: independent moral agents who depend on one another to flourish.

What can we say about Sara's happiness? Sara would never have chosen to incur a spinal cord injury and would go back in time if she could (or take a cure tomorrow). Even so, her experiences have provided her with insights into living well that she may never have discovered otherwise. And even without drawing on formal empirical measures, we can speak of her flourishing in terms similar to that set out by the virtue tradition. Although living with ongoing pain and physical limitations, she is a woman of deep spirituality and character, who knows what it is to love deeply and give of herself to her husband and child, and to others encouraged by her spirit.

9

Disability, Grace, and the Virtue of Letting Go of Control
Wild and Unruly Currents

One of the central emphases of this book is the importance of individual moral agency—the right and capacity of every person to control the shape of their own future. Without relenting on that emphasis, the fallacy of the West is that our environment can be mastered. But if disability teaches us anything, it is that life cannot be controlled. Paradoxically, our very selves, our bodies, are especially out of our control. Our bodies, "leaky messy things" that they are, confront us with our limits.[1] These limits are clearly revealed in Sara's narrative, and it is her experience and intuition that helped me to see that flourishing depends on opening ourselves to the out-of-controlledness of life, on learning to find peace in the flow of its wild and unruly currents. To that end, there is value in reclaiming the forgotten and often maligned virtue of humility, and relating that virtue to pride, anger, and forgiveness.

HUMILITY

The first step in letting go of control is learning the virtue of humility. At the time of my injury, I was an (almost) forty-year-old man proud of my capacity and success, a tall, blonde, and lean husband, father, published scholar, and active sportsman with every reason to feel in control of my life. But pride can be undone in an instant, as it was with me.

My confrontation with humility began with personal care. I was in and out of consciousness for the first couple of weeks after the accident, and it was only when things stabilized that I began to pay attention to what was being done for me and to me. I vividly remember the first time I realized that, having no control of my bowels, I was excreting in bed. When the smell brought the nurse's attention, he rolled me over and carefully wiped the mess off my bottom and groin. Not since infancy had I experienced another person caring for this part of my body, only now the experience was occurring with cognizance and awareness. It is hard to describe the realization, not only that you no longer have control of something as basic as bladder and bowel, but that nurses or carers would ever after be required to clean your private parts. I recall, just as vividly, the first time I had a catheter change, which involved a female nurse holding my penis and inserting a tube. It is a clarifying experience to realize that the body you once thought sexy meant nothing to nurses for whom dealing with your penis was just another procedure. In the years that have followed, even outside of my daily care, there have been times I have needed to ask passersby for help getting in and out of bathrooms. Once I had to ask three different strangers for assistance with a stuck catheter bag before finding someone willing; the first two having stared at me like I was a pervert before scurrying away. I have had workmates stick their hands down my pants to help fix a leak (and yes, when this happens, everything is on show). Twice I have traveled on a train after my bowels had given way, stinking so badly that people walked into the carriage, glanced my way, and immediately turned heel and headed back out.[2]

Incontinence is what separates infants from "big boys and girls," and to piss one's pants is humiliating.[3] Marcy Epstein, a Jewish scholar who writes from the experience of living in the in-between world of incomplete spinal cord injury (she can walk with a cane, but her sometimes hidden disability greatly complicates her life), recalls an experience similar to my own when, after soiling herself and calling for help, she was struck by the humility and solicitude of the carer, who taught her that "the taking of urine and feces from another person can be a holy act." And what she learned from the sanctification of this cleansing (to paraphrase her description) was of her need to "transform humiliation into humbleness."[4] She observes:

> Feeling humiliated is not an entirely horrible or isolated event for me. It's good to get over ourselves. For everything I've lost that I've loved,

there's another thing I'm glad to get rid of. Plus there are probably a few folks out there who think I have needed to come down a peg or two. I appear as a strong-willed and privileged person, a thin veneer that covers my sensitive, nearly dogfish pack mentality. . . . One could say I both lack and embody humility. Perhaps humiliation and humbleness both relate to humility, the former in the suffering and the latter in serenity. My ISCI has inspired humility in me.

. . .

There's a whole realm of disability that I am somewhat fearful to inhabit. But I am also so glad to be part of it. If I am mortified in this contested territory of experience and identity, it is only because I am truly alive and made aware of the subtler differences between life and death. The horizon between this state and the next is ever moving forward before me, and I know just enough to see the value of our humility. I keep thinking of us people with spinal cord injuries as people who have moved ahead. Literally, we all have our heads. We are useful. We have the ability to speak to the most magnificent and most small of themes: losing and finding, movement and stillness. In humility we are carrying ourselves, carrying others, having ourselves carried through this mortal expanse.[5]

Her description provides a beautiful interplay between humiliation and humility, suffering and serenity, carrying and being carried. Humility is brought to the fore for disability in more than just the messiness of incontinence (although incontinence is a potent symbol). It emerges in bodies that do not look and behave in ideal ways, in the need for support that goes beyond the norm, in social situations and behaviors that stand out and that are sometimes uncomfortable and embarrassing. Epstein, as with Chesterman in our previous chapter, suggests that the only way to respond is to let go and be at peace with one's vulnerability, its rhythm and graces. This mirrors, but I think also deepens, traditional constructions of the virtue of humility.

In earlier chapters I noted that humility was the central Christian virtue, embodied most fully in Christ who "made himself nothing . . . and humbled himself even to death on a cross" (paraphrase of Phil 2:6-8). In this light, in his *Summa*, Aquinas does less with humility than might be expected, perhaps too influenced by Aristotle,[6] for whom the pinnacle of virtue was to be great-souled (*megalopsychos*, a person of great virtue who does great things), and in the light of which, the virtue of humility rates no mention.[7] Aquinas, structuring his account of the virtues according to Aristotle, treats humility late in his list and subsumed under the cardinal virtue of temperance (the virtue of temperance moderates the passions for the good of reason). In so doing, he places humility within the rubric of self-control.[8] For him, humility is chiefly about reverence to God, from which flows our humility to our neighbors and every human creature, for God's sake.[9] In this comparison, next to God's goodness we are vile, lowly, and abject, mere dust and ashes (Gen 18:27). And even though Aquinas attends to it too late and too briefly, he nevertheless insists that humility is foundational to spirituality. He says that "almost the whole of Christian teaching is humility," and notes that it grounds submission and opens a person to the influx of divine grace, paving the way for the gifts of faith, hope, and love.[10] Humility requires one to be truthful about oneself, and is located in the mean between thinking too highly of oneself (pride) and too lowly (false humility). And because humility entails honest self-understanding and recognizes our reliance on God and others, it is central to our social relationships, and so informs political and social life, our willingness to submit to authority and obey the law.

It is noteworthy that MacIntyre, whose argument has been central to this book throughout, makes no specific mention of the virtue of humility in *Dependent Rational Animals*. One might imagine that his account of the virtues of acknowledged dependence would reference humility, especially because he emphasizes the fact that all of our powers and abilities are a gift, and that any virtues we possess have been learned from others; that once we were utterly dependent on our parents and communities, and that anything we achieve thereafter depends upon what we receive from our teachers and the traditions in which we are embedded.[11] No doubt MacIntyre, like Aquinas, has taken his lead from Aristotle, and at the least, his description of the virtues of acknowledged dependence values the gifts and abilities of others, both God and neighbor, and leads to gratitude and self-giving. But he does not take this insight far enough, perhaps because his focus is on the virtues of caregiving, and he fails to pay substantive attention to the humility that goes with being the one who is disabled and receiving care.

For both Aquinas and MacIntyre, and for positive psychologists, the emphasis of virtue is generally on self-control, where the habits of virtue steer the passions toward their proper ends. The virtue of humility (when and if we think of it) is understood the same way, as the habit that controls how we think of ourselves in relation to God and others. The experience of disability, however, is a reminder that life does not always allow such control.[12] I imagine that Aquinas would readily concede the point, although he might also respond that our inevitable loss of self-control is vice (or sin). But rather than understand humility within the rubric of temperance and success, might we see it as the willingness to let go of control? Positive psychology takes a dualistic view of the matter, where a person either has "a locus of control" or feels himself to be "out of control." But Epstein and Chesterman envisage a third option, and that is to have the humility to let go of control, or better, to hold it loosely. It is to realize that control is only ever partial and limited, and so to be at peace with the limits of virtue and achievement.

Understood this way, humility is about vulnerability. To be vulnerable goes hand in hand with what it is to be a creature of the earth, and to face one's vulnerability is not to capitulate to weakness but, on the contrary, to have the courage to accept that life is risky. It means that I take the train into the college where I work, knowing that I have experienced incontinence in the past and might again today. But when I allow myself to be vulnerable in this way, I refuse to be shamed if the worst happens. And my irregular incontinence is nothing next to the countless ways in which people with disabilities confront their vulnerability on a day-to-day basis.

To exercise the virtue of humility is to move toward authenticity, which begins with honest self-evaluation. We can speak of authenticity in two ways. At its simplest, to be authentic is to be honest with oneself about one's strengths and weaknesses, capacities and dependencies, virtues and vices, and thereafter refuse to pretend (at least to oneself, although it may still be necessary to wear a mask around others) that one is anything other than what one in fact is. Moral authenticity goes one step further. It aims for self-transcendence, since honest self-evaluation includes judgments of value about the good and the bad, the true and the false, the strong and the weak, and intends to do something about it.[13] I make this point with some reservation, since dominant power structures too often frame judgments about what is bad, false, and sinful. But the issue is not sin per se, but that vice undermines flourishing, which creates a particular dilemma in the context of discrimination. Indeed, "Something grim emerges when one tries to work with a *eudaimonistic* moral theory while examining oppression, for one centers the importance of flourishing and then confronts the terrible fact of its distortions or absence under conditions of oppression."[14] Oppression can distort the moral self, preventing the development of certain virtues that facilitate flourishing. In the context of feminism, for example, oppression can generate traits such as low self-esteem, misplaced gratitude, fear of standing out, obsequiousness, and so on, all of which make it more difficult to engage in the political action needed for one's own liberation.[15] Facing up to the fact that moral damage may well have been done to people with disabilities is not to blame them if they fail to flourish as they might, but to recognize the ultimate evil of oppression, and acknowledge the need for personal transformation.[16] The virtue of humility provides a means for individuals to come to terms with their moral brokenness, to look to change what can be changed, and to seek help, if need be, in doing so. For this reason, in theological parlance, we might think of humility as giving in to grace.

In Christian theological tradition, grace is the interior dimension of the love of God at work in the life of the individual.[17] It is "the love of God poured into our hearts through the Holy Spirit" (Rom 5:5) that heals and transforms a person so that she might be free from the captivity and distortion of sin. The tradition has long debated the relationship between grace and our capacity to do the good. The reformers concluded that human nature was utterly corrupt and so, without grace, incapable of any good. Aquinas and the subsequent Catholic tradition distinguished between the good of grace and nature, asserting that God gives humanity the natural capacity to move toward the good, but that due to the problem of sin, a person needs supernatural grace to achieve the meritorious good of a supernatural virtue that accomplishes salvation.[18] But if we leave the question of salvation to church theologians, might we also draw on the notion of grace to describe the healing and peace that come from the letting go, the vulnerability and authenticity, that is at the heart of humility? To let go of the need for control is to move from humiliation to humility, and so to open oneself to the healing and peace that are the essence of grace—even the peace that comes with facing the worst life has to give (ultimately, death), and discovering the truth of the psalmist, "Yea, though I walk through the valley of the shadow of death, I will fear no evil: for thou art with me; thy rod and thy staff they comfort me" (Ps 23:4, KJV). Sara Chesterman, similarly, found a peace that might be labeled grace in the spiritual and meditative practices that enabled her to accept the limitations of her disability.

The danger of advocating the virtue of humility in the context of disability is that it works to entrench the status quo, as is apparent in Aquinas' assertion that humility supports submission to authorities. But the virtue of humility is even more important for those in power, and in this light, disabled people have every right to expect to find humility in others. I mentioned earlier Epstein's observation of the humility that went with the intimacies of caregiving, but it is a virtue less often encountered in the myriad interactions of disabled people with the professional experts who oversee their health care and other needs. It goes without saying, for example, that patients must trust in the expertise of clinicians, but as feminists have noted in the context of reproductive care, power dynamics in patient-physician relationships can inhibit women's (and disabled people's) freedom.[19] The issue is not only that clinicians need the humility to recognize that their expertise has its limits and that they are fallible, but also that disabled people are the experts on their own bodies and lives. Medical treatment is always a collaboration between professionals and people with impairments, even if this is not always acknowledged.[20] Reflecting on a thirty-year career in neurology working with people with spina bifida, a doctor describes what he has learned about the attitude he needs to embody with his patients:

> I find that I have progressed from ignorance to paternalism through arrogance to a new humility. I have become more tolerant, perhaps more compassionate, less judgmental, somewhat wiser, more confused. I am still learning how deep my own biases run, and how little I really know about the lives of those with disabilities. I no longer know the ethically correct answer to the specific questions posed by the patients' problems.

It is the willingness to acknowledge how little one really knows, and accept the consequent confusion and ambiguity that evidences the letting go of humility for those in positions of power. Of course, the exercise of virtue demands wisdom. A patient is unlikely to trust a surgeon who, trying to be humble, embraces ambiguity and confusion before a major operation. The virtue of humility does not eliminate the need for expertise, but it places that expertise in a context that appreciates that it is the disabled person herself (as with any patient) that has ultimate responsibility for the medical interventions that shape her life.

Beyond medical care, paternalism—even more than outright discrimination—is the primary target of the social model of disability:

> Paternalism lies at the center of the oppression of people with disabilities. Paternalism starts with the notion of superiority: We must and can take control of these "subjects" in spite of themselves, in spite of their individual will, or culture and tradition, or their sovereignty. The savages need to be civilized (for their own good). The cripples need to be cared for (for their own good). The pagans need to be saved (for their own good). Paternalism is often subtle in that it casts the oppressor as benign, as protector.[21]

Paternalism arises in the presumption of superiority, and humility is its antidote. And if we endorse the humility of individual disabled people and their carers, and insist upon the humility of experts, we can also look for humility as a social and political virtue. It is manifest, for example, when politicians decide to listen to the disabled voice, and when funding programs—such as Australia's recent National Disability Insurance Scheme—are implemented in such a way that people with disabilities are not told what support they need, but are given choice and control over the services they receive.[22] The paradox of humility is that when it is shared, it is both letting go of control and handing it over, which simultaneously releases and empowers and so facilitates flourishing.

PRIDE

Incontinence is a symbol of humiliation and shame. It marks a person as the ultimate outsider, disgusting, unclean, pitiable. It is one thing to advance a move from humiliation to humility, but something more is needed to empower people to flourish, namely pride:

> At the jagged edge where self-hatred meet[s] pride lies an essential question: how do we construct and reconstruct self-love in the

face of the corrosive dehumanization and abusiveness oppression inflicts? How do we sift our dramatic histories for what we can celebrate and be proud of, the nuggets of inspiration, affirmation, self-respect? When can a derogatory term be repurposed into a vehicle of self-affirmation, and when does the stench of its history prove too intolerable?[23]

Disability pride takes shame and imagines a new future, where stories of alienation, discrimination, and humiliation become narratives of justice, power, and community formation.[24] In doing so, it learns especially from the pride of feminism. Consider, for example, the Blood Brigade—the Bloodsisters—who take an eternity of the shame, shunning, and uncleanness of menstruation and turn it into a symbol of feisty rage and pride; recognizing that the personal is political, and that messy bodies can be celebrated as symbols of power.[25]

In Christian tradition, however, pride is considered to be a sin. Augustine thought pride the cardinal sin, so that fallen Angels were

> delighted with their own power, as though they were their own good. Thus have they fallen away from that supreme good which is common to all, which brings felicity, and they have devoted themselves to their own ends. They have chosen pride in their own elevation in exchange for the true exaltation of eternity; empty cleverness in exchange for the certainty of truth; the spirit of faction instead of unity and love; and so they have become arrogant, deceitful, and envious.[26]

Aquinas, likewise, holds that pride stands over and above other vices. It is the immoderate and unreasonable elevation of our own excellence, without the acknowledgment that everything we have comes from God and others.[27] For him, pride is the arrogant and false claim that we are "self-made" people.[28] It is opposed to humility and results in self-interested action, since it is an inordinate desire for preeminence, and so ultimately leads to rebellion (as is symbolized in the original rebellion of Adam and Eve).[29]

I noted earlier that humility is a virtue that goes unmentioned in Aristotle, who elevated the *megalopsychos*, the great-souled man whose virtuous character makes him worthy of great things. Not only is he worthy of greatness, but he knows himself to be so, and thus deserves and claims honor.[30] It is readily apparent why subsequent interpreters were suspicious of this account, and why Aquinas did very little with it.

MacIntyre, for example, finds the *megalopsychos* appalling, because "the great-souled man's characteristic attitude requires a society of superiors and inferiors in which he can exhibit his particular brand of condescension. He is essentially a member of a society of unequals. In such a society he is self-sufficient and independent."[31] Note, though, that the problem is not that the *megalopsychos* thinks too highly of himself, since he judges his own virtue truthfully, but that he fails to acknowledge his dependency, taking pleasure in his service to others, but no pleasure in receiving.

Aristotle could never imagine the great-souled man as disabled, since disabled people lack the capacities that Aristotle thinks are the prerequisite to greatness, and are too often on the receiving end of other people's generosity. But if we take away the assumption of social superiority, and appreciate that greatness itself is a gift so that there is no shame in receiving, the notion of the *megalopsychos* can speak to what we mean by disability pride, although it might be better to reverse the equation. The great souls of people with disabilities can speak to what the *megalopsychos* is all about. To celebrate disability pride is not to dispense with humility, but to recognize the great souls of disabled people, and to insist that they deserve honor.

Disability pride mirrors and sometimes draws on the practices of other liberationist movements: indigenous pride in colonized nations, black pride in nations with a history of slavery and hate that continues into the present, and feminist and queer pride in the context of universal discrimination against women and diverse genders and sexualities. Disability pride stands as both an ally and an occasional antagonist of these movements, since disabled people have been marginalized by almost everyone at one time or another. Disability pride is about individual capacity, but it is also about community action, and so is inherently political.

It is best left to others with more right than I to describe the history, practices, and spirit of disabled activism. As I readily admitted from the outset, I am something of an interloper in the field. I am a white, middle-class, well-educated, Western, man who comes to disability relatively late in life—and without giving up these other privileges—so I have little right to speak of dehumanizing marginalization.

And yet. At my lowest point, when loss and humiliation had shattered my pretense, I took up Paul Longmore's *Why I Burned My*

Book and Other Essays on Disability, and felt the hints of a welcome, an invitation to join a community that had previously been invisible to me. I discovered stories of great-souled people, individuals who had experienced shame and exclusion, and transformed their experiences into stories of power and pride, and with those stories went on and changed the world. These were people to be proud of, and in learning that I could join them (not as a champion but as a nobody just doing my best to get through the day), the pride that gradually arose in me changed the way I thought about my spinal cord injury. Rather than continuing to lament what I had lost, or bide my time waiting for a cure, disability became something I could embrace. Disability pride is an identity. "Like homosexuals [*sic*] in the early 1970s, many disabled people are rejecting the 'stigma' that there is something sad or to be ashamed of in their condition. They are taking pride in their identity as disabled people, parading it instead of closeting it."[32] Disabled identity is fluid, with ever-changing horizons.[33] And like flourishing, it is storied; "the truth about stories is that's all we are."[34] It is in our stories that we can take experiences of loss, humiliation, and shame and infuse them with the meaning and political power that pride offers.

Once again, care is needed, because disability pride is easily confused with inspiration porn. The latter is an expression of able-bodied pity, assuming that disabled people are praiseworthy for doing nothing more than what any person does to make it through the day. Disability pride does not arise from the fact that a person in a wheelchair has the "courage" to get out of the house and go to work or do the shopping. That is nothing more than the choice to live, which is not really a choice at all. Rather, pride emerges from the fact that a person has the courage to resist the prejudice that thinks her getting out and about is an amazing accomplishment. And that pride is not just an individual emotion, but a collective empowerment.

The Positivity Myth

Disability pride is sometimes contrasted with the general logic of virtue, and for good reason. Critics take aim at the use of stories of people with impairments—such as "Superman" Christopher Reeve and one-armed surfer Bethany Hamilton—to show how individuals exercising positive virtues rise above their disability. Too often, "disability appears as an individual physical problem that can be best overcome (and should be overcome) through strength of character and adherence to an established set of community values."[35] These stories tend to depoliticize disability, setting aside vital discussions of social and political responsibility for disablement, and blaming people who do not "overcome" their disability for their lack of character and failure.

The positivity myth is a prevailing cultural attitude that draws on the arguments of positive psychology (and shallow readings of virtue theory) to insist that a positive attitude (or virtue) is the certain pathway to achievement. The dark side of this myth has been made clear to me in the countless inspirational stories of people with an SCI, usually sent to me by well-meaning friends looking to provide encouragement. The stories follow a predictable two-part pattern; first showing the horror of a disabling accident, and second, elevating a person's inspirational recovery and their refusal to give in to disability.

Consider the example of a *60 Minutes* report on Curtis Landers.[36] Curtis is a fifteen-year-old boy who injured his third and fourth cervical vertebrae while playing rugby league. While at the time the story was aired it was still too early to know the full extent of his recovery, the program documented his notable improvement. Curtis had been able to regain function in his arms, fingers, and legs. The program rightly celebrated the rapidity and extent of his recovery, with the reporter claiming that doctors had originally asserted that Curtis would never walk again, but that "in his mind, it was never a matter of if, but when." As is typical in these stories, Curtis was asked, "Was there ever a moment, in all honesty, when you thought 'I will never walk again'?" He gave the expected response (although with some reluctance), "Not really, I was planning to play [football] this season again, so walking wasn't a worry." This exchange was followed by video of Curtis at work in the gym, taking tentative steps, while John Newman and Alex Clare's inspirational song, "Not Giving in," played in the background. The report ended with Curtis stepping out of his wheelchair as he left the hospital.

Of course, Curtis' recovery is wonderful news, and we should celebrate it. The problem is not Curtis, but that the story about him was framed to perpetuate the positivity myth; that if a person has faith in himself and never gives up, then nothing is impossible—including overcoming an SCI. In fact, however, positive thinking has very little to do with recovery from an SCI. When a person incurs such an injury, the long-term damage to the neurological system is indeterminate, and it takes months and years to find out the extent of the damage caused by the initial trauma. The nature, location, and extent of the injury (especially whether it is complete or incomplete) is the principal determinant of neurological recovery.[37] In Curtis' case, he regained movement in his arms and legs within a week of his accident and was walking within months. This means that his spinal cord had incurred less damage than his doctor initially thought when they (apparently) suggested that he would never walk again. Curtis' wonderful recovery had little to do with his expectation, faith, or positivity, nor is it a product of his "defying his doctors." These attitudes might well have helped him deal with the emotional trauma of the injury. But mostly, he was fortunate. If the damage to his neurological system had been more severe, no amount of positive thinking would have kept him out of a wheelchair.

Responding to the story, quadriplegic Paul Mariager observed:

> It makes out that walking is a panacea for happiness. It's everything. It's treated like an option, as though if you don't recover you don't have will power. It's unfair, it's untrue and it's dangerous. These kind of hero worship stories make out that you're either a god, or you're a quad.[38]

Given my personal focus on SCI at the time of the *60 Minutes* report, I had not previously thought about the issue from the perspective of other types of disability. But a few days after the Curtis Landis story, another television station reported on the achievement of Lia Sintras.[39] The story was introduced as follows: "Now for a courageous teenager overcoming huge physical disabilities to inspire others to make every step count." And the story that subsequently emerged was impressive. Lia was born with cerebral palsy and has lived with a wheelchair all of her life. Her mother noted that at birth Lia's diagnosis was grim, with the family told that she would never walk nor be able to communicate with other kids. With good reason "Mum" proudly stated that "she proved them wrong." The story went on to describe Lia's fierce determination to succeed, evidenced when she accomplished the seemingly impossible goal of walking into the graduation ceremony when she completed her schooling. It was no small victory, achieved after 574 hours of training. To top it off, Lia shared her story as part of Steptember, a charity that raises funds to support people living with cerebral palsy. The report finished by summarizing the lesson we are meant to learn from Lia's narrative: "It's mind over matter. We are often really self-limiting, and she just pushed through it."

Again, let me be clear. I have nothing but admiration for Lia and her family. Hers is a story that should be reported. But it is also about time we faced up to the dark side of the positivity myth. The way that the contemporary media reports stories of triumphing over disability impacts upon those who do not manage to walk again, and who live permanently with the challenge of disability. The issue is not only the nonsensical fear of wheelchairs and the general public's obsession with walking (for many with disabilities, the wheelchair provides freedom). It is that disability cannot be thought away; mind does not trump matter but is itself an embodied reality.

The positive thinking myth has attained the status of being the central ideology of global culture's civil faith. It is believed and propagated with religious conviction, and as such, is unquestioned and unquestionable. It has its parallel in the Christian prosperity and faith healing movement. Both place too much emphasis on individual faith. Both focus on those who experience healing, ignoring and implicitly denigrating those who do not. And both fail to recognize that suffering and disability are inevitable facts of human life, not something that can be believed away.

The positivity myth has found its way into every sector of society. It is the standard fodder of the self-help industry, shapes political ideologies, and informs our cultural values; as such, it is celebrated in every medium of popular culture (television, film, music, and the like). But when the winner of the TV show *The Voice* looks back on her success and opines that "if you believe in yourself, your dream will come true," it is conveniently forgotten that this did not prove true for the other contestants.

In its application to disability, the positivity myth is an attempt to tame and control the bodies and minds of people whose lives we do not understand, and so fear. Cultural discourse and media celebrate only those who are able to transform themselves into their image—their normality—free from disability. We all want to believe that unyielding faith will cure cancer, determined effort will overcome the limits of cerebral palsy, and strength of will can enable the quadriplegic to walk again, because we cannot imagine that it is possible to live well in the midst of suffering, sickness, and disability. Yet, in praising individuals who "succeed" we damn those who do not (at least according to the normative measure of success, which is to live without, or at least beyond, impairment), and we conveniently forget that disability is a social problem that requires a political response and social transformation, and that responsibility for such transformation rests not on the individual "victim," but on our shared political will.

Disability pride, then, is radically different to the typical construction of personal pride—to the positivity myth's "believe in yourself." Many people with an acquired injury such as SCI will adopt the latter and not the former, because their self-understanding was formed prior to their injury, and depending on their subsequent experiences, it may or may not undergo substantive alteration. In my research into the flourishing of people with quadriplegia, it became apparent that some people understand their personal flourishing over and against their view of the disabled majority, who they take to have capitulated to the constraints of their impairment.[40] Disability pride is not compulsory, and one can celebrate a person's decision to adopt positive attitudes and values in the effort to make the most of life, even while lamenting the extent to which those attitudes might unreasonably judge others and fail to appreciate the extent to which disability advocates have transformed the world we live in for the better (even if there is still more to do).

Honoring Great-Souled People

While disability pride stands in direct opposition to the positivity myth, it does not undermine the logic of the virtue tradition—at least as I have tried to frame it throughout this book. Indeed, the point of the virtue tradition is to reflect on the virtues needed for a person to flourish, not to overcome disability. And while an individualist focus on disability mistakes its social construction and demeans people who cannot meet ableist norms, to ignore individual capacity and responsibility is equally demeaning, precisely because it fails to elevate the contribution disabled people make to their own flourishing.

If, as suggested, disability pride includes an appreciation of the achievements of the disabled community, and the formation of a disabled identity learned through hearing the stories of disabled resistance to marginalization, thereafter it entails learning to love oneself. It is to recognize oneself as great-souled; as being virtuous and worthy of honor.

Of course, honest self-evaluation might lead to an alternate judgment. Disabled people are as virtuous, sinful, and inauthentic as the rest, and as in need of personal transformation, of facing up to brokenness, of being willing to say sorry and change our ways, as being in desperate need of grace. Disabled people are both victims and perpetrators of hatred, discrimination, and exclusion. Many are those who reject Christianity on the grounds that it is fundamentally about judgment (and too often Christians prove this is not an unfounded objection); however, the heart of the Christian gospel is not judgment but transformative grace. The life, death, and resurrection of Jesus symbolize the divine willingness graciously to encircle us in our brokenness, redeem us from the cycle of sin, help us to become more authentic, and welcome us into communities of love and acceptance that empower us to live just and generous lives.

But, while disability pride does not celebrate vice, some of what Western culture thinks of as weak, disgusting, and sinful needs to be reevaluated. The virtue of humility can be part of the process of this reevaluation, as it replaces humiliation and shame with self-acceptance. As those of us who live with disability (and illness, aging, and other bodily limitations) come to accept that we are fragile, weak, and often out of control—and that messiness, inefficiency, and limitation are part and parcel of what it is to be human—that very acceptance has transformative power, since it involves learning to rely on grace (whether found in Christian faith, or in other meditative and spiritual practices). Thereafter, we have the opportunity to live proudly, to take control where we can (even while holding it loosely), celebrating the beauty of strangely shaped disabled bodies and differently functioning minds, valuing the resilience that goes with negotiating a society that is often structured to exclude us (and being gratified in the innumerable ways we are made to feel welcome), celebrating the sorts of achievements that are valued by anybody who works hard (in my case, publishing an article, teaching a class, raising children), and taking pride in activities we share with other crips who are transforming the world by making it a more inclusive place. In so doing, we not only become humble and great-souled people who live well, but we participate in the disabled narratives that are reframing what it is to be a person who is worthy of honor.

RAGE

In speaking of humility and grace in the way that I have done in this chapter thus far, I am reminded of a series of blog entries I wrote following a two-week period in which I had ongoing issues with incontinence. When the problem first emerged, I responded in a manner that reflects the letting go that attends to the virtue of humility, asserting that "if all of life is understood as a gift, as a wondrous spark amidst the fragility and finitude of the universe, then there is reason for thankfulness, for the small moments of grace."[41] But a few days later, after two more bouts of diarrhea, my response was less sanguine:

> Last week I wrote a blog entry describing problems with my bowel and "small moments of grace." As I reread that blog from a different vantage point today, it really does seem like super-spiritual, sanctimonious tripe. "Look at the man who wrote that; isn't he wonderful? Such a man of faith in the face of hard times." Vomit.
>
> I wonder whether "he" and "me" are the same person. Has an alien exchanged our brains? Today, I can't see any grace in the midst of this half-life. I spent three days last week in bed, and thought my bowel issues were over. I felt well, chirpy even. On Monday, I went to POW and exercised with [my physical therapist] Fernanda, no problems. On Tuesday (yesterday), I went to college and taught a class in the morning, no problems, felt fine. But at 2 p.m., I was in my office working on a lecture when my tummy did its thing, and out came the shite.
>
> You'd think it'd get easier, but I don't know how to convey how frustrated and angry I felt. It was like an explosion in my brain, my thoughts an angry whirl of violence; I wanted to jump out of my skin, to run my wheelchair through the window, to smash my computer, to scream and curse and shout out to God: "Enough is enough!"[42]

In her brilliant "Blind Rage: An Open Letter to Helen Keller," Georgina Kleege, who shares Keller's blindness, writes of her frustration at having to deal with the legacy of Keller's perfect attitude.

Describing the various difficulties that result from her being blind, she says, "I rage against the world for being inaccessible to me," and asks of Keller "what did you do with that rage, Helen? Because you must have felt it. . . . But you never let it show."[43] The rage that Kleege describes is a visceral response to the unfairness of disability, which encompasses the hardship that results from the impairment itself, but is principally a result of day-to-day socialized disablement; of having to deal with an environment that is too often inaccessible, and to interact with people who are ignorant, paternalistic, and thoughtless.

How might this rage be understood in the context of the virtue tradition? Aristotle holds that anger is a passion that needs to be steered by wisdom and virtue. Following the logic of virtue in the mean, he says that the good-tempered (or gentle) person gets angry at the things and with whom he ought, anger that is appropriate to the occasion and controlled by reason. In comparison, the irascible person is angered too easily and carries his anger too far, whereas the slavish person fails to defend himself and others when he should.[44]

The Bible itself maintains a tension between anger and forgiveness. God exercises wrath toward human evil, and is often portrayed in ways that reflect the impulsive everyday anger that is common to human experience. Jesus tends to emphasize forgiveness and grace as alternatives to anger, and asserts that "anyone who is angry with a brother or sister will be subject to judgment" (Matt 5:22). Even so, Jesus gets angry at the corruption and commercialization of religion, condemning pharisaical hypocrisy and overturning the tables of the money changers at the door to the temple (Matt 21:12). In chapter 2 of this book, I explored the importance of the anger of Jesus as a symbol of liberation. Subsequent Christian tradition came to understand Jesus' seemingly ambiguous attitude to anger by distinguishing between anger directed at the person (unacceptable) and the sin (acceptable). It is a distinction generally attributed to Augustine, and is still used today in conservative responses to gays and lesbians—"love the sinner hate the sin."[45] As Aquinas later realized, however, the distinction does not hold up (since it is always the person who sins[46]), so he draws on both Aristotle and Jesus to assert that anger is properly directed toward others when it is based on justice—on giving a person what he or she deserves. Anger becomes evil when it is more or less than right reason demands.[47] Rage, for Aquinas, is uncontrolled anger, and so sinful.

As with all emotions, anger is genetically coded, having its ground in our evolutionary history, and as such is a universal passion that serves survival purposes, in particular, to frame individual responses to situations of conflict, and so orchestrate social relationships. But while anger is universal, its responses and behaviors are culturally framed, varying from one culture to another.[48] This means that what we come to learn as "properly directed anger" is socialized, and normally serves the status quo of familial, social, and political hierarchies.[49] Feminists have noted, for example, that "when women express anger they engage in emotional deviance," are punished for daring to do so, and are thus kept in their place.[50]

"Nobody likes a grumpy cripple" observes Kleege, identifying the emotional deviance of disabled rage. Crip anger is both a necessary response to the frustrations of disability, but also potentially self-destructive.[51] In his paper "Public Transport," John Hockenberry writes about the experience of catching a taxi in New York during the 1990s, where cab drivers often refused to stop for a person in a wheelchair. He describes one freezing Christmas Eve when, after being ignored by a half a dozen cabs, he managed to corner a taxi; but, after transferring himself into the back seat of the car, the cabbie refused to help out by loading the chair into the trunk of the vehicle. Hockenberry recalls his reaction:

> "Just put the chair in the trunk right now. It's Christmas Eve, pal. Why don't you just pretend to be Santa for five fucking minutes?" His smile vanished. I had crossed a line by being angry. But he also looked relieved, as though now he could refuse me in good conscience. It was all written clearly on his face. "You're crazy, man. I don't have to do nothing for you." I looked at him once more and said, "If you make me get back into this chair, you are going to be very sorry." It was a moment of visceral anger. There was no turning back now. "Go away, man. It's too cold."
>
> I got back into the chair. I placed my backpack with my wallet in it on the back of my chair for safekeeping. I grabbed his door and, with all of my strength, pushed it back on its hinges until I heard a loud snap. It was now jammed open. I rolled over to his passenger window, and two insane jabs of my right fist shattered it. I rolled around to the

front of the cab, and with my fist in my white handball glove took out first one, then the other headlight. The light I was bathed in from the front of the cab vanished. The face of the driver could now be seen clearly, illuminated by the dashboard's glow.

I could hear myself screaming at him in a voice that sounded far away. I knew the voice, but the person it belonged to was an intruder in this place. He had nothing to do with this particular cabbie and his stupid, callous insensitivity; rather, he was the overlord to all such incidents that had come before. Whenever the gauntlet was dropped, it was this interior soul, with that screaming voice and those hands, who felt no pain and who surfed down a wave of hatred to settle the score. This soul had done the arithmetic and chosen the weapons. I would have to live with the consequences.[52]

The consequences turned out to be severe lacerations to his hand, and a visit to accident and emergency for repair (and it is likely that was the last time that particular cab driver picked up a person in a wheelchair). On the one hand, as Hockenberry himself admits, his rage was all out of proportion and out of control, and ended up being self-destructive. On the other hand, we understand his anger, and can recognize it as symbolically proportionate to the discriminatory attitudes of cab drivers at the time. I have no substantive information as to whether things have changed in the decades since Hockenberry's rage, although I had very good experiences with taxi drivers in my visit to New York in 2015. And I wonder, to what extent do I owe the ease with which I could get around the city to the rage that led Hockenberry and others to advocate for change?

Morality in contexts of oppression is inevitably ambiguous. Adverse conditions can create a situation where exercising virtue for a politics of resistance carries a cost to the bearer. Resistance sometimes requires actions that are self-sacrificial—even morally corrosive—which might be labeled as "burdened virtues."[53] While "those who are not angry at the things they should be are fools,"[54] even so anger is liable to go wrong; to be targeted at the wrong people (including oneself), to have dangerous consequences, and to enact a psychological cost.[55]

If rage is an inevitably human response to hardship and injustice and, at the same time, potentially self-destructive (and damaging to others), transmuting that rage from the individual to collective action may be able to protect the person and help to direct the anger toward an appropriate and achievable goal. Of course, collective rage also has its burdens and can be self-destructive, either because those in power respond with force to cement oppression, or because revolution has chaotic and unpredictable consequences. But the collective action of the disability rights movement worldwide has resulted in real change in cultural perceptions of disability, in environmental access, and in substantive changes to social and political institutional power structures. Movement participants drew insight from the actions of feminists and the civil rights movement to develop strategies that harnessed their anger and gave it power. Earlier, I noted that disability pride leads to disability identity—and this is a group identity that facilitates group action, and in so doing empowers individuals. Most people are familiar with the Americans with Disabilities Act of 1990, as well as the continued struggle to render it effective in people's everyday lives. Such achievements have occurred globally (such as in Australia's Disability Discrimination Act of 1992), and have been enacted in global policy (such as in the United Nations' Convention on the Rights of Persons with Disabilities of 2006).

Typical of the achievements of the collective actions of people with disabilities is the recent implementation of the National Disability Insurance Scheme 2013 (NDIS) in Australia.[56] The scheme is directed by the vision of "optimising social and economic independence and full participation for people with disability," with the goal to ensure that "people with disability are in control and have choices, based on the UN Convention on the Rights of Persons with Disabilities."[57] In essence, the scheme reframes the way disability support is arranged, shifting from a paternalistic framework to giving people with disabilities the right to choose the nature and source of their own support. In this way, it reflects the importance of independent agency for which we have argued in earlier chapters.

The NDIS exists only because of the potent advocacy of people with disabilities. When the scheme was launched by Prime Minister Julia Gillard and the Labour Party in 2013, Labour's Family and Community Services Minister Jenny Macklin commented that it was "one of the best grassroots campaigns I have seen."[58] As noted in the 2009 report, "Shut Out: The Experience of People with Disabilities and Their Families in Australia,"

People with disabilities may be present in our community, but too few are actually part of it. Many live desperate and lonely lives of exclusion and isolation. The institutions that once housed them may be closed, but the inequity remains. Where once they were physically segregated, many Australians with disabilities now find themselves socially, culturally and politically isolated. They are ignored, invisible and silent. They struggle to be noticed, they struggle to be seen, they struggle to have their voices heard. What you will read in this report is their attempt to break down the walls of silence and finally have their story told.[59]

To break this silence, a variety of disability groups across the nation came together to form the National Disability and Carer Alliance (NDCA), established to campaign for the NDIS. Adopting the slogan "every Australian counts," the campaign focused on amplifying the voices of people with a disability,[60] organizing for them to meet with their local MPs, to tell their stories and to encourage politicians to champion their cause in Parliament.[61] The NDCA also interviewed people across the country, publishing their findings in "Shut Out" (cited above). Although much of what was learned was shocking, the report also highlighted the character of people who were not passive victims of their circumstances but, rather, angry, determined, strong, creative, and dignified. These were people fighting for a fair go. As the report concludes, "They have fought hard to achieve their goals. They have refused to take no for an answer."[62] The power of the collective disabled voice was apparent from the fact that the NDIS legislation, with a budgeted cost of more than $20 billion a year, was passed with bipartisan support during a period of extreme turmoil and acrimony in the Australian parliament (especially between the then Prime Minister Julia Gillard and opposition leader Tony Abbott).

FORGIVENESS

While anger is inevitable and sometimes necessary, still, no one wants to be a grumpy cripple—at least not most of the time. Wisely directed anger serves individual and collective flourishing, but it needs to dissipate if happiness is the goal. One way in which this can occur is through the offer of forgiveness, an act and attitude central to Christian faith (and to many other religious traditions). In the Gospels, Jesus' teaching is replete with exhortations to forgive, most potently illustrated in the parable of the prodigal son (Luke 15:11-35), made spiritually central in the Lord's Prayer, "forgive us our debts, as we also have forgiven our debtors" (Matt 6:12), and modeled on the cross in the offer of forgiveness to those who have been involved in the crucifixion: "Father, forgive them, for they do not know what they are doing" (Luke 23:34). In this act of forgiveness, Jesus intends to end the cyclical repetition of acts of violence and revenge.[63]

Forgiveness is the act of giving up or letting go of feelings of anger, resentment, bitterness, and vengeance, and of claims to a debt owed. Depending on the nature of the wrong, forgiveness is a process rather than a one-off event, and as a result, it can be facilitated by religious ritual and therapeutic care. Forgiveness can be understood as a virtue. As Aristotle observes, "bitter human beings carry a heavy weight" whereas "the gentle person is given not to revenge but rather to forgiveness."[64] In Aquinas, similarly, the virtue of forgiveness is subsumed within temperance, and involves the tendency to let go of anger and to mitigate punishment (clemency).[65] Because forgiveness entails the letting go of anger and other negative sentiments, it has been found to benefit psychological well-being, health (negative emotions have physiological consequences), and stable relationships, and is also negatively correlated with depression and anxiety.[66] For this reason, Seligman and other positive psychologists advocate "forgiveness as a powerful tool that can transform feelings of anger and bitterness into neutrality, or even, for some, into positive emotions."[67]

Exercising the virtue of forgiveness is not as straightforward as it first seems, and as with any virtue, demands the exercise of wisdom. This is especially true in any suggestion that victims of abuse, oppression, and discrimination should forgive. To forgive an abuser is understandably difficult for people who suffer the psychological effects long after the abuse has ceased, and this difficulty is magnified for disabled people whose experience of oppression and discrimination is systemic and ongoing. A person's whole life will be influenced by abuse and oppression, to the extent that the capacity to forgive may well be outside of one's control—or at the very least, a lengthy and difficult process.[68] There is an inherent danger in insisting that victims forgive their victimizers and oppressors, since it has the potential to diminish the horror of their experience and, worse, reinforce the status quo. This danger has been all too apparent in the scandal of clerical sexual abuse, where victims, asked to forgive and forget punishment, were silenced, and abusive priests offered absolution and thereafter allowed to remain in positions of power. The price of easy forgiveness is similarly apparent in religious institutions where the preaching of forgiveness, alongside theologies of female submission, has kept victimized women in abusive marriages.[69] To urge disabled people to forgive the individuals, institutions, and broader society that have oppressed them is to court a similar danger.

It is noteworthy that in the Gospels, the charge to forgive is not specifically directed at victims of abuse and oppression, but aimed primarily at those in power: the master forgives the debtor; the father forgives the prodigal son, and asks the older brother to do the same; and when Jesus forgives, it is a sign of his power and authority (Mark 2:5-12).[70] This is because forgiveness is not just a psychological tool, intended to help a victim feel better. Rather, it serves a social purpose, which is to effect peace and reconciliation between individuals and in society more generally. Because this is so, justice and forgiveness are not opposed to one another, but are intended to work together to effect both social transformation (justice) and healing (forgiveness). The wise person has the capacity to hold justice and forgiveness in tension when deciding how and when to act in any particular situation of injustice. Dietrich Bonhoeffer famously distinguished between cheap and costly grace, where cheap grace is "the preaching of forgiveness without requiring repentance" and costly grace compels a person to the difficult path of following Christ, and so of submitting to change.[71] In a similar manner, cheap and quick forgiveness allows those responsible for abuse and oppression to escape responsibility for their actions, and when this occurs nothing is done to shift relations of power. This is especially the case when those in power refuse to face up to the damage they have caused, and so fail to ask for or want forgiveness.

The situation is different where disability pride and collective action empower people in the various ways described earlier. When so empowered, disabled people have the opportunity to be agents of healing and reconciliation, and to offer transformative forgiveness to individuals and the society that has wronged them, as those individuals and groups begin to face that wrong and seek to work for change (even if there is still much more to be done). In such a context, forgiveness is a mark of power, and an invitation of welcome coming from the very people that were once excluded.[72] Since the meaning of disability is socially constructed and concerns the universality of human frailty, disabled identity is flexible and open, and intends to break down—rather than entrench—the barriers between the disabled and nondisabled. The fluidity and openness of disability involves "collective affinities," and the imagining of a "we" that includes people who identify with disability even though they themselves do not have one (partners, families, friends, theorists, activists, and support workers), that embraces those with illnesses or impairments that are not generally recognized as a disability, and that extends to the impairment and social exclusion that go with aging.[73] In this way, forgiveness becomes the agent of a better future, one in which simplistic binaries are done away with (disabled/nondisabled). Such a future will require a response from those who currently under-stand themselves as nondisabled, but it will also depend on disabled people themselves taking the journey of forgiveness, letting go of the weight of their justified anger, and forging new social networks that welcome and celebrate human difference.

Of course, there is no guarantee that an individual's situation will improve, nor that social disablement will be addressed. In circum-stances that feel hopeless, anger is often directed at God (or at some contemporary metaphysical equivalent, such as "The Universe"). The Bible records a number of instances where people express their anger to God: Moses complains about Yahweh's failure to deliver Israel from the Pharaoh (Exod 5:22-23), the book of Job is an extended complaint to God about injustice, and the Psalms recount Israel's anger at the suffering it has experienced and at God's failure to protect the nation.[74] Even so, it is one thing to be angry at God, but another thing altogether to determine to forgive God. We generally understand that the need for repentance is ours, and that it is God's task to forgive, but rarely will we admit that the God we hold to be "perfect, loving, and good" has a case to answer for the hurt inflicted on us, especially if that hurt has proven intractable, as is too often the case with disability. My friend Jay McNeill, whose experiences have informed much of the argument of this book, illuminates the task of forgiveness, as well as its aftermath, writing:

> I have told God a few times that I forgive Him for the injustice in
> my life. It might be my imagination, but I have sensed that He was
> sorry that I got caught in the crossfire as an innocent casualty, but He
> is making a promise that He will ultimately conquer evil and bring
> heaven to earth . . . and He wants me to help that happen. The more
> God and I forgive each other, the more trust I have in the relation-
> ship . . . the more honest I am with Him and the more we recon-
> cile . . . the more I value my friendship with Him.[75]

Whatever the metaphysical realities or propriety of our forgiving
God (and imagining God's apology), the point of such an exchange is to
find a way to let go of the bitterness of anger. In this experience of letting
go, there is a possibility of a move from forgiveness to gratitude, from
hardship to discovery.[76] The disabled journey is one that gives special
insight into the relationship between forgiveness and gratitude, since
for many people disability is "a road I did not choose, but now, on it, I
am making all kinds of important discoveries," whether they be new
purposes and meanings, new friendships, or new spiritual horizons.[77]
Again, to quote Jay McNeill:

> I have paid a price to be Sunshine's father. It would be pretentious of
> me not to acknowledge that I do lament the challenges, but I have
> earned a privilege that you can't buy. Sunshine trusts me; she knows
> that I will be there and because of that she gives me a life-changing
> love in return. . . . I think we would all benefit from having a "Sun-
> shine" in our life. I am not saying I would wish my journey on any-
> body, but I wonder if the world would be in less turmoil if we were all
> forced to lay down our selfishness to make someone else's life better.
> I know beyond a shadow of a doubt that without the crisis of Sun-
> shine's journey crashing my party, the extra freedom and disposable
> time I would have had would have been directed to making me feel
> better about myself through experiences and buying lots of stuff.
> Instead, through no noble choice, disability has been wedged into my
> world and I am a far better human because of it.[78]

In describing forgiveness as the letting go of anger, we have
returned to where we started this chapter—with humility, which was
defined in terms of the letting go of control. It is when humility, pride,
anger, and forgiveness come together in creative tension that a person
is graced to live and flourish with the difficulties that attend to disability. The biological realities of impairment and the social injustice of

disablement present a challenge to conceptions of the virtue tradition and positive psychology that overemphasize individual control and positive thinking, giving rise to the positivity myth, which only exacerbates the alienation of disabled people unable to satisfy Western culture's false ideals. Humility helps us to admit the limits of our fragility and vulnerability, to have the courage to accept that life is risky, to move toward authenticity, and to look for the same in the experts and support services responsible for our care.

Humility, though, is not opposed to pride, at least where the latter is not hubris, but a recognition that those of us who claim crip can be great-souled people, worthy of honor, who live well, and who proudly identify with the community and world-changing legacy of people with disabilities, past and present. Disability pride helps us to see that the anger we feel at the discrimination, exclusion, and oppression of disabled people is justified, that we have reason to be grumpy cripples, and that our rage can be harnessed to bring social change. And yet anger is not the end of our story. Disabled identity reaches for healing and reconciliation; and forgiveness, wisely offered, is one of the mechanisms to help bring this about. Sublating them all, grace (wherever it is found) provides the inner healing that is needed to help us to be humble, authentic, strong, and forgiving, and so to flourish in and through the wild out-of-control journey of our disabled lives.

Conclusion
A Disabled Account of Faith

To write about disability, flourishing, and virtue is to take on a theory of everything, and for that reason, it is doomed to failure. Indeed, what I have written in this book is sure to have disappointed its readers along the way. It will not have been godly enough for Christians, evidence-based enough for scientists, deep enough for philosophers, and worst of all, it has left far too many experiences of disability inadequately covered or untouched altogether, so that the people for whom I have written will justly complain that I have not treated their experience adequately. And they will be right. My only defense is that it seems somehow appropriate for a book grounded in the fact of human fragility and vulnerability, which elevates humility and grace, to fail to meet the standards that others (and I) might set it.

Of the omissions, the one that stands out most to me is my fail-ure to explore the *eudaimonia* of people with a mental illness. How do we understand flourishing for a person whose disability, among other things, targets happiness? This is a topic to which the virtue tradition might make a valuable contribution, but it is a task that I feel ill equipped to undertake. I can imagine that living with severe and disabling mental illness can provide unique insights and important challenges to the virtue tradition's vision of flourishing, but lacking both mental health expertise and the personal experience of mental illness, I fear that any conclusions I might reach would do more harm than good. The same might be said of any of the topics addressed in the previous pages, but while I have chosen to take on fields of knowledge that are beyond the ken of my training as a theologian, for me at least the complex field of mental illness is a step too far.[1] But I hope that in making this point, someone better suited than I might take up the challenge.

Some might wonder why I devoted a whole chapter to sexuality but spent less time talking about friendship. I can only reply that the importance of friendship permeated the book from start to end, forming an implicit undercurrent rather than an explicit chapter. In any event, Hans Reinders—a dialogue partner in earlier chapters—has already written the definitive theology of disability and friendship. I wholeheartedly refer my readers to his insightful book *Receiving the Gift of Friendship*, and hope their reading of each of us is edified by the other. This book's sustained attention to sex is my attempt to offer a gift to the church and its members, as well as to the academic practice of theology. Sex may be given too much attention in the media of contemporary popular culture, but it is rarely faced honestly and openly by the church. Moreover, the sexual losses that attend to SCI have been at the forefront of my search for happiness following my injury, so taking on this topic has had personal significance. It may come as no surprise to hear I wrote the first draft of the chapter on disabled sexuality before any of the rest of the book. My hope is that this chapter will aid the church in its much-needed dialogue about sex and sexuality, as well as be my offering to my sisters and brothers who need the church to hear their voices and their experience of disability and sexuality.

And what about race and poverty, and their disproportionate impact on people with a disability? As this book took shape, America was in the midst of an ugly, racially charged presidential election cycle, and Black Lives Matter advocates were protesting extrajudicial killings and dehumanization of black people by police and the wider society. Just as black and brown bodies bear much of society's violence in general, it is also the case that black and Latino/a persons with disabilities suffer most, and it is their experiences that remain largely untold.[2] This is even more true outside the West. In the Middle East and Africa, the consequences of war, terrorism, and long-term political instability have created populations where tens of millions now suffer with impairments in places where inadequate infrastructure is doubly disabling.[3] Even in wealthy countries such as my own, Aboriginal Australians are twice as likely to be disabled than are nonindigenous Australians, and they also face disadvantage in accessing support services.[4] These were issues beyond this work's explicit focus, but while my concern was happiness and virtue in general, I hope it has become clear that the virtue tradition has political significance, and that virtues can contribute to political advocacy and social change.

The list of lacunae could go on. Should I have paid more attention to sensory disability, or focused more on establishing the biblical foundations of happiness and flourishing? Very possibly. But I said at the outset that I could not hope to provide a comprehensive account of the rich diversity of disability, nor a complete history of *eudaimonian* ethics in its philosophical and theological context. My hope, though, is that readers might take on these various tasks in the light of their own experiences and contexts. The virtue tradition is less concerned with detailed content, fixed conclusions, and specific political injunctions than it is with providing a framework for moral thinking and agency. To that end I hope readers are encouraged to wrestle with what flourishing might look like for them, in the light of their impairments and vulnerabilities, social and cultural opportunities and constraints, and personal visions and passions.

My goals were limited and creative. I intended to reflect as a Christian theologian on the significance of the virtue tradition for the happiness of people with disabilities, and to see whether disability itself offered fresh insight into how we should understand flourishing. As to the first goal, a concept of virtue freed from elitist conceptions of human nature is as relevant to people with a disability as it is to anyone else. Those of us with disabilities are enriched by an understanding of happiness that includes but runs deeper than mere pleasure. We are as susceptible as anyone to short-term and self-destructive behaviors (sin), and do well to be reminded that practicing the virtues and orienting our vision toward meaningful goals can help us to lead full and rich lives. The world we live in often thinks little of us, and so expects little from us. And if we unconsciously buy into those low expectations, we face the danger of frittering away our time and so failing to reach our potential. That we are pitied, and that people are amazed that we do the mundane things of everyday life, does not mean that we should live pitifully. And most people with disabilities do not. As for those for whom happiness proves to be elusive, more often than not their hardships are a product of injustice. In advocating the importance of virtue, we must take care not to blame victims for their failure to flourish.

In respect to the second goal, the disabled community teaches us that it is possible to live well—to enjoy pleasure, gratification, and meaning—while putting up with unwieldy and contumacious bodies and brains and fighting against prejudice and paternalism. The experience of disabled interdependence is a reminder that no one flourishes on their own, and that deep friendships and capacity-enhancing support are foundational to the achieving of our potential. The sensuality and sexuality of disabled people confront our limited conception of sexual potency and capacity, the small-mindedness of our image of the body beautiful, and the shallowness of our conception of masculinity and femininity. The humility, pride, and rage of the disabled community challenges our assumption that weakness and power are opposites, and shows us what it is to be great-souled and virtuous while also broken and vulnerable. And through it all, grace emerges as the remedy to doubt, hopelessness, vice, failure, prejudice, and paternalism. It is grace that enables us to let go of the need for control and to open ourselves to the healing and peace that come from trusting in the love of God poured into our hearts through the Holy Spirit.

FAITH, HOPE, AND LOVE

In the course of this book, I considered the contribution of the theological virtues—faith, hope, and love—to our journey through the suffering that often attends to disability. As St. Paul asserts,

> [12]For now, we see only a reflection as in a mirror; then we shall see face to face. Now I know in part; then I shall know fully, even as I am fully known. [13]And now these three remain: faith, hope, and love. But the greatest of these is love. (1 Cor 13:12-13)

The theological virtues are gifts of grace that transform and enrich the intellectual and moral life, and so direct a person toward their telos, ultimately to God. They have both theological and anthropological reference, as Spirit and spirit, as utterly beyond us and as virtues of character worth striving for. Faith, hope, and love are inextricably entwined with one another, and together they inject life with meaning, motivate perseverance, and encourage generous and mutual self-giving. But if the theological virtues can contribute to our flourishing with a disability, does disability offer revelation into what it is to exercise faith, hope, and love?

If Lonergan is correct in his argument that faith is "knowledge born of religious love," a response to the love of God flooding our hearts, which thrusts us to self-transcendence in the mystery of love and awe, then faith remains an interim virtue.[5] Because death brings certainty, faith is a virtue for this side of heaven ("for now we see only a reflection as in a mirror").[6] Far from being a liability, this means that faith is a thoroughly earthy virtue, grounded in experience and reasoned judgment. It is needed most when life gets messy, which is why faith and hope go hand in hand. Faith is trust in the power of love, and hope enables a person to persevere through seemingly impossible circumstances.

Every person exercises faith at many levels. It is clichéd but no less true that we need to have faith in ourselves. Such faith may be little more than shallow egoism when the boast of the athlete, tycoon, or movie star, but it has a deeper meaning when a person with a disability trusts in their own capacity to succeed in the face of the doubts and small-mindedness of others. The evils of pity and paternalism are that they undermine trust in oneself, and so diminish a person's potential. But in rejecting pity and paternalism in the strongest of terms, disabled people reveal both the strengths and limits of self-belief. Disability is a sign of the paradox that we are capable of much more than is expected of us but, even so, there are many things we cannot do. And that is not pitiable; it is just the way things are for everyone, even for those who are in denial, having bought the false hopes of the purveyors of the positivity myth. Realistic self-belief generates hope that is neither naively optimistic or hopelessly despairing. Indeed, disability leaves no room for either naiveté or despair. But it does remind us that faith in ourselves is not enough. Faith needs a larger object.

Faith in our family, friends, and care workers (if we have them) is not the antidote to the failure of self-belief, but its partner. Our faith in others sublates our faith in ourselves, incorporating and expanding its horizons. Nondisabled individualists too often forget this, but as disability intertwines our bodies and minds with others, we discover that life can be deeper, wider, higher, and richer than we had realized. Of course, disability can also constrain and shrink us, when built environments, social structures, and cultural values alienate and discriminate. But even then, we can reach out for the support of peers and advocates, who lift our vision and give us the faith to see that the world need not be the way it is now. In their persistent struggle for justice, crip advocates model the power of hope; that even though obstacles seem to be overwhelming, the fight for a better future is worth persevering for.

It is this vision of a different future that hints at the value of religious faith. Political advocacy rarely if ever attains its goals, because prejudice and disgust are deeply rooted in the human psyche, and are thereby entrenched in the structures of social and cultural power (including, sadly, in the church). In the face of endemic disabling prejudice, it is easy enough to give in to meaninglessness. Once again, faith needs a larger object.

If faith in God is the knowledge born of religious love, then *what* it believes and trusts in is the gospel of Christ, the good news that the kingdom of God will be established in the power of the Spirit, that God's love can and will prevail over deathly and disabling evil in all its manifestations. Thus faith enables us to trust in the love of God, to love others in return, and to live out of the gift of that love by refusing to accept that life is meaningless.

In a Christian context, the object of faith is Jesus Christ. The message and life of Jesus establish the vision of the good life for believers, as well as the virtues that enable a person to achieve it. Both were countercultural in Jesus' time, and remain so today. That is to say, Jesus is not the heroic, virtuous man of Greco-Roman ideals, nor the Davidic Warrior of Jewish messianic expectation, and in emphasizing love of enemies, humility, forgiveness, self-sacrifice, and other virtues normally judged as weakness, his life continues to challenge our assumptions about human ideals. While there is always the danger of projecting our presuppositions of what constitutes perfect humanity and full divinity onto Jesus, I share with Nancy Eiesland the view that disability offers unique insight.[7] It is not only that Jesus embraces and elevates disability as a sign of the kingdom of God (Luke 14), but that he was jeered at and abused, and on the cross, he takes onto himself the suffering and alienation that have too often been central to the experience of disability.

Indeed, the cross, in its historical context, is a symbol of humiliation, and unlike so much of mainstream middle-class Christianity today (for whom the cross is merely Christian branding), people with disabilities are uniquely placed to see its radical abnormality. It is noteworthy also that we label the events of the crucifixion "the Passion," and thus recognize that while virtues moderate the passions, and temperance is a cardinal virtue, nevertheless, faith in Jesus resists moderation and passivity. Jesus was passionately angry at injustice, compassionate to anyone who suffered, and impassioned in his insistence that God's kingdom was oriented especially to the flourishing of the poor, the captive, and the disabled.

It is easy enough to write about faith in God as I am doing now (after all, these are just words on the page), but another thing altogether for faith to have substance. In the first chapter of this book, Jay McNeill observed that before the birth of his daughters, he had become habituated into a Christianity that functioned autonomously. Confronted with the reality of Sunshine's condition, he realized that his faith was empty and powerless. Jay is not just raising the problem of theodicy. Rather, he is saying that disability leaves no room for nonsense:

> Once I started evaluating all the things I thought were true about my faith by the light of the brutal reality of my daily life with Sunshine, the intricate and self-serving theology that I had created turned out to be redundant. I realized that I had built my life on sand.

For him, faith is not about theological precision or distinction, nor many of the shallow and self-serving religious constructs and practices that make up too much of the church's theology and its life. In fact, he says, faith that is not available to Sunshine—that "relies on understanding a set of complex ideas such as atonement"—cannot be what saving faith is all about.[8]

> So what, then, if my daughter Sunshine is not able to comprehend the life of Jesus or even the concept of a God? If faith genuinely relies on some level of intellect or reasoning, then the most vulnerable in our community are at a disadvantage. It makes Jesus' call to have faith like a child a far more provocative idea. So how important is a conclusive view on Christianity then? The more people argue about an intricate theology that promises to unlock a new profound

understanding, the more removed I feel from Christianity because it excludes my daughter.

Jay offers a profound challenge not simply to a theology of salvation, but to the practice of theology itself. By turning to Sunshine as the beloved of God, Jay insists that those who live with disability are not the outliers or even the least common denominator of salvation. Rather, they live at the heart of salvation, at the center of Christ's call to a certain kind of faith. Sunshine, then, is not simply an exception we must consider but a full picture of the humanity the Son came to save.

If this is so, then Sunshine's faith has something to say, something to offer those who speak about love of God and about the life of faith. Jay concludes that Sunshine's faith is about the love that is the product of the life they share together, and that is received from and reaches toward God, whether Sunshine knows it or not. This echoes Lonergan's notion of faith as knowledge born of religious love, where religion references not the external form, but the essential experience of divine love.[9] This love transcends our conscious knowing. It possesses us and takes us beyond ourselves. Such a love "brings a deep-set joy that can remain despite humiliation, failure, privation, pain, betrayal, and desertion," and brings with it a radical peace that bears fruit in virtuous love of one's neighbor.[10]

Faith, at every level, facilitates flourishing, and disability is a potent symbol of the possibility of faithful flourishing in a messy world.

Notes

INTRODUCTION: A DISABLED ACCOUNT OF FLOURISHING

1 Alasdair MacIntyre, *Dependent Rational Animals: Why Human Beings Need the Virtues* (Chicago: Open Court Publishing, 1999), chap. 8.

2 Stella Young, "We're Not Here for Your Inspiration," *The Drum*, Australian Broadcasting Corporation, first posted and updated July 2, 2012, accessed June 8, 2015, http://www.abc.net.au/news/2012-07-03/young-inspiration -porn/4107006.

3 Young, "We're Not Here for Your Inspiration."

4 Young, "We're Not Here for Your Inspiration."

5 Shane Clifton, *Husbands Should Not Break: A Memoir about the Pursuit of Happiness after Spinal Cord Injury* (Eugene, Ore.: Resource Publications, 2015).

6 Clifton, *Husbands Should Not Break*, 114.

7 MacIntyre, *Dependent Rational Animals*, 2.

8 Paul K. Longmore, *Why I Burned My Book and Other Essays on Disability* (Philadelphia: Temple University Press, 2003); Tom Shakespeare, *Disability Rights and Wrongs* (New York: Taylor & Francis, 2006).

9 See, for example, Roger Crisp, ed., *How Should One Live? Essays on the Virtues* (Oxford: Oxford University Press, 1996); Philippa Foot, *Virtues and Vices: And Other Essays in Moral Philosophy* (Oxford: Oxford University Press, 2003); Lisa Tessman, *Burdened Virtues: Virtue Ethics for Liberatory Struggles* (Oxford: Oxford University Press, 2005); Daniel C. Russell, ed., *The Cambridge Companion to Virtue Ethics* (Cambridge: Cambridge University Press, 2013).

10 World Health Organization, "Towards a Common Language for Functioning, Disability and Health: The International Classification of Functioning, Disability and Health" (Geneva: World Health Organization, 2002), http:// www.who.int/classifications/icf/en/.

11 Victor Finkelstein, *Attitudes and Disabled People* (New York: World Rehabilitation Fund, 1980); Paul Abberley, "The Concept of Oppression and the
Development of a Social Theory of Disability," *Disability, Handicap & Society*
2, no. 1 (1987): 5–19, doi:10.1080/02674648766780021; Colin Barnes, *Disabled
People in Britain and Discrimination: A Case for Anti-Discrimination Legislation* (London: C. Hurst, 1991); Gary L. Albrecht, Katherine D. Seelman, and
Michael Bury, *Handbook of Disability Studies* (London: SAGE, 2001).

12 Longmore, *Why I Burned My Book*, 1; Tom Shakespeare, *Disability Rights and
Wrongs Revisited*, 2nd ed. (New York: Routledge, 2014), 21–25.

13 Longmore, *Why I Burned My Book*, 2.

14 I have used the metaphor of blindness deliberately in this sentence to see
whether it gets noticed, and so invite us to think about whether its usage is
appropriate.

15 The construct of "society" that follows draws on Bernard Lonergan's scale
of values. See Bernard J. F. Lonergan, *Method in Theology* (London: Darton,
Longman & Todd, 1972), 31–32; Robert M. Doran, *Theology and the Dialectics of History* (Toronto: University of Toronto Press, 1990), 10; Neil Ormerod
and Shane Clifton, *Globalization and the Mission of the Church* (London: T&T
Clark, 2009), chap. 2.

16 The literature outlining the social injustice faced by people with disabilities globally is summarized in the "World Report on Disability" (Geneva:
World Health Organization, 2011), http://www.who.int/disabilities/world
_report/2011/.

17 For a critical disability reading of the virtue tradition and the Bible, refer to
chapter 3 of this book, as well as Amos Yong, *The Bible, Disability, and the
Church: A New Vision of the People of God* (Grand Rapids: Eerdmans, 2011);
Sarah J. Melcher, Mikeal C. Parsons, and Amos Yong, *The Bible and Disability:
A Commentary*, Studies in Religion, Theology, and Disability (Waco, Tex.: Bay-
lor University Press, 2017). More broadly, see Rosemarie Garland-Thomson,
*Extraordinary Bodies: Figuring Physical Disability in American Culture and Lit-
erature* (New York: Columbia University Press, 1996); David T. Mitchell and
Sharon L. Snyder, "Representation and Its Discontents: The Uneasy Home of
Disability in Literature and Film," in Albrecht, Seelman, and Bury, *Handbook
of Disability Studies*, 195–218; Sally Chivers, *The Silvering Screen: Old Age and
Disability in Cinema* (Toronto: University of Toronto Press, 2011).

18 Patrick Devlieger et al., eds., *Rethinking Disability: World Perspectives in Culture and Society* (Antwerp: Garant, 2016), 19.

19 Shakespeare, *Disability Rights and Wrongs Revisited*, 2.

20 Stella Young, "To My Eighty-Year-Old Self," in *Between Us: Women of Letters*,
ed. Marieke Hardy and Michaela McGuire (Melbourne: Penguin, 2014). See
also "Stella Young's Letter to Herself at 80 Years Old," *Sydney Morning Herald*,
November 22, 2014, http://www.smh.com.au/lifestyle/celebrity/stella-youngs
-letter-to-herself-at-80-years-old-20141113-11llol.html.

21   Deborah J. Gallagher, "On Using Blindness as Metaphor and Difficult Ques-
      tions: A Response to Ben-Moshe," *Disability Studies Quarterly* 26, no. 2 (2006),
      http://dsq-sds.org/article/view/690.
22   Hans S. Reinders, *Receiving the Gift of Friendship: Profound Disability, Theolog-
      ical Anthropology, and Ethics* (Grand Rapids: Eerdmans, 2008), 46.
23   Simon J. Williams, "Is Anybody There? Critical Realism, Chronic Illness and
      the Disability Debate," *Sociology of Health & Illness* 21, no. 6 (1999): 797–819,
      doi:10.1111/1467-9566.00184; Nick Watson, "Researching Disablement," in
      Routledge Handbook of Disability Studies, ed. Nick Watson, Alan Roulstone,
      and Carol Thomas (New York: Taylor & Francis, 2012), 93–106; Shakespeare,
      Disability Rights and Wrongs Revisited.
24   Shakespeare, *Disability Rights and Wrongs Revisited*, 72.
25   Alison Kafer, *Feminist, Queer, Crip* (Bloomington: Indiana University Press,
      2013), 13.
26   Lonergan, *Method in Theology*, 292.
27   Martin Seligman, "The New Era of Positive Psychology," TED.com, accessed
      March 28, 2017, https://www.ted.com/talks/martin_seligman_on_the_state_of
      _psychology.
28   Tom Shakespeare, Kath Gillespie-Sells, and Dominic Davies, *The Sexual Pol-
      itics of Disability: Untold Desires* (London: Cassell, 1996).
29   See, for example, David Serlin, "Pissing without Pity: Disability, Gender, and
      the Public Toilet," in *Toilet: Public Restrooms and the Politics of Sharing*, ed.
      Harvey Molotch and Laura Noren (New York: New York University Press,
      2010), 167–85. Similarly, the 2017 theme for the disability stream of the Amer-
      ican Academy of Religion was "Toilet Justice: Peeing and the Politics of Mar-
      ginalized Bodies."

1: THE EXPERIENCE OF DISABILITY

1   Jay McNeill, *Growing Sideways* (blog), https://jaymcneill.com/. Jay finished
     blogging on January 21, 2017, but his series of posts remains online.
2   For an illuminating look at the issues at stake in disability, deafness, and
     cochlear implants, see Robert Sparrow, "Implants and Ethnocide: Learning
     from the Cochlear Implant Controversy," *Disability & Society* 25, no. 4 (2010):
     455–66, doi:10.1080/09687591003755849.

2: DISABILITY, THEODICY, AND THE PROBLEM OF PAIN

1   This chapter draws from Shane Clifton, "Theodicy, Disability, and Fragility:
     An Attempt to Find Meaning in the Aftermath of Quadriplegia," *Theological
     Studies* 76, no. 4 (2015): 765–84, doi:10.1177/0040563915605263.
2   For an illuminating examination of the modern turn from abstraction to the
     particular experiences of marginalized people, see Mark Stephen Murray
     Scott, "Theodicy at the Margins: New Trajectories for the Problem of Evil,"
     Theology Today 68, no. 2 (2011): 150, doi:10.1177/0040573611405878.

3   Cynthia S. W. Crysdale and Neil Ormerod, *Creator God, Evolving World* (Minneapolis: Fortress, 2013), 92.

4   Eleonore Stump, *Wandering in Darkness: Narrative and the Problem of Suffering* (Oxford: Oxford University Press, 2012), 8.

5   Stump, *Wandering in Darkness*, 11.

6   For an insight into the challenge of adjusting to spinal cord injury, see Shane Clifton, "Grieving My Broken Body: An Autoethnographic Account of Spinal Cord Injury as an Experience of Grief," *Disability and Rehabilitation* 36, no. 21 (2014): 1823–29.

7   Longmore, *Why I Burned My Book*, 150.

8   It is also the case that every human life entails the experience of suffering, which is inevitably incomparable, so that one person's burden cannot and should not be weighed against another's.

9   MacIntyre, *Dependent Rational Animals*.

10 Marius C. Felderhof, "Evil: Theodicy or Resistance?" *Scottish Journal of Theology* 57, no. 4 (2004), doi:10.1017/S0036930604000328.

11 John Swinton, *Raging with Compassion: Pastoral Responses to the Problem of Evil* (Grand Rapids: Eerdmans, 2007), 42–43.

12 For this helpful distinction, see Hans S. Reinders, *Disability, Providence, and Ethics: Bridging Gaps, Transforming Lives*, Studies in Religion, Theology, and Disability (Waco, Tex.: Baylor University Press, 2014), Kindle location 473.

13 Hence, science and theology are not competing disciplines, as is too often assumed by creationists on the one hand and scientific atheists on the other.

14 Aquinas, *Contra Gentiles* 3.69.15.

15 Neil Ormerod, *A Public God: Natural Theology Reconsidered* (Minneapolis: Fortress, 2015).

16 Augustine, *Confessions* 3.12.

17 See, for example, D. A. Carson, *How Long, O Lord? Reflections on Suffering and Evil*, 2nd ed. (Grand Rapids: Baker Academic, 2006), 40; William Dembski, *The End of Christianity* (Nashville: B&H Academic, 2009).

18 Such is the view of Carson and Dembski, and literal six-day-creation proponents such as *Answers in Genesis* (website). See Tommy Mitchell, "Why Does God's Creation Include Death and Suffering?" *Answers in Genesis*, January 31, 2008, https://answersingenesis.org/suffering/why-does-gods-creation-include-death-and-suffering/.

19 Peter van Inwagen, *The Problem of Evil* (Oxford: Oxford University Press, 2008), 86. Van Inwagen claims to be offering a defense, rather than theodicy—a possible explanation for suffering that may or may not reflect God's actual reason. But his argument only carries weight if his possible explanation is convincing. In my view, it is not.

20 Van Inwagen, *Problem of Evil*.

21 Creationists take this logic to its absurd conclusion, arguing that prior to the fall, "there was no survival of the fittest, . . . both humans and animals were

vegetarians"—thus Tyrannosaurus Rex, the plant eater. See Mitchell, "Why Does God's Creation Include Death and Suffering?"

22   See Carson, *How Long, O Lord?* 45.

23   Amos Yong takes up the inherently demeaning character of this identification in *Theology and Down Syndrome: Reimagining Disability in Late Modernity*, Studies in Religion, Theology, and Disability (Waco, Tex.: Baylor University Press, 2007), 162; see also Thomas E. Reynolds, *Vulnerable Communion: A Theology of Disability and Hospitality* (Grand Rapids: Brazos, 2008), 27–28.

24   Shane Clifton, "The Dark Side of Prayer for Healing: Toward a Theology of Well-Being," *Pneuma* 36, no. 2 (2014): 204–25.

25   Reynolds, *Vulnerable Communion*, 33.

26   Stump, *Wandering in Darkness*, 384; although this reading of Aquinas is subject to debate—see Agustín Echavarría, "Thomas Aquinas and the Modern and Contemporary Debate on Evil," *New Blackfriars* 94, no. 1054 (2013): 733–54, doi:10.1111/nbfr.12034.

27   Aquinas on Rom 8:6, cited in Stump, *Wandering in Darkness*, 385.

28   Inwagen, *Problem of Evil*, 88.

29   Stump, *Wandering in Darkness*, 156, 396.

30   Michael Stoeber, *Reclaiming Theodicy: Reflections on Suffering, Compassion and Spiritual Transformation* (New York: Palgrave Macmillan, 2006).

31   Stoeber, *Reclaiming Theodicy*, 28.

32   Stoeber, *Reclaiming Theodicy*, 53.

33   Marilyn McCord Adams, *Horrendous Evils and the Goodness of God* (Ithaca, N.Y.: Cornell University Press, 2000), 26.

34   Adams, *Horrendous Evils and the Goodness of God*, 26–28.

35   In response to these horrors, Adams develops both an aesthetic conception of suffering—noting that victims and perpetrators of evil suffer seemingly irreversible degradation into the subhuman—and an aesthetic theodicy, which finds that even horrendous evil can offer a unique vision of God that can facilitate a divine embrace and thus deep beauty. Adams, *Horrendous Evils and the Goodness of God*, 106–7, 161–62.

36   Marilyn McCord Adams, *Christ and Horrors: The Coherence of Christology* (Cambridge: Cambridge University Press, 2006), 47–48.

37   Adams, *Christ and Horrors*, 205–41.

38   Adams, *Horrendous Evils and the Goodness of God*, 167.

39   Stump, *Wandering in Darkness*, 420.

40   Clifton, "Grieving My Broken Body."

41   See Mark Tonga's story later in this book.

42   R. N. Barker et al., "The Relationship between Quality of Life and Disability across the Lifespan for People with Spinal Cord Injury," *Spinal Cord* 47, no. 2 (2009): 149–55, doi:10.1038/sc.2008.82; Terri A. deRoon-Cassini et al., "Psychological Well-Being after Spinal Cord Injury: Perception of Loss and Meaning Making," *Rehabilitation Psychology* 54, no. 3 (2009): 306–14, doi:10.1037/a0016545; Irmo Marini and Noreen M. Glover-Graf, "Religiosity

and Spirituality among Persons with Spinal Cord Injury: Attitudes, Beliefs, and Practices," *Rehabilitation Counseling Bulletin* 54, no. 2 (2011): 82–92, doi:10.1177/0034355210368868; Eleanor Weitzner et al., "Getting On with Life: Positive Experiences of Living with a Spinal Cord Injury," *Qualitative Health Research* 21, no. 11 (2011): 1455–68, doi:10.1177/1049732311417726.

43 N. Levy, "Deafness, Culture, and Choice," *Journal of Medical Ethics* 28, no. 5 (2002): 284–85, doi:10.1136/jme.28.5.284.

44 This insight is from personal correspondence with Rob Nichols of CBM (an organization that works to improve the lives of people with disabilities in the poorest places in the world).

45 Jean Vanier, *Becoming Human*, 2nd ed. (Mahwah, N.J.: Paulist, 2008), 45.

46 Reynolds, *Vulnerable Communion*, 118.

47 To be fair, most academic treatments of theodicy do not make this mistake, and Stump, Stoeber, and Adams cannot be accused of doing so.

48 Jay McNeill, personal correspondence with author, April 8, 2015.

49 Andrew Gleeson, *A Frightening Love: Recasting the Problem of Evil* (London: Palgrave Macmillan, 2011), 5.

50 Gleeson, *Frightening Love*, 51–57.

51 Ormerod, *Public God*, 167.

52 Ormerod, *Public God*, 167.

53 Alvin Plantinga, *God, Freedom, and Evil* (Grand Rapids: Eerdmans, 1973); Richard Swinburne, *Providence and the Problem of Evil* (Oxford: Oxford University Press, 1998).

54 Ormerod, *Public God*, 166.

55 Lonergan, *Method in Theology*, 117.

56 Van Inwagen argues, "Natural evil, according to the expanded free-will defense, is a special case of evil that is caused by the abuse of free will; the fact that human beings are subject to destruction by earthquakes is a consequence of an aboriginal abuse of free will"(*Problem of Evil*, 91). To arrive at this conclusion, he envisages a point in evolutionary history when primates reached the point of achieving free will, but before the fall—at which time, they possessed "preternatural powers" that enabled them to live in perfect love and protect themselves from wild beasts, disease, and destructive natural events (86). I find this argument unconvincing.

57 Matias Casás-Selves and James DeGregori, "How Cancer Shapes Evolution, and How Evolution Shapes Cancer," *Evolution: Education and Outreach* 4, no. 4 (2011): 624–34, doi:10.1007/s12052-011-0373-y.

58 Reinders, *Disability, Providence, and Ethics*, Kindle loc. 3684.

59 Crysdale and Ormerod, *Creator God, Evolving World*, 45; Neil Ormerod, "Chance and Necessity, Providence and God," *Irish Theological Quarterly* 70, no. 3 (2005): 263–78.

60 Gleeson, *Frightening Love*, 105.

61 It is feminism that has most forcefully reminded us that theology needs to take embodiment seriously, and this emphasis is given further weight in feminist

reflection on disability. Deborah Creamer, for example, draws on the experience of disability to highlight the fact that human life is always subject to limits—that bodies are "leaky, messy things"—and that reflection on the distinct and diverse experiences of embodiment allow for creative meaning making. Deborah B. Creamer, *Disability and Christian Theology: Embodied Limits and Constructive Possibilities* (Oxford: Oxford University Press, 2008), 115–17.

62 E.g., Stoeber, *Reclaiming Theodicy*, chap. 3.

63 Adams, *Christ and Horrors*, 72.

64 Adams, *Christ and Horrors*, 207–11.

65 Nancy L. Eiesland, *The Disabled God: Toward a Liberatory Theology of Disability* (Nashville: Abingdon, 1994), 89. Whether or not a quadriplegic uses a sip and puff wheelchair will depend on the level of their injury. Most (including myself) do not.

66 Peter Laughlin, *Jesus and the Cross: Necessity, Meaning, and Atonement* (Eugene, Ore.: Pickwick, 2014), 83.

67 Jürgen Moltmann, *The Crucified God: The Cross of Christ as the Foundation and Criticism of Christian Theology* (London: SCM Press, 1974).

68 Laughlin, *Jesus and the Cross*, 33.

69 For a fuller discussion see Crysdale and Ormerod, *Creator God, Evolving World*, 99.

70 Bernard J. F. Lonergan, "The Redemption," in *Collected Works: 1958–1964*, ed. Robert C. Croken, Frederick E. Crowe, and Robert M. Doran (Toronto: University of Toronto Press, 1996); Mark T. Miller, "Imitating Christ's Cross: Lonergan and Girard on How and Why," *Heythrop Journal* 54, no. 5 (2013): 859–79, doi:10.1111/j.1468-2265.2012.00786.x.

71 Aquinas, *Summa Theologica* 1.2.Q62. Also Joseph P. Wawrykow, "The Theological Virtues," in *The Oxford Handbook of Aquinas*, ed. Brian Davies and Eleonore Stump (Oxford: Oxford University Press, 2012).

72 Brian D. McLaren, *Finding Faith: A Self-Discovery Guide for Your Spiritual Quest* (Grand Rapids: Zondervan, 1999), 201.

73 See Aquinas, *Summa Theologica* 2.2.QQ1–8. See also Eleonore Stump, *Aquinas* (London: Routledge, 2003), 361–68.

74 Lonergan, *Method in Theology*, 117.

75 Aquinas, *Summa Theologica* 2.2.Q4.A8.

76 Stump, *Wandering in Darkness*, 163.

77 Clifton, "Dark Side of Prayer for Healing."

78 Lizette Larson-Miller, "Healing: Sacrament or Prayer?" *Anglican Theological Review* 88, no. 3 (2006): 370.

79 Cindy L. Buchanan and Shane J. Lopez, "Understanding Hope in Individuals with Disabilities," in *The Oxford Handbook of Positive Psychology and Disability*, ed. Michael L. Wehmeyer (Oxford: Oxford University Press, 2013).

80 Pat Dorsett, "The Importance of Hope in Coping with Severe Acquired Disability," *Australian Social Work* 63, no. 1 (2010): 83–102.

81   Benedict XVI, *Spe Salvi*, Encyclical Letter, last modified 2007, http://www. vatican.va/holy_father/benedict_xvi/encyclicals/documents/hf_ben-xvi _enc_20071130_spe-salvi_en.html.

82   Jay McNeill, *Growing Sideways* (Melbourne: self-published on Kindle, 2011).

3: DISABILITY, VIRTUE, AND THE MEANING OF HAPPINESS

  1   See for example Philippa Foot, *Virtues and Vices*; Alasdair MacIntyre, *After Virtue: A Study in Moral Theory*, 3rd ed. (Notre Dame: University of Notre Dame Press, 2007); Martha Nussbaum, "Non-Relative Virtues: An Aristotelian Approach," in *The Quality of Life*, ed. Martha Nussbaum and Amartya Sen (Oxford: Oxford University Press, 1993).

  2   Luther H. Martin, "The Hellenisation of Judaeo-Christian Faith or the Christianisation of Hellenic Thought," *Religion and Theology* 12, no. 1 (2005): 13.

  3   Thomas F. Torrance, *Trinitarian Faith: The Evangelical Theology of the Ancient Catholic Faith*, 2nd ed. (London: T&T Clark, 1997), 68; Lonergan, *Method in Theology*, chap. 8.

  4   Russell, *Cambridge Companion to Virtue Ethics*, 7.

  5   Dylan M. Smith et al., "Health, Wealth, and Happiness: Financial Resources Buffer Subjective Well-Being after the Onset of a Disability," *Psychological Science* 16, no. 9 (2005): 663–66.

  6   Aristotle, *Nicomachean Ethics* 1095b.

  7   Young, "We're Not Here for Your Inspiration."

  8   Aristotle, *Nicomachean Ethics* 1095b.

  9   Aristotle, *Nicomachean Ethics* 1098a.

10   Aristotle, *Nicomachean Ethics* 1097b.

11   Russell, *Cambridge Companion to Virtue Ethics*, 10.

12   Rosalind Hursthouse, *On Virtue Ethics* (Oxford: Oxford University Press, 1999), 222; MacIntyre, *Dependent Rational Animals*, 11.

13   Aristotle, *Nicomachean Ethics* 1098a.

14   Hursthouse, *On Virtue Ethics*, 222.

15   Hursthouse, *On Virtue Ethics*, 221–22.

16   Longmore, *Why I Burned My Book*, 7.

17   Aristotle, *Nicomachean Ethics* 1106a.

18   Aristotle, *Nicomachean Ethics* 1107a.

19   While this list is from *Nicomachean Ethics*, Aristotle has a more expansive list of virtues in his *Eudemian Ethics*.

20   MacIntyre, *After Virtue*, 187. Aristotle uses the term "activity" but MacIntyre refers to "practices," since it enables him to reference specific practices that have meaning beyond everyday activities. Practices are "cooperative human activities through which goods internal to that form of activity are realized."

21   Russell, *Cambridge Companion to Virtue Ethics*, 15.

22   MacIntyre, *After Virtue*, 198.

23   MacIntyre, *After Virtue*, 150.

24   Aristotle, *Nicomachean Ethics* 1099a.

25 Aristotle, *Nicomachean Ethics*, book 6.

26 MacIntyre, *After Virtue*, 194.

27 MacIntyre, *After Virtue*, 222.

28 Aristotle, *Nicomachean Ethics* 1156a.

29 Aristotle, *Nicomachean Ethics* 1157–59.

30 Aristotle, *Politics* 1260a.

31 Aristotle, *Nicomachean Ethics* 1099b.

32 Aristotle, *Nicomachean Ethics* 1124b.

33 For a more detailed discussion, see the chapter "Virtue, Character, Moral Formation, and the Ends of Life," in John Barton, *Ethics in Ancient Israel* (Oxford: Oxford University Press, 2015), 157–84.

34 Stephen Pope, "Virtues in Theology," in *Virtues and Their Vices*, ed. Kevin Timpe and Craig A. Boyd (Oxford: Oxford University Press, 2014), 397.

35 Barton, *Ethics in Ancient Israel*, 162.

36 Barton, *Ethics in Ancient Israel*, 167.

37 Barton, *Ethics in Ancient Israel*, 171.

38 MacIntyre holds that narrative is central to the virtue tradition, because we learn about virtues through stories (*After Virtue*, 205).

39 David M. Gunn and Danna Nolan Fewell, *Narrative in the Hebrew Bible*, Oxford Bible Series (Oxford: Oxford University Press, 1993), 204.

40 Ronald Hendel, *Remembering Abraham: Culture, Memory, and History in the Hebrew Bible* (Oxford: Oxford University Press, 2005).

41 Ellen T. Charry, *God and the Art of Happiness* (Grand Rapids: Eerdmans, 2010), 193.

42 See, for example, "Sin, Impurity, and Forgiveness," chap. 7 in Barton, *Ethics in Ancient Israel*.

43 This is typified in passages such as Prov 11:19, "Truly the righteous attain life, but whoever pursues evil finds death."

44 Carol A. Newsom, "Positive Psychology and Ancient Israelite Wisdom," in *The Bible and the Pursuit of Happiness: What the Old and New Testaments Teach Us about the Good Life*, ed. Brent A. Strawn (Oxford: Oxford University Press, 2012), 133.

45 Newsom, "Positive Psychology and Ancient Israelite Wisdom," 134.

46 Saul M. Olyan, *Disability in the Hebrew Bible: Interpreting Mental and Physical Differences* (Cambridge: Cambridge University Press, 2008). Some good efforts are being made to rectify the lacunae, including Melcher, Parsons, and Yong, *Bible and Disability*.

47 Olyan, *Disability in the Hebrew Bible*, 5.

48 Olyan, *Disability in the Hebrew Bible*, 28, 140–41. A similar ban applied to barren women: Susan Ackerman, "The Blind, the Lame, and the Barren Shall Not Come into the House," in *Disability Studies and Biblical Literature*, ed. Candida R. Moss and Jeremy Schipper (New York: Palgrave Macmillan, 2011).

49 Saul M. Olyan, *Rites and Rank: Hierarchy in Biblical Representations of Cult* (Princeton: Princeton University Press, 2000), 62.

50 Barton, *Ethics in Ancient Israel*, 6.

51 Saul M. Olyan, "The Ascription of Physical Disability as a Stigmatizing Strategy in Biblical Iconic Polemics," in Moss and Schipper, *Disability Studies and Biblical Literature*, 92.

52 For a more detailed discussion, see the analysis of Jesus' healing ministry below.

53 See John Wesley's explanatory notes on Lev 21:17, Wesley Center Online, Wesley Center for Applied Theology, Northwest Nazarene University, accessed August 25, 2017, http://wesley.nnu.edu/john-wesley/john-wesleys-notes-on-the-bible/notes-on-the-third-book-of-moses-called-leviticus/#Chapter%2BXXI.

54 John E. Hartley, *Leviticus*, Word Biblical Commentary 4 (Grand Rapids: Zondervan, 1992), 349–50.

55 Samuel E. Balentine, *Leviticus*, Interpretation: A Bible Commentary for Teaching and Preaching (Louisville, Ky.: Westminster John Knox, 2003), 169.

56 I owe this insight to personal correspondence with Caroline Batchelder.

57 Olyan, *Disability in the Hebrew Bible*, 11.

58 Yong, *Bible, Disability, and the Church*, Kindle loc. 451; Olyan, *Disability in the Hebrew Bible*, 10.

59 Jeremy Schipper, "Reconsidering the Imagery of Disability in 2 Samuel 5:8b," *Catholic Biblical Quarterly* 67, no. 3 (2005): 422–34; Jeremy Schipper, *Disability Studies and the Hebrew Bible: Figuring Mephibosheth in the David Story* (New York: T&T Clark, 2009).

60 An excellent disabled reading of this text is given by Jeremy Schipper, *Disability and Isaiah's Suffering Servant* (Oxford: Oxford University Press, 2011).

61 David J. Bosch, *Transforming Mission: Paradigm Shifts in the Theology of Mission* (Maryknoll, N.Y.: Orbis Books, 1991), 32.

62 Joel B. Green, "'We Had to Celebrate and Rejoice!': Happiness in the Topsy-Turvy World of Luke-Acts," in Strawn, *Bible and the Pursuit of Happiness*, 183.

63 Green, "'We Had to Celebrate and Rejoice!'" 171.

64 Crysdale and Ormerod, *Creator God, Evolving World*, 101.

65 As Stanley Hauerwas observes, "There is no way to know the Kingdom except by learning of the story of this man Jesus. For his story defines the nature of how God rules and how such a rule creates a corresponding world and society." See Hauerwas, *A Community of Character: Toward a Constructive Christian Social Ethic* (Notre Dame: University of Notre Dame Press, 1991), 45.

66 Michael G. Lawler and Todd A. Salzman, "Virtue Ethics: Natural and Christian," *Theological Studies* 74, no. 2 (2013): 465.

67 Lawler and Salzman, "Virtue Ethics."

68 MacIntyre, *After Virtue*, 182.

69 MacIntyre, *After Virtue*, 184.

70 Yong, *Bible, Disability, and the Church*, Kindle loc. 716.

71 Yong, *Bible, Disability, and the Church.*

72 Allan Anderson, *To the Ends of the Earth: Pentecostalism and the Transformation of World Christianity* (Oxford: Oxford University Press, 2012), 149; Philip Jenkins, *The Next Christendom: The Coming of Global Christianity* (New York: Oxford University Press, 2011), 159.

73 Joni Eareckson Tada, *A Place of Healing: Wrestling with the Mysteries of Suffering, Pain, and God's Sovereignty* (Colorado Springs, Colo.: David C. Cook, 2015), 47–48 (emphasis in original).

74 Elisabeth Schüssler Fiorenza, *Rhetoric and Ethic: The Politics of Biblical Studies* (Minneapolis: Fortress, 1999), 14.

75 Elisabeth Schüssler Fiorenza, *But She Said: Feminist Practices of Biblical Interpretation* (Boston: Beacon Press, 1992).

76 Susan Haber, "A Woman's Touch: Feminist Encounters with the Hemorrhaging Woman in Mark 5.24-34," *Journal for the Study of the New Testament* 26, no. 2 (2003): 171–92.

77 As N. T. Wright observes, "It is prudent, methodologically, to hold back from too hasty a judgement on what is actually possible and what is not within the space-time universe. There are more things in heaven and earth than are dreamed of in post-Enlightenment philosophy." Wright, *Jesus and the Victory of God*, Christian Origins and the Question of God 2 (Minneapolis: Fortress, 1996), Kindle loc. 4156.

78 Marcus Borg, *Jesus: Uncovering the Life, Teachings, and Relevance of a Religious Revolutionary* (New York: HarperCollins, 2006), 62.

79 Wright, *Jesus and the Victory of God*, Kindle loc. 63750.

80 Wright, *Jesus and the Victory of God*, Kindle loc. 4247.

81 Louise Gosbell, "Banqueting and Disability: Reconsidering the Parable of the Banquet (Luke 14:15-24)," in *Theology and the Experience of Disability*, ed. Andrew Picard and Myk Habets (Burlington, Vt.: Ashgate, 2016).

82 Gosbell, "Banqueting and Disability."

83 Elisabeth Schüssler Fiorenza, *Jesus, Miriam's Child, Sophia's Prophet: Critical Issues in Feminist Christology* (New York: Continuum, 1994), chap. 4; Darby Kathleen Ray, *Deceiving the Devil: Atonement, Abuse, and Ransom* (Cleveland, Ohio: Pilgrim, 1998); Joanne C. Brown, Carole R. Bohn, and Elizabeth Bettenhausen, eds., *Christianity, Patriarchy, and Abuse: A Feminist Critique* (Cleveland, Ohio: Pilgrim, 1989); J. Denny Weaver, *The Nonviolent Atonement*, 2nd ed. (Grand Rapids: Eerdmans, 2011).

84 John Dominic Crossan, *The Power of Parable: How Fiction by Jesus Became Fiction about Jesus*, reprint ed. (New York: HarperOne, 2013), 142, 186.

85 Wright, *Jesus and the Victory of God*, 44–66.

86 See, for example, Rosemary Radford Ruether, *Sexism and God-Talk: Toward a Feminist Theology* (Boston: Beacon Press, 1993); Elizabeth Johnson, *She Who Is: The Mystery of God in Feminist Theological Discourse*, 10th anniversary expanded ed. (New York: Crossroad, 2001); Lisa Isherwood, *Introducing Feminist Christologies* (New York: Continuum, 2001), 15–32.

87 Bonnie Kent, "Augustine's Ethics," in *The Cambridge Companion to Augustine*, ed. Eleonore Stump and Norman Kretzmann (Cambridge: Cambridge University Press, 2001), 208. See Augustine, *The Happy Life*, in *Trilogy of Faith and Happiness*, trans. Roland J. Teske, Michael Campbell, and Ray Kearney, intro. and notes by Michael Fiedrowicz and Roland J. Teske, ed. Boniface Ramsey (New York: New City Press, 2010).

88 Augustine, *City of God* 15.22; Kent, "Augustine's Ethics," in Stump and Kretzmann, *Cambridge Companion to Augustine*, 215.

89 MacIntyre, *After Virtue*, 184.

90 Aquinas, *Summa Theologica* 1.2.Q4.7. Joseph Stenberg, "Aquinas on Happiness" (Ph.D. diss., University of Colorado at Boulder, 2016), 119.

91 Aquinas, *Summa Theologica* 1.2.3.

92 Stenberg, "Aquinas on Happiness," 8.

93 Aristotle, *Nicomachean Ethics* 1099a. See also discussion of Aristotle and the continent person earlier in this chapter.

94 Aquinas, *Summa Theologica* 2.2.Q123.8.

95 Aquinas, *Summa Theologica* 1.2.Q4.6.

96 Aquinas, *Summa Theologica* 1.2.26.

97 Aquinas, *Summa Theologica* 2.2.Q29.A3. For a more detailed discussion of Aquinas' treatment of love, see Stump, *Wandering in Darkness*, 127.

98 Aquinas, *Summa Theologica* 2.2.Q23.A1.

99 Aquinas, *Summa Theologica* 2.2.Q4.A8.

100 Aquinas, *Summa Theologica* 2.2.Q25.A8.

101 Aquinas, *Summa Theologica* 2.2.Q30.A1.

102 Aquinas, *Summa Theologica* 2.2.Q30.A2.

103 Rachel Hurst, "Forget Pity or Charity: Disability Is a Rights Issue," Media Action WACC, 1998; Shakespeare, *Disability Rights and Wrongs Revisited*, 13.

104 Joseph P. Shapiro, *No Pity: People with Disabilities Forging a New Civil Rights Movement* (New York: Broadway Books, 1994), 22.

105 Sharon V. Betcher, *Spirit and the Politics of Disablement* (Minneapolis: Fortress, 2007), 107. Betcher labels this type of pity as "conspicuous compassion."

106 Aquinas, *Summa Theologica* 2.2.

107 MacIntyre, *After Virtue*, 178.

108 Friedrich Wilhelm Nietzsche, *Beyond Good and Evil: Prelude to a Philosophy of the Future*, ed. Rolf-Peter Horstmann, trans. Judith Norman (Cambridge: Cambridge University Press, 2002), 85.

109 The greatest works emerging from this renewed interest inform the whole of this work, from first to last. However, interested readers might look to the following as places to begin to follow the thread of this resurgence: Stanley Hauerwas and Charles R. Pinches, *Christians among the Virtues: Theological Conversations with Ancient and Modern Ethics* (Notre Dame: University of Notre Dame Press, 1997); Roger Crisp and Michael Slote, eds., *Virtue Ethics*, Oxford Readings in Philosophy (Oxford: Oxford University Press, 1997); Martin E. P. Seligman, *Authentic Happiness: Using the New Positive Psychology*

to Realize Your Potential for Lasting Fulfillment (New York: Simon and Schuster, 2002); Nancy E. Snow, ed., *Cultivating Virtue: Perspectives from Philosophy, Theology, and Psychology* (Oxford: Oxford University Press, 2014); Timpe and Boyd, *Virtues and Their Vices.*

4: DISABILITY, ADVOCACY, AND THE GOOD LIFE

1 Carolyn C. Morf and Walter Mischel, "The Self as a Psycho-Social Dynamic Processing System: Toward a Converging Science of Selfhood," in *Handbook of Self and Identity*, ed. Mark R. Leary and June Price Tangney (New York: Guilford Press, 2012).

2 Robert A. Neimeyer, ed., *Meaning Reconstruction and the Experience of Loss* (Washington, D.C.: American Psychological Association, 2001), 263–64.

3 Shane Clifton, Gwynnyth Llewellyn, and Tom Shakespeare, "Quadriplegia and the Good Life," qualitative research project conducted under the auspices of the University of Sydney, the Centre for Disability Research and Policy. Some of the logic of this book emerges from that study. Publications arising from that study include Shane Clifton, Gwynnyth Llewellyn, and Tom Shakespeare, "Quadriplegia, Virtue Theory, and Flourishing: A Qualitative Study Drawing on Self-Narratives," *Disability and Society*, forthcoming, 2017.

4 Mark was the only person in our study who took this view. Others said they had had a good life, but would have much preferred to live without the injury.

5 Ron Amundson, "Disability, Ideology, and Quality of Life: A Bias in Biomedical Ethics," in *Quality of Life and Human Difference: Genetic Testing, Health Care, and Disability*, ed. David T. Wasserman, Robert Samuel Wachbroit, and Jerome Edmund Bickenbach (New York: Cambridge University Press, 2005).

5: DISABILITY, PSYCHOLOGY, AND THE SCIENCE OF HAPPINESS

1 G. L. Albrecht and P. J. Devlieger, "The Disability Paradox: High Quality of Life against All Odds," *Social Science & Medicine* 48, no. 8 (1999): 977–88.

2 David Lykken and Auke Tellegen, "Happiness Is a Stochastic Phenomenon," *Psychological Science* 7, no. 3 (1996): 186–89, doi:10.1111/j.1467-9280.1996. tb00355.x; Ed Diener, Richard E. Lucas, and Christie Napa Scollon, "Beyond the Hedonic Treadmill: Revising the Adaptation Theory of Well-Being," *American Psychologist* 61, no. 4 (2006): 305–14; Sonja Lyubomirsky, "Hedonic Adaption to Positive and Negative Experiences," in *The Oxford Handbook of Stress, Health, and Coping*, ed. Susan Folkman (New York: Oxford University Press, 2010); Robert A. Cummins and Mark Wooden, "Personal Resilience in Times of Crisis: The Implications of SWB Homeostasis and Set-Points," *Journal of Happiness Studies* 15, no. 1 (2013): 223–35, doi:10.1007/s10902-013-9481-4.

3 Philip Brickman, Dan Coates, and Ronnie Janoff-Bulman, "Lottery Winners and Accident Victims: Is Happiness Relative?" *Journal of Personality and Social Psychology* 36, no. 8 (1978): 917–27.

4 Shane Frederick and George Loewenstein, "Hedonic Adaptation," in *Well-Being: Foundations of Hedonic Psychology*, ed. Daniel Kahneman, Edward

Diener, and Norbert Schwarz (New York: Russell Sage Foundation, 1999), 302–29.

5 Diener, Lucas, and Scollon, "Beyond the Hedonic Treadmill."

6 Lyubomirsky, "Hedonic Adaption to Positive and Negative Experiences," 203.

7 Lyubomirsky, "Hedonic Adaption to Positive and Negative Experiences," 204.

8 Sharanjit Uppal, "Impact of the Timing, Type and Severity of Disability on the Subjective Well-Being of Individuals with Disabilities," *Social Science & Medicine* 63, no. 2 (2006): 525–39, doi:10.1016/j.socscimed.2006.01.016.

9 S. A. Kilic, D. S. Dorstyn, and N. G. Guiver, "Examining Factors That Contribute to the Process of Resilience following Spinal Cord Injury," *Spinal Cord* 51, no. 7 (2013): 553–57, doi:10.1038/sc.2013.25.

10 Kennon M. Sheldon and Richard E. Lucas, eds., *Stability of Happiness: Theories and Evidence on Whether Happiness Can Change* (London: Academic Press, 2014), 30.

11 Ed Diener and Carol Diener, "Most People Are Happy," *Psychological Science* 7, no. 3 (1996): 181–85; Diener, Lucas, and Scollon, "Beyond the Hedonic Treadmill."

12 Peter Singer, "Why We Must Ration Health Care," *New York Times Magazine*, July 15, 2009, http://www.nytimes.com/2009/07/19/magazine/19healthcare-t.html.

13 Ron Amundson, "Quality of Life, Disability, and Hedonic Psychology," *Journal for the Theory of Social Behaviour* 40, no. 4 (2010): 374–92, doi:10.1111/j.1468-5914.2010.00437.x.

14 Amundson, "Quality of Life, Disability, and Hedonic Psychology," 381.

15 Dan W. Brock, "Justice and the ADA: Does Prioritizing and Rationing Health Care Discriminate against the Disabled?" *Social Philosophy & Policy* 12, no. 2 (1995): 182.

16 Amundson, "Disability, Ideology, and Quality of Life, in Wasserman et al., *Quality of Life and Human Difference*."

17 Alex C. Michalos, "Education, Happiness and Wellbeing," *Social Indicators Research* 87, no. 3 (2008): 350, doi:10.1007/s11205-007-9144-0. For further discussion, see M. Joseph Sirgy, *The Psychology of Quality of Life: Hedonic Well-Being, Life Satisfaction, and Eudaimonia*, 2nd ed. (Dordrecht: Springer, 2012), 31–33.

18 Amundson, "Disability, Ideology, and Quality of Life," in Wasserman et al., *Quality of Life and Human Difference*, 112.

19 Seligman, *Authentic Happiness*, xi.

20 Seligman, *Authentic Happiness*.

21 Martin E. P. Seligman, *Flourish: A Visionary New Understanding of Happiness and Well-Being* (repr., New York: Free Press, 2012), 1.

22 Seligman, *Authentic Happiness*, 8.

23 Seligman, *Authentic Happiness*, 14.

24 Making this point, Nancy Snow refers to Kant's aphorism, "virtue ethics is not an ethics for Angels." Nancy E. Snow, "Virtue and Flourishing," *Journal of Social Philosophy* 39, no. 2 (2008): 227, doi:10.1111/j.1467-9833.2008.00425.x.

25 Ed Diener, Heidi Smith, and Frank Fujita, "The Personality Structure of Affect," *Journal of Personality and Social Psychology* 69, no. 1 (1995): 130–41, doi:10.1037/0022-3514.69.1.130; Sirgy, *Psychology of Quality of Life*, 8; Seligman, *Flourish*, 16.

26 Luc Lecavalier and Marc J. Tassé, "An Exploratory Study of the 'Personality' of Adolescents and Adults with Down Syndrome," *Journal of Intellectual and Developmental Disability* 30, no. 2 (2005): 67–74, doi:10.1080/13668250500124976.

27 J. G. Wishart and F. H. Johnston, "The Effects of Experience on Attribution of a Stereotyped Personality to Children with Down's Syndrome," *Journal of Intellectual Disability Research* 34, no. 5 (1990): 409–20, doi:10.1111/j.1365-2788.1990.tb01551.x.

28 Michael A. Cohn and Barbara L. Fredrickson, "Positive Emotions," in *The Oxford Handbook of Positive Psychology*, ed. Shane J. Lopez and C. R. Snyder, 2nd ed. (Oxford: Oxford University Press, 2009).

29 Marek Spinka, Ruth C. Newberry, and Marc Bekoff, "Mammalian Play: Training for the Unexpected," *Quarterly Review of Biology* 76, no. 2 (2001): 141–68.

30 Matthew Gervais and David Sloan Wilson, "The Evolution and Functions of Laughter and Humor: A Synthetic Approach," *Quarterly Review of Biology* 80, no. 4 (2005): 395–430, doi:10.1086/498281.

31 Cohn and Fredrickson, "Positive Emotions," in Lopez and Snyder, *Oxford Handbook of Positive Psychology*, 14.

32 Robert Emmons, "Gratitude, Subjective Well-Being, and the Brain," in *The Science of Subjective Well-Being*, ed. Michael Eid and Randy J. Larsen (New York: Guilford Press, 2008).

33 Laurence Clark, "Disabling Comedy: 'Only When We Laugh!'" paper presented at the Finding the Spotlight conference, Liverpool Institute for the Performing Arts, May 30, 2003, http://disability-studies.leeds.ac.uk/files/library/Clark-Laurence-clarke-on-comedy.pdf; Gervais and Wilson, "Evolution and Functions of Laughter and Humor," 402.

34 D. Kim Reid, Edy Hammond Stoughton, and Robin M. Smith, "The Humorous Construction of Disability: 'Stand-Up' Comedians in the United States," *Disability & Society* 21, no. 6 (2006): 629–43, doi:10.1080/09687590600918354.

35 Michele M. Tugade and Barbara L. Fredrickson, "Resilient Individuals Use Positive Emotions to Bounce Back from Negative Emotional Experiences," *Journal of Personality and Social Psychology* 86, no. 2 (2004): 320–33.

36 Cohn and Fredrickson, "Positive Emotions," in Lopez and Snyder, *Oxford Handbook of Positive Psychology*, 18.

37 Clifton, "Grieving My Broken Body."

38 Catherine E. Foote and Arthur W. Frank, "Foucault and Therapy: The Disciplining of Grief," in *Reading Foucault for Social Work*, ed. Adrienne S. Chambon, Allan Irving, and Laura Epstein (New York: Columbia University Press, 1999), 170.

39 Cohn and Fredrickson, "Positive Emotions," in Lopez and Snyder, *Oxford Handbook of Positive Psychology*, 21.

40 Eric L. Garland and Barbara L. Fredrickson, "Mindfulness Broadens Awareness and Builds Meaning at the Attention-Emotion Interface," in *Mindfulness, Acceptance, and Positive Psychology: The Seven Foundations of Well-Being*, ed. Todd B. Kashdan and Joseph V. Ciarrochi (Oakland: New Harbinger, 2013), 41.

41 Seligman, *Flourish*, 33–35; Kashdan and Ciarrochi, *Mindfulness, Acceptance, and Positive Psychology*; Itai Ivtzan and Tim Lomas, eds., *Mindfulness in Positive Psychology: The Science of Meditation and Wellbeing* (Florence, Ky.: Taylor & Francis, 2016); Kristen Neff and Dennis Tirch, "Self-Compassion and ACT," in Kashdan and Ciarrochi, *Mindfulness, Acceptance, and Positive Psychology*, 78–106; Sharna St Leon, Desiree Kozlowski, and Stephen Provost, "Resilience and the Role of Savouring Pleasure," *Frontiers in Psychology* 6 (2015), doi:10.3389/conf.fpsyg.2015.66.00010.

42 Tim Lomas, "Nourishment from the Roots: Engaging with the Buddhist Foundations of Mindfulness," in Ivtzan and Lomas, *Mindfulness in Positive Psychology*, 265–79.

43 Seligman, *Authentic Happiness*, 103; Sirgy, *Psychology of Quality of Life*, 161.

44 Seligman, *Flourish*, 11.

45 Sirgy, *Psychology of Quality of Life*, 13–15.

46 The measurement of QOL is complex and has been the focus of substantive literature. For a summary, see Robert Costanza et al., "Quality of Life: An Approach Integrating Opportunities, Human Needs, and Subjective Well-Being," *Ecological Economics* 61, nos. 2–3 (2007): 267–76, doi:10.1016/j.ecolecon.2006.02.023; Sirgy, *Psychology of Quality of Life*, 31–35.

47 Ivan Brown, Chris Hatton, and Eric Emerson, "Quality of Life Indicators for Individuals with Intellectual Disabilities: Extending Current Practice," *Intellectual and Developmental Disabilities* 51, no. 5 (2013): 316–32, doi:10.1352/1934-9556-51.5.316.

48 People looking for a solid overview of this literature might consider Wehmeyer, *Oxford Handbook of Positive Psychology and Disability*.

49 Michael L. Wehmeyer and Todd D. Little, "Self-Determination," in Wehmeyer, *Oxford Handbook of Positive Psychology and Disability*, 116–36.

50 For a summary of the literature, see Ashley Craig, "Resilience in People with Physical Disabilities," in *The Oxford Handbook of Rehabilitation Psychology*, ed. Paul Kennedy (Oxford: Oxford University Press, 2012), 479–91; Kilic, Dorstyn, and Guiver, "Examining Factors That Contribute to the Process of Resilience."

51 Nan Zhang Hampton, "Subjective Well-Being among People with Spinal Cord Injuries: The Role of Self-Efficacy, Perceived Social Support, and Perceived Health," *Rehabilitation Counseling Bulletin* 48, no. 1 (2004): 31–37; Kilic, Dorstyn, and Guiver, "Examining Factors That Contribute to the Process of Resilience," 556; James Middleton, Yvonne Tran, and Ashley Craig,

"Relationship between Quality of Life and Self-Efficacy in Persons with Spinal Cord Injuries," *Archives of Physical Medicine and Rehabilitation* 88, no. 12 (2007): 1643–48, doi:10.1016/j.apmr.2007.09.001.

52 Kathleen B. Kortte et al., "Positive Psychological Variables in the Prediction of Life Satisfaction after Spinal Cord Injury," *Rehabilitation Psychology* 55, no. 1 (2010): 43, doi:10.1037/a0018624; C. Peter et al., "Psychological Resources in Spinal Cord Injury: A Systematic Literature Review," *Spinal Cord* 50, no. 3 (2012): 190, doi:10.1038/sc.2011.125; Martha H. Chapin and Donald Holbert, "Employment at Closure Is Associated with Enhanced Quality of Life and Subjective Well-Being for Persons with Spinal Cord Injuries," *Rehabilitation Counseling Bulletin* 54, no. 1 (2010): 6–14, doi:10.1177/0034355210367685.

53 Hampton, "Subjective Well-Being among People with Spinal Cord Injuries"; Anette Johansen Quale and Anne-Kristine Schanke, "Resilience in the Face of Coping with a Severe Physical Injury: A Study of Trajectories of Adjustment in a Rehabilitation Setting," *Rehabilitation Psychology* 55, no. 1 (2010): 12–22, doi:10.1037/a0018415; Elizabeth N. Matheis, David S. Tulsky, and Robert J. Matheis, "The Relation between Spirituality and Quality of Life among Individuals with Spinal Cord Injury," *Rehabilitation Psychology* 51, no. 3 (2006): 265–71, doi:10.1037/0090-5550.51.3.265; Brian White, Simon Driver, and Ann Marie Warren, "Resilience and Indicators of Adjustment during Rehabilitation from a Spinal Cord Injury," *Rehabilitation Psychology* 55, no. 1 (2010): 23–32; K. R. Monden et al., "Resilience following Spinal Cord Injury: A Phenomenological View," *Spinal Cord* 52, no. 3 (2014): 199, doi: 10.1038/sc.2013.159.

54 Quale and Schanke, "Resilience in the Face of Coping with a Severe Physical Injury"; Weitzner et al., "Getting On with Life"; Kilic, Dorstyn, and Guiver, "Examining Factors That Contribute to the Process of Resilience."

55 Kortte et al., "Positive Psychological Variables in the Prediction of Life Satisfaction after Spinal Cord Injury"; Dorsett, "Importance of Hope"; Ioanna Tzonichaki and George Kleftaras, "Paraplegia from Spinal Cord Injury: Self-Esteem, Loneliness, and Life Satisfaction," *OTJR* 22, no. 3 (2002): 96–103; Peter et al., "Psychological Resources in Spinal Cord Injury."

56 Christopher Peterson, Nansook Park, and Martin E. P. Seligman, "Greater Strengths of Character and Recovery from Illness," *Journal of Positive Psychology* 1, no. 1 (2006): 17–26, doi:10.1080/17439760500372739.

57 Peterson, Park, and Seligman, "Greater Strengths of Character," 25.

58 Peterson, Park, and Seligman, "Greater Strengths of Character," 17.

59 Peterson, Park, and Seligman, "Greater Strengths of Character," 24. See also Dana S. Dunn, Gitendra Uswatte, and Timothy R. Elliott, "Happiness, Resilience, and Positive Growth following Physical Disability: Issues for Understanding, Research, and Therapeutic Intervention," in Lopez and Snyder, *Oxford Handbook of Positive Psychology*, 117–32.

60 Cretien van Campen and Jurjen Iedema, "Are Persons with Physical Disabilities Who Participate in Society Healthier and Happier? Structural Equation

Modelling of Objective Participation and Subjective Well-Being," *Quality of Life Research* 16, no. 4 (2007): 635–45.

61 Ariel Miller and Sara Dishon, "Health-Related Quality of Life in Multiple Sclerosis: The Impact of Disability, Gender and Employment Status," *Quality of Life Research* 15, no. 2 (2006): 259–71; Chapin and Holbert, "Employment at Closure"; David W. Hess et al., "Psychological Well-Being and Intensity of Employment in Individuals with a Spinal Cord Injury," *Topics in Spinal Cord Injury Rehabilitation* 9, no. 4 (2004): 1–10; Eric Emerson et al., "Becoming Disabled: The Association between Disability Onset in Younger Adults and Subsequent Changes in Productive Engagement, Social Support, Financial Hardship and Subjective Wellbeing," *Disability and Health Journal* 7, no. 4 (2014): 448–56, doi:10.1016/j.dhjo.2014.03.004.

62 Jane E. Dutton, Laura Morgan Roberts, and Jeff Bednar, "Prosocial Practices, Positive Identity, and Flourishing at Work," in *Applied Positive Psychology: Improving Everyday Life, Health, Schools, Work, and Society*, ed. Stewart I. Donaldson, Mihaly Csikszentmihalyi, and Jeanne Nakamura (New York: Routledge, 2011), 158.

63 World Health Organization, "World Report on Disability," 238.

64 D. Rowell and L. B. Connelly, "Personal Assistance, Income and Employment: The Spinal Injuries Survey Instrument (SISI) and Its Application in a Sample of People with Quadriplegia," *Spinal Cord* 46, no. 6 (2008): 417–24, doi:10.1038/sj.sc.3102157. The situation is similar elsewhere: see for example James S. Krause, Joseph V. Terza, and Clara E. Dismuke, "Factors Associated with Labor Force Participation after Spinal-Cord Injury," *Journal of Vocational Rehabilitation* 33, no. 2 (2010): 89–99, doi:10.3233/JVR-2010-0518.

65 Seligman, *Flourish*, 224.

66 Daniel W. Sacks, Betsey Stevenson, and Justin Wolfers, "The New Stylized Facts about Income and Subjective Well-Being," *Emotion* 12, no. 6 (2012): 1181–87, doi:10.1037/a0029873.

67 James S. Krause and K. S. Reed, "Barriers and Facilitators to Employment after Spinal Cord Injury: Underlying Dimensions and Their Relationship to Labor Force Participation," *Spinal Cord* 49, no. 2 (2011): 288, doi:10.1038/sc.2010.110.

68 World Health Organization, "World Report on Disability," 239–40.

69 Martha H. Chapin and Donald G. Kewman, "Factors Affecting Employment following Spinal-Cord Injury: A Qualitative Study," *Rehabilitation Psychology* 46, no. 4 (2001): 400–416; John Rose et al., "Factors Affecting the Likelihood That People with Intellectual Disabilities Will Gain Employment," *Journal of Intellectual Disabilities* 9, no. 1 (2005): 9–23, doi:10.1177/1744629505049725; Gregory C. Murphy and Amanda E. Young, "Employment Participation following Spinal Cord Injury: Relation to Selected Participant Demographic, Injury and Psychological Characteristics," *Disability & Rehabilitation* 27, no. 21 (2005): 1297–1306; Lisa Ottomanelli and Lisa Lind, "Review of Critical Factors Related to Employment after Spinal Cord Injury: Implications

for Research and Vocational Services," *Journal of Spinal Cord Medicine* 32, no. 5 (2009): 503–31; Shaun Michael Burns et al., "Psychosocial Predictors of Employment Status among Men Living with Spinal Cord Injury," *Rehabilitation Psychology* 55, no. 1 (2010): 81–90, doi:10.1037/a0018583.

70 Kamil Yazicioglu et al., "Influence of Adapted Sports on Quality of Life and Life Satisfaction in Sport Participants and Non-Sport Participants with Physical Disabilities," *Disability and Health Journal* 5, no. 4 (2012): 249–53, doi:10.1016/j.dhjo.2012.05.003; Rongzhi Li, "The Effect of Community-Based Group Music Therapy on Quality of Life for Individuals with Developmental Disabilities" (master's thesis, East Carolina University, 2010), http://libres.uncg.edu/ir/uncg/listing.aspx?styp=ti&id=6668.

71 Eric Emerson, "The Quality of Life of Disabled Children," in *Enhancing the Quality of Life of People with Intellectual Disabilities*, ed. Ralph Kober, Social Indicators Research Series 41 (Dordrecht: Springer, 2010), 223–37, doi:10.1007/978-90-481-9650-0_14.

72 World Health Organization, "World Report on Disability," 10.

73 Emerson, "Quality of Life of Disabled Children," in Kober, *Enhancing the Quality of Life*, 233.

74 Seligman, *Authentic Happiness*, 14.

75 Seligman, *Authentic Happiness*, 258–60.

76 Abbott L. Ferriss, "Religion and the Quality of Life," *Journal of Happiness Studies* 3, no. 3 (2002): 199–215; Sirgy, *Psychology of Quality of Life*, 115–17.

77 Bruce Headey et al., "Authentic Happiness Theory Supported by Impact of Religion on Life Satisfaction," *Journal of Positive Psychology* 5, no. 1 (2010): 73–82, doi:10.1080/17439760903435232.

78 Ferriss, "Religion and the Quality of Life."

79 Ed Diener, Louis Tay, and David G. Myers, "The Religion Paradox: If Religion Makes People Happy, Why Are So Many Dropping Out?" *Journal of Personality and Social Psychology* 101, no. 6 (2011): 1278–90, doi:10.1037/a0024402.

80 Diener, Tay, and Myers, "The Religion Paradox," 1278.

81 Roy K. Chen and Nancy M. Crewe, "Life Satisfaction among People with Progressive Disabilities," *Journal of Rehabilitation* 75, no. 2 (2009): 50–58.

82 Brick Johnstone, Bret A. Glass, and Richard E. Oliver, "Religion and Disability: Clinical, Research and Training Considerations for Rehabilitation Professionals," *Disability and Rehabilitation* 29, no. 15 (2007): 1153–63, doi:10.1080/09638280600955693; White, Driver, and Warren, "Resilience and Indicators of Adjustment"; Monden et al., "Resilience following Spinal Cord Injury."

83 Johnstone, Glass, and Oliver, "Religion and Disability," 1156.

84 George Lindbeck, *The Nature of Doctrine: Religion and Theology in a Postliberal Age* (Louisville, Ky.: Westminster, 1984), 18.

85 Nietzsche, *Beyond Good and Evil*, 54–55 (emphasis in original).

86 William Gaventa, "Forgiveness, Gratitude, and Spirituality," in Wehmeyer, *Oxford Handbook of Positive Psychology and Disability*, 229.

87 Clifton, "Dark Side of Prayer for Healing," 204–25.
88 Michael E. McCullough et al., "Forgiveness," in Lopez and Snyder, *Oxford Handbook of Positive Psychology*, 427.
89 Young, "To My Eighty-Year-Old Self."
90 Seligman, *Flourish*, 1.

6: PROFOUND DISABILITY, INDEPENDENCE, AND FRIENDSHIP

1 Aristotle, *Nicomachean Ethics* 1124a–1125a.
2 Garret Merriam, "Rehabilitating Aristotle: A Virtue Ethics Approach to Disability and Human Flourishing," in *Philosophical Reflections on Disability*, ed. D. Christopher Ralston and Justin Hubert Ho, Philosophy and Medicine 104 (Dordrecht: Springer, 2009), 133–51.
3 Merriam, "Rehabilitating Aristotle," 134.
4 Merriam, "Rehabilitating Aristotle," 135.
5 Merriam, "Rehabilitating Aristotle," 137.
6 The case studies and their interpretation are that of Merriam, "Rehabilitating Aristotle."
7 Merriam, "Rehabilitating Aristotle," 138.
8 Merriam, "Rehabilitating Aristotle."
9 Anencephaly is a commonly used case study in the field of disability studies, although descriptions of the impairment vary from one presentation to another. Here, I follow the findings and interpretation of Merriam. Like most disabilities, the impairment is manifest in many different ways. Anencephaly is the absence of a major portion of the brain, and the outcome of the impairment depends upon the region of the brain affected. Merriam goes on to use the case studies of Keller and anencephaly as a basis for discussing the ethics of preventing the birth of disabled children, as well as exploring the fascinating situation of deliberate disablement; asking whether it is ethical for disabled people to seek to produce children that share in their disability.
10 For more information, see "Anencephaly," NIH National Library of Medicine, US Department of Health and Human Services, accessed January 5, 2017, https://ghr.nlm.nih.gov/condition/anencephaly.
11 Merriam, "Rehabilitating Aristotle," 139–41.
12 MacIntyre, *Dependent Rational Animals*.
13 MacIntyre, *Dependent Rational Animals*, 4.
14 For this reason, *Dependent Rational Animals* includes an extended discussion of dolphin intelligence and sociality, noting that many characteristics once deemed exclusively human are shared by dolphins and other intelligent animals. MacIntyre, *Dependent Rational Animals*, chaps. 3–7.
15 Contra to the proposed reconstruction of virtue by Merriam that was outlined above.
16 MacIntyre, *Dependent Rational Animals*, 1–2.
17 Eva Feder Kittay, *Love's Labor: Essays on Women, Equality and Dependency* (New York: Routledge, 1999); Eva Feder Kittay and Ellen K. Feder, eds., *The*

Subject of Care: Feminist Perspectives on Dependency (Lanham, Md.: Rowman & Littlefield, 2003).

18 MacIntyre, *Dependent Rational Animals*, 90.

19 MacIntyre, *Dependent Rational Animals*, 91.

20 MacIntyre, *Dependent Rational Animals*, chaps. 7–8.

21 MacIntyre is assuming a western view of parenting, here, but although the aims of parenting vary from one culture to another, it is generally true that parents aim for their children to live the good life—even if the shape of that life is culturally diverse. See Beatrice Blyth Whiting and Carolyn Pope Edwards, *Children of Different Worlds: The Formation of Social Behavior* (Cambridge, Mass.: Harvard University Press, 1992).

22 MacIntyre, *Dependent Rational Animals*, 100.

23 MacIntyre, *Dependent Rational Animals*, 100.

24 MacIntyre, *Dependent Rational Animals*, chap. 11.

25 MacIntyre, *Dependent Rational Animals*, 126.

26 MacIntyre, *Dependent Rational Animals*, 125.

27 In the field of disability, the language of "support" is generally preferred to that of "dependency." Since I am explaining MacIntyre, I follow his language for the moment, but will prefer the term "support" later in the argument.

28 MacIntyre, *Dependent Rational Animals*, 94.

29 Lonergan, *Method in Theology*, 11.

30 Lonergan, *Method in Theology*, 20.

31 Lonergan, *Method in Theology*, 104.

32 Lonergan, *Method in Theology*, 117.

33 Lonergan, *Method in Theology*, 105.

34 Lonergan, *Method in Theology*, 110.

35 Lonergan, *Method in Theology*, 240–41.

36 Definition of "intellectual disability," World Health Organization, accessed March 23, 2016, http://www.euro.who.int/en/health-topics/noncommunicable-diseases/mental-health/news/news/2010/15/childrens-right-to-family-life/definition-intellectual-disability.

37 Even the label "intellectual disability" reflects this failure, and almost no definition makes the distinction. This is an observation affirmed by Kelley Johnson, Jan Walmsley, and Marie Wolfe, *People with Intellectual Disabilities: Towards a Good Life?* (Bristol: Policy Press, 2010), 54.

38 Martha Nussbaum, *Upheavals of Thought: The Intelligence of Emotions* (Cambridge: Cambridge University Press, 2001).

39 "Independence is not an all or nothing concept but a concept that admits of degrees." John Vorhaus, "Disability, Dependency and Indebtedness?" *Journal of Philosophy of Education* 41, no. 1 (2007): 36, doi:10.1111/j.1467-9752.2007.00537.x.

40 Gwynnyth Llewellyn et al., eds., *Parents with Intellectual Disabilities: Past, Present and Futures* (Chichester: Wiley-Blackwell, 2010), 4.

41 The field is emerging, but studies looking at the physical and psychological welfare, linguistic and educational status, and quality of life and life satisfaction of

children of parents with an intellectual disability have found that one cannot generalize about the parenting abilities of parents with intellectual disabilities. Indeed, it is the case that, on average, children of mothers with an intellectual disability exhibited poorer measures of educational achievement, but even so, many did well. Of interest for our purposes is that the majority of such children recall having happy childhoods. Interested readers should consult Llewellyn et al., *Parents with Intellectual Disabilities* (especially the concluding chapter).

42   Llewellyn et al., *Parents with Intellectual Disabilities*, 247; M. Tucker and Orna Johnson, "Competence Promoting vs. Competence Inhibiting Social Support for Mentally Retarded Mothers," *Human Organization* 48, no. 2 (1989): 95–107, doi:10.17730/humo.48.2.d64q452755008t54. Tucker and Johnson describe "competence promoting" support, but I follow Nussbaum in concentrating on capacity rather than competence.

43   Anne-Marie Callus, *Becoming Self-Advocates: People with Intellectual Disability Seeking a Voice* (Oxford: Peter Lang, 2013), 170.

44   Ruth Northway, "What Does Independence Mean?" *Journal of Intellectual Disabilities* 19, no. 3 (2015): 204, doi:10.1177/1744629515593659.

45   This is the label she chooses to describe her daughter's impairment. Kittay, *Love's Labor*, xi.

46   Kittay, *Love's Labor*, 154, 5.

47   Kittay, *Love's Labor*, 77; it is noteworthy that disableism (alternately called "ableism" in some contexts) impacts a child with a disability and their family. See also Carmen Frances Jarrett, Rachel Mayes, and Gwynnyth Llewellyn, "The Impact of Disablism on the Psycho-Emotional Well-Being of Families with a Child with Impairment," *Scandinavian Journal of Disability Research* 16, no. 3 (2014): 195–210, doi:10.1080/15017419.2013.865671.

48   Kittay, *Love's Labor*, 92.

49   Kittay, *Love's Labor*, 70.

50   For a noteworthy discussion of the significance of motherhood, see Sara Ruddick, *Maternal Thinking: Toward a Politics of Peace* (Boston: Beacon Press, 1995).

51   Nancy Gibbs, "Pillow Angel Ethics," *Time*, January 7, 2007, http://content.time.com/time/nation/article/0,8599,1574851,00.html.

52   Gibbs, "Pillow Angel Ethics."

53   Genevieve Field, "Should Parents of Children with Severe Disabilities Be Allowed to Stop Their Growth?" *New York Times Magazine*, March 22, 2016, http://www.nytimes.com/2016/03/27/magazine/should-parents-of-severely -disabled-children-be-allowed-to-stop-their-growth.html.

54   "Involuntary or Coerced Sterilisation of People with Disabilities in Australia," The Senate of the Commonwealth of Australia, Community Affairs References Committee, July 17, 2013, http://www.aph.gov.au/Parliamentary _Business/Committees/Senate/Community_Affairs/Involuntary_Sterilisation/ First_Report;seealsoOHCHRetal.,"EliminatingForced,CoerciveandOtherwise

Involuntary Sterilization," World Health Organization, May 2014, http://www.who.int/reproductivehealth/publications/gender_rights/eliminating-forced-sterilization/en/.

55 OHCHR et al., "Eliminating Forced, Coercive and Otherwise Involuntary Sterilization," 9.

56 See Stuart Blume, *The Artificial Ear: Cochlear Implants and the Culture of Deafness* (New Brunswick, N.J.: Rutgers University Press, 2009). For further insight, see Sparrow, "Implants and Ethnocide."

57 Jay McNeill, "When Someone Asked Whether It Would Be Better if My Daughter Passed Away," *Growing Sideways* (blog), last modified January 16, 2016, accessed October 4, 2017, http://jaymcneill.com/2016/01/15/when-someone-asked-whether-it-would-be-better-if-my-daughter-passed-away/ (emphasis in original).

58 This is a point that lies at the heart of MacIntyre's argument (*Dependent Rational Animals*, 75).

59 Ruddick, *Maternal Thinking*, chaps. 6–7.

60 MacIntyre, *After Virtue*, 205.

61 MacIntyre, *After Virtue*, 216.

62 Nussbaum and Sen, *Quality of Life*.

63 It is interesting to note that Nussbaum's first published book was a translation and commentary of Aristotle's explanation of animal activity, which grounded his ethical theory. Martha C. Nussbaum, *Aristotle's "De Motu Animalium"* (Princeton, N.J.: Princeton University Press, 1978).

64 Nussbaum, "Non-Relative Virtues," contra Merriam, "Rehabilitating Aristotle."

65 In the decade since her original outline of the capabilities, she allowed herself some minor amendments and expansions on the original list. Indeed, she presents the list of capabilities as an open rather than closed proposal, one intended for discussion and debate. This current list is from Martha Nussbaum, *Frontiers of Justice: Disability, Nationality, Species Membership*, The Tanner Lectures on Human Values (Cambridge, Mass.: Harvard University Press, 2006), 76–78.

66 Nussbaum, *Frontiers of Justice*, 179.

67 Martha Nussbaum, "The Capabilities of People with Cognitive Disabilities," in *Cognitive Disability and Its Challenge to Moral Philosophy*, ed. Eva Feder Kittay and Licia Carlson (Malden, Mass.: Wiley-Blackwell, 2010), 79–82.

68 Whether Australia has achieved equal access is debatable. There is some evidence that the income gradient of health is much smaller in Australia than in the United States—Rasheda Khanam, Hong Son Nghiem, and Luke B. Connelly, "Child Health and the Income Gradient: Evidence from Australia," *Journal of Health Economics* 28, no. 4 (2009): 805–17, doi:10.1016/j.jhealeco.2009.05.001. On the other hand, the Australian indigenous population continues to suffer substantively lower health outcomes than the rest of the population—see Carrington C. J. Shepherd, Jianghong Li, and Stephen R. Zubrick, "Social

Gradients in the Health of Indigenous Australians," *American Journal of Public Health* 102, no. 1 (2012): 107–17, doi:10.2105/AJPH.2011.300354.

69 After establishing the capabilities approach with Sen, Nussbaum went on to apply the logic to the empowerment of women, and explored its potential contribution to three serious and unsolved problems of justice: the marginalization of people with physical and mental impairments; the challenge of global citizenship (of transcending the nation-state); and issues of justice in our treatment of nonhuman animals. Nussbaum, *Frontiers of Justice*, 160; Martha C. Nussbaum and Jonathan Glover, eds., *Women, Culture, and Development: A Study of Human Capabilities* (Oxford: Oxford University Press, 1995).

70 Nussbaum, *Frontiers of Justice*, 168.

71 Nussbaum, *Frontiers of Justice*, 187.

72 It is interesting that this type of speculation is always about children, as if because they have not yet grown into adults they may be less than human, whereas adults in a prolonged coma, or with advanced dementia, do not have their humanity questioned because they have previously lived human lives.

73 Nussbaum, *Frontiers of Justice*, 409.

74 Ormerod and Clifton, *Globalization and the Mission of the Church*, chap. 6.

75 Nussbaum, *Frontiers of Justice*, 413.

76 Martha Nussbaum, *Cultivating Humanity: A Classical Defense of Reform in Liberal Education* (Cambridge, Mass.: Harvard University Press, 1997), 9.

77 Nussbaum, *Frontiers of Justice*, 355.

78 Nussbaum, *Cultivating Humanity*, 90.

79 Jonathan Sacks, *The Dignity of Difference: How to Avoid the Clash of Civilizations* (London: Continuum, 2002), 7.

80 Cephalic disorders result from abnormal development of or damage to the brain. Microcephaly is thus a similar disability to anencephaly (considered by Merriam and Nussbaum), except that, in this case, the circumference of the head is smaller than average, resulting in brain damage. The functional impact depends upon the exact nature of the shrinkage and its impact on the brain, but although a microcephalic lives longer than an anencephalic, lifespan is still normally short. "Cephalic Disorders Fact Sheet," NIH National Institute of Neurological Disorders and Stroke, accessed January 6, 2017, https://www.ninds.nih.gov/Disorders/Patient-Caregiver-Education/Fact-Sheets/Cephalic-Disorders-Fact-Sheet.

81 Reinders, *Receiving the Gift of Friendship*, 89.

82 Reinders, *Receiving the Gift of Friendship*, 95, 101, 103.

83 Reinders, *Receiving the Gift of Friendship*, 273.

84 Reinders is not alone in focusing on relational constructions of the image of God and the importance of friendship. See also Reynolds, *Vulnerable Communion*, 180–88; Yong, *Theology and Down Syndrome*, 184–91; Molly C. Haslam, ed., *A Constructive Theology of Intellectual Disability: Human Being as Mutuality and Response* (New York: Fordham University Press, 2012).

85 Stephen G. Dempster, *Dominion and Dynasty: A Biblical Theology of the Hebrew Bible* (Downers Grove, Ill.: IVP Academic, 2003), 60; J. Richard Middleton, *The Liberating Image: The Imago Dei in Genesis 1* (Grand Rapids: Brazos, 2005), 26.

86 See the earlier discussion of Sen and Nussbaum's capabilities approach.

87 Molly Haslam makes a similar observation in her response to Reinders, noting that our humanity requires mutual responsiveness, but she goes on to argue that responsiveness can occur in "prelinguistic nonagential" ways (*Constructive Theology of Intellectual Disability*, 9–10). I share her basic insight, but not her rejection of agency and capacity.

88 Shakespeare, *Disability Rights and Wrongs Revisited*, 192.

89 Jed Boardman, "Social Exclusion and Mental Health—How People with Mental Health Problems Are Disadvantaged: An Overview," *Mental Health and Social Inclusion* 15, no. 3 (2011): 112–21, doi:10.1108/20428301111165690.

90 Micah O. Mazurek, "Loneliness, Friendship, and Well-Being in Adults with Autism Spectrum Disorders," *Autism* 18, no. 3 (2014): 223–32, doi:10.1177/1362361312474121; Rachel Robertson, "'Misfitting' Mothers: Feminism, Disability and Mothering," *Hectate* 40, no. 1 (2014): 10.

91 Keith R. McVilly et al., "'I Get by with a Little Help from My Friends': Adults with Intellectual Disability Discuss Loneliness," *Journal of Applied Research in Intellectual Disabilities* 19, no. 2 (2006): 191–203, doi:10.1111/j.1468-3148.2005.00261.x.

92 Rosemarie Garland-Thomson, "Misfits: A Feminist Materialist Disability Concept," *Hypatia* 26, no. 3 (2011): 593, doi:10.1111/j.1527-2001.2011.01206.x.

93 Garland-Thomson, "Misfits"; Robertson, "'Misfitting' Mothers."

94 Garland-Thomson, "Misfits," 604.

95 Aquinas, *Summa Theologica* 1.2.26.

96 Shakespeare, *Disability Rights and Wrongs Revisited*, 203.

7: DISABILITY, SEXUALITY, AND INTIMACY

1 Shakespeare, *Disability Rights and Wrongs Revisited*, 209.

2 It is a question that is particularly in play in the context of spinal cord injury. When the topic comes up, I can tell by their embarrassment that people are curious about my sexual (in)capacity.

3 Clifton, *Husbands Should Not Break*, 83.

4 K. D. Anderson et al., "Long-Term Effects of Spinal Cord Injury on Sexual Function in Men: Implications for Neuroplasticity," *Spinal Cord* 45, no. 5 (2007): 338–48, doi:10.1038/sj.sc.3101978.

5 See, for example, the forum discussion of sexuality by members of Apparelyzed, http://www.apparelyzed.com/forums/ (site discontinued).

6 Kenneth C. W. Kammeyer, *A Hypersexual Society* (Basingstoke: Palgrave Macmillan, 2008).

7   Jackie D. Cramp, Frédérique J. Courtois, and David S. Ditor, "Sexuality for Women with Spinal Cord Injury," *Journal of Sex & Marital Therapy* 41, no. 3 (2015): 238–53, doi:10.1080/0092623X.2013.869777.

8   Eleanor Richards et al., "Women with Complete Spinal Cord Injury: A Phenomenological Study of Sexuality and Relationship Experiences," *Sexuality and Disability* 15, no. 4 (1997): 280, doi:10.1023/A:1024773431670.

9   "Spinal-Cord Injury Fact Sheet," World Health Organization, last modified November 2013, http://www.who.int/mediacentre/factsheets/fs384/en/.

10   Linda Mona et al., "Prescription for Pleasure: Exploring Sex-Positive Approaches in Women with Spinal Cord Injury," *Topics in Spinal Cord Injury Rehabilitation* 15, no. 1 (2009): 18, doi:10.1310/sci1501-15.

11   Dina Hassouneh et al., "Abuse and Health in Individuals with Spinal Cord Injury and Dysfunction," *Journal of Rehabilitation* 74, no. 3 (2008): 3–9; Margaret A. Nosek et al., "Disability, Psychosocial, and Demographic Characteristics of Abused Women with Physical Disabilities," *Violence against Women* 12, no. 9 (2006): 838–50, doi:10.1177/1077801206292671.

12   For a poignant illustration of the challenge of dealing with the need for personal care, read Mark O'Brien's descriptions of the embarrassment of unintentional orgasm when being bathed, alongside his desire to ask nurses to help him with sexual services—which he is unable to do for many years. Mark O'Brien, with Gillian Kendall, *How I Became a Human Being: A Disabled Man's Quest for Independence* (Madison: University of Wisconsin Press, 2012).

13   Richards et al., "Women with Complete Spinal Cord Injury."

14   Richards et al., "Women with Complete Spinal Cord Injury," 279.

15   Rania Abi Rafeh, "Sex-Ability," *Columbia Spectator*, October 14, 2015, http://columbiaspectator.com/eye/2015/10/14/sex-ability.

16   Shakespeare et al., *Sexual Politics of Disability*, 43.

17   Margrit Shildrick, *Dangerous Discourses of Disability, Subjectivity and Sexuality* (London: Palgrave Macmillan, 2012), 64.

18   OHCHR et al., "Eliminating Forced, Coercive and Otherwise Involuntary Sterilization," 5. Similarly, a 2013 report by an Australian Federal Government Senate committee expressed its abhorrence of the treatment of too many Australian women with disabilities who suffered "involuntary or coerced sterilisation as a way to, for example, deal with menstrual management, control fertility, or avoid pregnancy as a result of rape." Community Affairs References Committee, "Involuntary or Coerced Sterilisation of People with Disabilities in Australia," 42.

19   Michael Carl Gill, *Already Doing It: Intellectual Disability and Sexual Agency* (Minneapolis: University of Minnesota Press, 2015), 5.

20   Miriam Taylor Gomez, "The 'S' Words: Sexuality, Sensuality, Sexual Expression and People with Intellectual Disability," *Sexuality and Disability* 30, no. 2 (2012): 238, doi:10.1007/s11195-011-9250-4.

21   Shakespeare, Gillespie-Sells, and Davies, *Sexual Politics*, 42–44; Shildrick, *Dangerous Discourses*, 66.

22 Shildrick, *Dangerous Discourses*, 71.

23 Mark O'Brien, "On Seeing a Sex Surrogate," *Sun Magazine*, May 1990, http://thesunmagazine.org/issues/174/on_seeing_a_sex_surrogate?print=al &url=issues/174/on_seeing_a_sex_surrogate&page=1.

24 O'Brien, *How I Became a Human Being*, 80.

25 O'Brien, *How I Became a Human Being*, 213.

26 TouchingBase.org, accessed November 1, 2015, http://www.touchingbase.org/.

27 Russell P. Shuttleworth, "The Search for Sexual Intimacy for Men with Cerebral Palsy," *Sexuality and Disability* 18, no. 4 (2000): 269, doi:10.1023/A:1005646327321.

28 I am not wanting to suggest that these activities and character traits are not part of a woman's experience but, rather, to highlight the fact that these types of characteristics are tied up with cultural constructions of masculinity. See Kurt Lindemann and James L. Cherney, "Communicating in and through 'Murderball': Masculinity and Disability in Wheelchair Rugby," *Western Journal of Communication* 72, no. 2 (2008): 107–25, doi:10.1080/10570310802038382.

29 Nicole Markotić and Robert McRuer, "Leading with Your Head: On the Borders of Disability, Sexuality, and the Nation," in *Sex and Disability*, ed. Robert McRuer and Anna Mollow (Durham, N.C.: Duke University Press, 2012), 166.

30 Shakespeare, Gillespie-Sells, and Davies, *Sexual Politics*, 61.

31 Shakespeare, Gillespie-Sells, and Davies, *Sexual Politics*, 62.

32 Riva Lehrer, "Golem Girl Gets Lucky," in McRuer and Mollow, *Sex and Disability*, 242.

33 Garland-Thomson, *Extraordinary Bodies*, 8, 16.

34 Garland-Thomson, *Extraordinary Bodies*, 28.

35 Shakespeare, Gillespie-Sells, and Davies, *Sexual Politics*, 200; Russell Shuttleworth and Teela Sanders, eds., *Sex and Disability: Politics, Identity and Access* (Leeds: Disability Press, 2010).

36 Shakespeare, Gillespie-Sells, and Davies, *Sexual Politics*, 76.

37 Nancy Mairs, "On Being a Cripple," in *Plaintext: Deciphering a Woman's Life (Essays, Feminist-Theory, Literary Criticism, Autobiography)* (Ph.D. diss., The University of Arizona, 1984), 48–66. Also freely available online at http://disabilitystudies.web.unc.edu/files/2016/01/mairs-on-being-a-cripple.pdf. Nancy Mairs died on January 16, 2017. For an obituary published online, see William Grimes, "Nancy Mairs, Who Wrote about Her Mental Illness and Multiple Sclerosis, Dies at 73," *New York Times*, December 7, 2016, https://www.nytimes.com/2016/12/07/books/nancy-mairs-dead-author.html.

38 Alison Kafer, "Desire and Disgust: My Ambivalent Adventures in Devoteeism," in McRuer and Mollow, *Sex and Disability*, 346.

39 Kafer, "Desire and Disgust," 347.

40 Anna Mollow and Robert McRuer, "Introduction," in McRuer and Mollow, *Sex and Disability*, 7.

41 I explore the struggle of the lack of privacy that I have had to deal with in my memoir. In one surreal experience, I had a doctor and nurse inject my penis

with a stimulant, and then asked my wife to massage the organ to see the effects—while they looked on. Clifton, *Husbands Should Not Break*, 169.

42 Kafer, *Feminist, Queer, Crip*, 9.

43 Schüssler Fiorenza, *But She Said*.

44 Tom Shakespeare, "Coming Out and Coming Home," *International Journal of Sexuality and Gender Studies* 4, no. 1 (1999): 50, doi:10.1023/A:1023202424014. See also Craig Blyth, "Members Only: The Use of Gay Space(s) by Gay Disabled Men," in Shuttleworth and Sanders, *Sex and Disability*, 41–58.

45 Anna Mollow, "Is Sex Disability?" in McRuer and Mollow, *Sex and Disability*, 286.

46 Lehrer, "Golem Girl Gets Lucky," in McRuer and Mollow, *Sex and Disability*, 245.

47 Kafer, *Feminist, Queer, Crip*, 15.

48 Shildrick, *Dangerous Discourses*, 6.

49 Shildrick, *Dangerous Discourses*, 9.

50 Teela Sanders, "Sexual Citizenship, Sexual Facilitation and the Right to Pleasure," in Shuttleworth and Sanders, *Sex and Disability*, 140.

51 Rachel Wotton and Saul Isbister, "A Sex Worker Perspective on Working with Clients with Disability and the Developments of Touching Base Inc.," in Shuttleworth and Sanders, *Sex and Disability*, 155–77.

52 Indeed, as our own employment should help us to realize, just because a relationship is commercial does not mean it is not real.

53 Anne Finger, "Helen and Frida," *Kenyon Review* 16, no. 3 (1994): 3. And before my readers complain about my usage of a text with such explicit language, the point of the artwork (and description) is to shake our sensibilities.

54 Ann Millett-Gallant, *The Disabled Body in Contemporary Art* (Basingstoke: Palgrave Macmillan, 2012), 7–12.

55 Millett-Gallant, *Disabled Body in Contemporary Art*, 20.

56 Lehrer, "Golem Girl Gets Lucky," in McRuer and Mollow, *Sex and Disability*, 233. I highly encourage the reader to explore some of Lehrer's work, including her self-portraits, at her website, RivaLehrer Art.com, accessed February 22, 2017, https://www.rivalehrerart.com/.

57 Tobin Siebers, "Disability Aesthetics and the Body Beautiful: Signposts in the History of Art," *Alter-European Journal of Disability Research* 2, no. 4 (2008): 330.

58 Siebers, "Disability Aesthetics and the Body Beautiful," 336.

59 Consider, for example, Dove's Campaign for Real Beauty. While commercial goals and feminist values are not easily aligned, at least the campaign reflected a growing movement that wants to see a new vision of beauty. For a feminist and sociological analysis of the campaign, see Judith Taylor, Josée Johnston, and Krista Whitehead, "A Corporation in Feminist Clothing? Young Women Discuss the Dove 'Real Beauty' Campaign," *Critical Sociology* 42, no. 1 (2016): 123–44, doi:10.1177/0896920513501355. For a critical reading from a disabled perspective, see Sarah Heiss, "Locating the Bodies of Women and Disability in

Definitions of Beauty: An Analysis of Dove's Campaign for Real Beauty," *Disability Studies Quarterly* 31, no. 1 (2011), http://dsq-sds.org/article/view/1367.

60   Harold Braswell, "Reclaiming the Faith: Review of Amos Yong, *The Bible, Disability, and the Church*," *Disability Studies Quarterly* 33, no. 2 (2013), http://dsq-sds.org/article/view/3715.

61   Eiesland, *Disabled God*; Yong, *Theology and Down Syndrome*; Yong, *Bible, Disability, and the Church*.

62   F. W. Dobbs-Allsopp, "The Delight of Beauty and Song of Songs 4:1-7," *Interpretation* 59, no. 3 (2005): 266. Christianity may have rejected the dualism of the Manicheans as so much heresy, but it remains shaped by this legacy in many ways. While Christian theology itself teaches a good creation (including created, human bodies), a bodily resurrection, and the renewal of all creation in an eschatological future, adherents to the faith remain open to the allurements of the dualist framework whereby the body is, at best, inessential and, at worst, a prison to be escaped. Throughout the Christian tradition, movements of asceticism and monasticism have likewise troubled the waters for thinking well about embodied theology and the goods of sexuality.

63   Marcella Althaus-Reid and Lisa Isherwood, *The Sexual Theologian: Essays on Sex, God and Politics* (London: A&C Black, 2004), 5–6.

64   Marcella Althaus-Reid, *The Queer God* (London: Routledge, 2003).

65   Siebers, "Disability Aesthetics and the Body Beautiful," 330.

66   Rosemary Radford Ruether, "Talking Dirty, Speaking Truth: Indecenting Theology," in *Dancing Theology in Fetish Boots*, ed. Lisa Isherwood and Mark D. Jordan (London: SCM Press, 2010), 266.

67   For an extended consideration of the theological significance of Christ's resurrected body bearing its cruciform woundedness, see Shelly Rambo, *Resurrecting Wounds: Living in the Afterlife of Trauma* (Waco, Tex.: Baylor University Press, 2017). Rambo takes these wounds and scars as sites of theological reflection, with real import for how we name and respond to trauma.

68   Richard Rohr, with Joseph Martos, *From Wild Man to Wise Man: Reflections on Male Spirituality*, 3rd ed. (Cincinnati, Ohio: St. Anthony Messenger Press, 2005), 8.

69   Matthew Del Nevo and Robyn Wrigley-Carr, "Spirituality in a Feminine Voice," in *Raising Women Leaders: Perspectives on Liberating Women in Pentecostal and Charismatic Contexts*, ed. Shane Clifton and Jacqueline Grey (Sydney: Australasian Pentecostal Studies, 2009), 254–73.

70   Consider *Self Portrait with Thorn Necklace and Hummingbird*, 1940 (oil on canvas), which has Kahlo portraying herself as a Christ-like victim, with the crown of thorns replaced by a necklace of thorns, and the dove, by a hummingbird—a fusion of Christian and Mexican culture.

71   Shakespeare, *Disability Rights and Wrongs Revisited*, 188.

72   Aquinas, *Summa Theologica* 2.2.QQ152–54.

73   Play is one of Nussbaum's universal human capabilities. Nussbaum, *Frontiers of Justice*, 77.

74 Here I am drawing on the insight of Margaret A. Farley, *Just Love: A Frame-work for Christian Sexual Ethics* (New York: Continuum, 2006).

75 Farley, *Just Love*, 127.

76 Farley, *Just Love*, 128.

77 Farley, *Just Love*, 244.

78 Aquinas, *Summa Theologica* 2.2.Q154.A1.

79 Aquinas, *Summa Theologica* 2.2.Q154.A2.

80 For discussion of reclaiming Aquinas' vision of chastity for the twenty-first century, see Jean Porter, "Chastity as a Virtue," *Scottish Journal of Theology* 58, no. 3 (2005): 285–301, doi:10.1017/S0036930605001444; Colleen McCluskey, "Lust and Chastity," in Timpe and Boyd, *Virtues and Their Vices*, 114–35.

81 Farley, *Just Love*, 215.

82 Aquinas, *Summa Theologica* 2.2.Q58.

83 For a fuller explanation of these principles, see Farley, *Just Love*, 215–31.

84 Farley argues that it does not, and reflects on the seven principles in the context of casual and premarital sex and GLTB relationships (*Just Love*, chap. 7).

85 Martha Nussbaum makes the case that conceptions of prostitution are framed by prejudice against women and sexuality, and seeks to develop an ethic that establishes justice for sex workers—Martha Nussbaum, " 'Whether from Reason or Prejudice': Taking Money for Bodily Services," *Journal of Legal Studies* 27, no. S2 (1998): 693–723, doi:10.1086/468040; Martha C. Nussbaum, *Sex and Social Justice* (New York: Oxford University Press, 2000).

86 For an argument that Christianity needs to rethink its attitude to sex work, see Lauren McGrow, "Doing It (Feminist Theology and Faith-Based Outreach) with Sex Workers—Beyond Christian Rescue and the Problem-Solving Approach," *Feminist Theology* 25, no. 2 (2017): 150–69, doi:10.1177/0966735016673258.

87 See, for example, Catherine Scott, *Scarlet Road*, documentary (2011); Meadhbh McGrath, " 'We Bring Happiness into Their Lives'—Meet the Sex Workers Providing Services for Clients with Disabilities," Independent.ie, September 12, 2016, http://www.independent.ie/life/health-wellbeing/health-features/we-bring-happiness-into-their-lives-meet-the-sex-workers-providing-services-for-clients-with-disabilities-34984671.html.

88 Christine Stark and Rebecca Whisnant, eds., *Not for Sale: Feminists Resisting Prostitution and Pornography* (Melbourne: Spinifex Press, 2005).

89 Tova Rozengarten and Heather Brook, "No Pity Fucks Please: A Critique of *Scarlet Road*'s Campaign to Improve Disabled People's Access to Paid Sex Services," *Outskirts* 34 (2016): 1–21.

90 Farley, *Just Love*, 224.

8: DISABILITY, LIMITATION, AND THE POSITIVITY MYTH

1 The following narrative is from the study mentioned in chapter 4 of this volume by Shane Clifton, Gwynnyth Llewellyn, and Tom Shakespeare, "Quadriplegia and the Good Life." I am grateful to Sara for telling her story, providing

editorial corrections and suggestions to subsequent write-ups, and allowing me to share this summary.

9: DISABILITY, GRACE, AND THE VIRTUE OF LETTING GO OF CONTROL

1 Creamer, *Disability and Christian Theology*, 116.

2 Clifton, *Husbands Should Not Break*.

3 Anna Stubblefield, "Living a Good Life . . . in Adult-Sized Diapers," in *Disability and the Good Human Life*, ed. Jerome E. Bichenbach, Franziska Felder, and Barbara Schmitz, Cambridge Disability Law and Policy Series (New York: Cambridge University Press, 2013), 219; Kafer, *Feminist, Queer, Crip*, 157.

4 Marcy Epstein, "On Humility," in *Deep: Real Life with Spinal Cord Injury*, ed. Marcy Epstein and Travar Pettway (Ann Arbor: University of Michigan Press, 2006), 123, 132.

5 Epstein, "On Humility," in Epstein and Pettway, *Deep*, 117, 133.

6 Sheryl Overmyer, in "Exalting the Meek Virtue of Humility in Aquinas," *The Heythrop Journal* 56, no. 4 (2015): 653, doi:10.1111/heyj.12009, suggests that Aquinas ought to have exalted humility to a higher place among the virtues.

7 Susan D. Collins and Robert C. Bartlett, "Interpretive Essay," in Aristotle, *Nicomachean Ethics* (trans. Collins and Bartlett), 237.

8 Aquinas, *Summa Theologica* 2.2.Q161.

9 Aquinas, *Summa Theologica* 2.2.Q161.A3. Also Overmyer, "Exalting the Meek Virtue of Humility," 654.

10 Aquinas, *Summa Theologica* 2.2.Q161.A2.

11 In his discussion of humility, Craig A. Boyd summarizes MacIntyre's account of the virtues of acknowledged dependence as though he is speaking about humility, but nowhere does MacIntyre actually refer specifically to that virtue. Craig A. Boyd, "Pride and Humility: Tempering the Desire for Excellence," in Timpe and Boyd, *Virtues and Their Vices*, 245–66.

12 I have noted throughout how the experience of disability is varied and cannot be subsumed under generalizations. Each experience is different, hence, the virtue of including in this text diverse voices who give attention to these experiences in their own words. On this particular point, however, I have especially in mind those experiences just described by Chesterman and Epstein.

13 Lonergan, *Method in Theology*, 37.

14 Tessman, *Burdened Virtues*, 5.

15 Tessman, *Burdened Virtues*, 19.

16 Tessman, *Burdened Virtues*, 34.

17 Neil Ormerod, *Creation, Grace and Redemption* (Maryknoll, N.Y.: Orbis, 2007), 109.

18 Aquinas, *Summa Theologica* 1.2.Q109.A2.

19 Carolyn McLeod, *Self-Trust and Reproductive Autonomy* (Cambridge, Mass.: MIT Press, 2002), 1.

20 Anita Ho, "Trusting Experts and Epistemic Humility in Disability," *International Journal of Feminist Approaches to Bioethics* 4, no. 2 (2011): 102–23, doi:10.2979/intjfemappbio.4.2.102.

21 James I. Charlton, *Nothing about Us Without Us: Disability Oppression and Empowerment* (Berkeley: University of California Press, 2000).

22 Australian Government, "2013–2016 Strategic Plan," National Disability Insurance Agency, 2013, accessed May 12, 2017, https://www.ndis.gov.au/html/sites/default/files/documents/strategic_plan_2.pdf.

23 Aurora Levins Morales, foreword to *Exile and Pride: Disability, Queerness, and Liberation*, by Eli Clare, 2015 ed. (Durham, N.C.: Duke University Press, 2015), xvi.

24 Eliza Chandler, "Sidewalk Stories: The Troubling Task of Identification," *Disability Studies Quarterly* 30, nos. 3–4 (2010), http://dsq-sds.org/article/view/1293.

25 Chris Bobel and Judith Lorber, *New Blood: Third-Wave Feminism and the Politics of Menstruation* (New Brunswick, N.J.: Rutgers University Press, 2010).

26 Augustine, *City of God* 12.1.

27 Aquinas, *Summa Theologica* 2.2.Q162.A4.

28 Boyd, "Pride and Humility," in Timpe and Boyd, *Virtues and Their Vices*, 255.

29 Aquinas, *Summa Theologica* 2.2.Q162.A5.

30 Howard J. Curzer, "Aristotle's Much Maligned Megalopsychos," *Australasian Journal of Philosophy* 69, no. 2 (1991): 132, doi:10.1080/00048409112344591.

31 Alasdair MacIntyre, *A Short History of Ethics* (Notre Dame: University of Notre Dame Press, 1998), 51.

32 Shapiro, *No Pity*, 20.

33 Kafer, *Feminist, Queer, Crip*, 16.

34 Chandler, "Sidewalk Stories."

35 Kafer, *Feminist, Queer, Crip*, 89.

36 "Curtis Rising," report by Peter Overton, produced by Hannah Stenning, *60 Minutes* (Australia), aired on August 24, 2014, available at https://www.youtube.com/watch?v=ZzQu29eH9KU.

37 Daniel Drazin and Maxwell Boakye, "Spontaneous Recovery Patterns and Prognosis after Spinal Cord Injury," in *Essentials of Spinal Cord Injury: Basic Research to Clinical Practice*, ed. Michael G. Fehlings and Alexander R. Vaccaro (New York: Thieme, 2012), chap. 7.

38 Cited in Corey Hague, "A God or a Quad: Time to Tell the Whole Truth about Spinal Cord Injuries," ABC Central Victoria, August 28, 2014, http://www.abc.net.au/local/stories/2014/08/28/4076206.htm?site=centralvic.

39 "Lia Walks into Her Year 10 Formal," Rove McManus, *The Project*, Channel 10, aired on September 3, 2014. View the Cerebral Palsy Alliance video on Lia, "Lia's Dream," at https://www.youtube.com/watch?v=JB9lkRhWQFY.

40 Clifton, Llewellyn, and Shakespeare, research project, "Quadriplegia and the Good Life," first mentioned in chapter 4 of this volume.

41 Clifton, *Husbands Should Not Break*, 155.

42 Clifton, *Husbands Should Not Break*, 156.

43 Georgina Kleege, "Blind Rage: An Open Letter to Helen Keller," *Southwest Review* 83, no. 1 (1998): 53–61.

44 Aristotle, *Nicomachean Ethics* 1125b.

45 William C. Mattison III, "Jesus' Prohibition of Anger (MT 5:22): The Person/Sin Distinction from Augustine to Aquinas," *Theological Studies* 68, no. 4 (2007): 839ff.

46 This explains why gays and lesbians find the cliché "love the sinner hate the sin" to be hateful.

47 Aquinas, *Summa Theologica* 2.2.Q158.A1.

48 David Matsumoto, Seung Hee Yoo, and Joanne Chung, "The Expression of Anger across Cultures," in *International Handbook of Anger*, ed. Michael Potegal, Gerhard Stemmler, and Charles Spielberger (New York: Springer, 2010), 125–37, doi:10.1007/978-0-387-89676-2_8.

49 Michael Potegal and Raymond W. Novaco, "A Brief History of Anger," in Potegal, Stemmler, and Spielberger, *International Handbook of Anger*, 19–21, doi:10.1007/978-0-387-89676-2_2.

50 Cheryl Hercus, "Identity, Emotion, and Feminist Collective Action," *Gender and Society* 13, no. 1 (1999): 37.

51 Kleege, "Blind Rage," 59.

52 John Hockenberry, "Public Transport," in *Voices from the Edge: Narratives about the Americans with Disabilities Act*, ed. Ruth O'Brien (Oxford: Oxford University Press, 2004), 140.

53 Tessman, *Burdened Virtues*, 107–32.

54 Aristotle, *Nicomachean Ethics* 1126a.

55 Tessman, *Burdened Virtues*, 121–24.

56 For my analysis of the significance of the NDIS for the church, see Shane Clifton, "NDIS, the Disabled Voice and the Church," *St Mark's Review*, no. 232 (2015): 65.

57 Australian Government, "2013–2016 Strategic Plan," 4.

58 Mike Steketee, "How a Forty-Year-Old Proposal Became a Movement for Change," *Inside Story: Current Affairs and Culture from Australia and Beyond*, InsideStory.org.au, October 22, 2013, accessed May 22, 2015, http://insidestory .org.au/how-a-forty-year-old-proposal-became-a-movement-for-change.

59 National Disability Strategy Consultation Report Prepared by The National People with Disabilities and Carer Council, "Shut Out: The Experience of People with Disabilities and Their Families in Australia," 2009, accessed May 22, 2015, https://www.dss.gov.au/our-responsibilities/disability-and -carers/publications-articles/policy-research/shut-out-the-experience-of-people -with-disabilities-and-their-families-in-australia, p. 1.

60 Cate Thill, "Listening for Policy Change: How the Voices of Disabled People Shaped Australia's National Disability Insurance Scheme," *Disability & Society* 30, no. 1 (2015): 16, doi:10.1080/09687599.2014.987220.

61 Steketee, "How a Forty-Year-Old Proposal Became a Movement for Change."

62 National Disability Strategy Consultation Report, "Shut Out," vi.

63 Ormerod, *Creation, Grace and Redemption*, 153.

64 Aristotle, *Nicomachean Ethics* 1126a.

65 Aquinas, *Summa Theologica* 2.2.Q157.A1.

66 Everett L. Worthington et al., "Forgiveness, Health, and Well-Being: A Review of Evidence for Emotional Versus Decisional Forgiveness, Dispositional Forgivingness, and Reduced Unforgiveness," *Journal of Behavioral Medicine* 30, no. 4 (2007): 291–302, doi:10.1007/s10865-007-9105-8; McCullough et al., "Forgiveness," in Lopez and Snyder, *Oxford Handbook of Positive Psychology*, 429.

67 Seligman, *Flourish*, 41.

68 Ormerod, *Creation, Grace and Redemption*, 154.

69 Sharon Lamb, "Women, Abuse, and Forgiveness: A Special Case," in *Before Forgiving: Cautionary Views of Forgiveness in Psychotherapy*, ed. Sharon Lamb and Jeffrie G. Murphy (Oxford: Oxford University Press, 2002), 155–73; Julia Baird, "Submission Is a Fraught Mixed Message for the Church," *Sydney Morning Herald*, February 13, 2015, http://www.smh.com.au/comment/submission-is-a-fraught-mixed-message-for-the-church-20150212-13d9nw.html.

70 Ormerod, *Creation, Grace and Redemption*, 156.

71 Dietrich Bonhoeffer, *The Cost of Discipleship* (London: SCM Press, 2015), 4–5.

72 Miroslav Volf provides a profound treatment of the challenge and potency of forgiveness in *Exclusion and Embrace: A Theological Exploration of Identity, Otherness, and Reconciliation* (Nashville: Abingdon, 1996).

73 Kafer, *Feminist, Queer, Crip*, 11–13.

74 Psalm 22, for example, asks, "My God, my God, why have you forsaken me?" And this complaint is taken up by Jesus himself on the cross (Mark 15:34).

75 Jay McNeill, "Forgive and Forget—Forgive God?" *Growing Sideways* (blog), March 27, 2012, https://jaymcneill.com/2012/03/27/forgive-forget-forgive-god/, accessed July 2016.

76 Gaventa, "Forgiveness, Gratitude, and Spirituality," in Wehmeyer, *Oxford Handbook of Positive Psychology and Disability*, 226–38.

77 Gaventa, "Forgiveness, Gratitude, and Spirituality," in Wehmeyer, *Oxford Handbook of Positive Psychology and Disability*, 234.

78 This citation is taken from chapter 1 of this volume, revisited here because it speaks powerfully to the new horizons made possible by living with disability.

CONCLUSION: A DISABLED ACCOUNT OF FAITH

1 The issue is not only that the label "mental illness" covers a wide range of diverse pathologies, but that great care is needed when relating notions of virtue and vice to illnesses that often target patterns of thought and behavior. If interdisciplinary engagement between the field of virtue ethics and the psychological sciences intends to be constructive rather than destructive, expertise in both disciplines is vital.

2 Sarah Griffith Lund, "Disabled Black Lives Matter," *Huffington Post*, September 1, 2015, last modified September 1, 2016, accessed November 3, 2016,

http://www.huffingtonpost.com/sarah-griffith-lund/disabled-black-lives -matt_b_8061040.html.

3 "Disability in Middle East and North Africa Region," The World Bank, "Disability and Development," last modified August 31, 2009, http://web.world bank.org/WBSITE/EXTERNAL/TOPICS/EXTSOCIALPROTECTION/ EXTDISABILITY/0,,contentMDK:20183396~menuPK:417332~pagePK: 148956~piPK:216618~theSitePK:282699,00.html.

4 "Disability within the Indigenous Community," Australian Indigenous Health Infonet, last modified October 20, 2015, accessed November 3, 2016, http:// www.healthinfonet.ecu.edu.au/related-issues/disability/reviews/disability -within-the-indigenous-community.

5 Lonergan, *Method in Theology*, 115.

6 Aquinas, *Summa Theologica* 1.2.Q67.A3–6.

7 Eiesland, *Disabled God*.

8 In this, he follows the inclination of Hans Reinders, in the latter's insistence that an anthropology that fails to embrace the profoundly disabled such as Kelly is inadequate (see the earlier discussion and Reinders, *Receiving the Gift of Friendship*).

9 Lonergan, *Method in Theology*, 105–6.

10 Lonergan, *Method in Theology*, 105. Lonergan did not have disability front and center when he made this observation, but he certainly could have done.

Bibliography

Abberley, Paul. "The Concept of Oppression and the Development of a Social Theory of Disability." *Disability, Handicap & Society* 2, no. 1 (1987): 5–19. doi:10.1080/02674648766780021.

Ackerman, Susan. "The Blind, the Lame, and the Barren Shall Not Come into the House." In Moss and Schipper, *Disability Studies and Biblical Literature*, 29–46.

Adams, Marilyn McCord. *Christ and Horrors: The Coherence of Christology.* Cambridge: Cambridge University Press, 2006.

————. *Horrendous Evils and the Goodness of God.* Ithaca, N.Y.: Cornell University Press, 2000.

Albrecht, G. L., and P. J. Devlieger. "The Disability Paradox: High Quality of Life against All Odds." *Social Science & Medicine* 48, no. 8 (1999): 977–88.

Albrecht, Gary L., Katherine D. Seelman, and Michael Bury. *Handbook of Disability Studies.* London: SAGE, 2001.

Althaus-Reid, Marcella. *The Queer God.* London: Routledge, 2003.

Althaus-Reid, Marcella, and Lisa Isherwood. *The Sexual Theologian: Essays on Sex, God and Politics.* London: A&C Black, 2004.

Amundson, Ron. "Disability, Ideology, and Quality of Life: A Bias in Biomedical Ethics." In *Quality of Life and Human Difference: Genetic Testing, Health Care, and Disability*, edited by David T. Wasserman, Robert Samuel Wachbroit, and Jerome Edmund Bickenbach. New York: Cambridge University Press, 2005.

————. "Quality of Life, Disability, and Hedonic Psychology." *Journal for the Theory of Social Behaviour* 40, no. 4 (2010): 374–92. doi:10.1111/j.1468-5914.2010.00437.x.

Anderson, Allan. *To the Ends of the Earth: Pentecostalism and the Transformation of World Christianity.* Oxford: Oxford University Press, 2012.

Anderson, K. D., J. F. Borisoff, R. D. Johnson, S. A. Stiens, and S. L. Elliott. "Long-Term Effects of Spinal Cord Injury on Sexual Function in Men: Implications for Neuroplasticity." *Spinal Cord* 45, no. 5 (2007): 338–48. doi:10.1038/sj.sc.3101978.

Aquinas, Thomas. *Summa Contra Gentiles.* Translated with an introduction and notes by Vernon J. Bourke. 4 vols. Notre Dame: University of Notre Dame Press, 1975.

————. *Summa Theologica.* Translated by Fathers of the English Dominican Province. 5 vols. Westminster, Md.: Christian Classics, 1981.

Aristotle. *Eudemian Ethics.* Edited and translated by Brad Inwood and Raphael Woolf. Cambridge: Cambridge University Press, 2013.

————. *Nicomachean Ethics.* Translated by Susan D. Collins and Robert C. Bartlett. Chicago: University of Chicago Press, 2011.

————. *Politics: Books I and II.* Translated with a commentary by Trevor J. Saunders. Clarendon Aristotle Series. Oxford: Clarendon, 1995.

Augustine. *City of God.* Translated by Henry Bettenson. London: Penguin, 2003.

————. *Confessions.* Translated by Henry Chadwick. Oxford: Oxford University Press, 1998.

————. *The Happy Life.* In *Trilogy of Faith and Happiness,* translated by Roland J. Teske, Michael Campbell, and Ray Kearney, introduction and notes by Michael Fiedrowicz and Roland J. Teske, edited by Boniface Ramsey. New York: New City Press, 2010.

Balentine, Samuel E. *Leviticus.* Interpretation: A Bible Commentary for Teaching and Preaching. Louisville, Ky.: Westminster John Knox, 2003.

Barker, R. N., M. D. Kendall, D. I. Amsters, K. J. Pershouse, T. P. Haines, and P. Kuipers. "The Relationship between Quality of Life and Disability across the Lifespan for People with Spinal Cord Injury." *Spinal Cord* 47, no. 2 (2009): 149–55. doi:10.1038/sc.2008.82.

Barnes, Colin. *Disabled People in Britain and Discrimination: A Case for Anti-Discrimination Legislation.* London: C. Hurst, 1991.

Barton, John. *Ethics in Ancient Israel.* Oxford: Oxford University Press, 2015.

Benedict XVI. *Spe Salvi.* Encyclical Letter, 2007. http://www.vatican.va/holy_father/benedict_xvi/encyclicals/documents/hf_ben-xvi_enc_20071130_spe-salvi_en.html.

Betcher, Sharon V. *Spirit and the Politics of Disablement.* Minneapolis: Fortress, 2007.

Blume, Stuart. *The Artificial Ear: Cochlear Implants and the Culture of Deafness.* New Brunswick, N.J.: Rutgers University Press, 2009.

Blyth, Craig. "Members Only: The Use of Gay Space(s) by Gay Disabled Men." In Shuttleworth and Sanders, *Sex and Disability*, 41–58.

Boardman, Jed. "Social Exclusion and Mental Health—How People with Mental Health Problems Are Disadvantaged: An Overview." *Mental Health and Social Inclusion* 15, no. 3 (2011): 112–21. doi:10.1108/20428301111165690.

Bobel, Chris, and Judith Lorber. *New Blood: Third-Wave Feminism and the Politics of Menstruation.* New Brunswick, N.J.: Rutgers University Press, 2010.

Bonhoeffer, Dietrich. *The Cost of Discipleship.* London: SCM Press, 2015.

Borg, Marcus. *Jesus: Uncovering the Life, Teachings, and Relevance of a Religious Revolutionary.* New York: HarperCollins, 2006.

Bosch, David J. *Transforming Mission: Paradigm Shifts in the Theology of Mission.* Maryknoll, N.Y.: Orbis Books, 1991.

Boyd, Craig A. "Pride and Humility: Tempering the Desire for Excellence." In Timpe and Boyd, *Virtues and Their Vices*, 245–66.

Braswell, Harold. "Reclaiming the Faith: Review of Amos Yong, *The Bible, Disability, and the Church.*" *Disability Studies Quarterly* 33, no. 2 (2013). http://dsq-sds.org/article/view/3715.

Brickman, Philip, Dan Coates, and Ronnie Janoff-Bulman. "Lottery Winners and Accident Victims: Is Happiness Relative?" *Journal of Personality and Social Psychology* 36, no. 8 (1978): 917–27.

Brock, Dan W. "Justice and the ADA: Does Prioritizing and Rationing Health Care Discriminate against the Disabled?" *Social Philosophy & Policy* 12, no. 2 (1995): 159–85.

Brown, Ivan, Chris Hatton, and Eric Emerson. "Quality of Life Indicators for Individuals with Intellectual Disabilities: Extending Current Practice." *Intellectual and Developmental Disabilities* 51, no. 5 (2013): 316–32. doi:10.1352/1934-9556-51.5.316.

Brown, Joanne C., Carole R. Bohn, and Elizabeth Bettenhausen, eds. *Christianity, Patriarchy, and Abuse: A Feminist Critique.* Cleveland, Ohio: Pilgrim, 1989.

Buchanan, Cindy L., and Shane J. Lopez. "Understanding Hope in Individuals with Disabilities." In Wehmeyer, *Oxford Handbook of Positive Psychology and Disability*, 154–65.

Burns, Shaun Michael, Briana L. Boyd, Justin Hill, and Sigmund Hough. "Psychosocial Predictors of Employment Status among Men Living with Spinal Cord Injury." *Rehabilitation Psychology* 55, no. 1 (2010): 81–90. doi:10.1037/a0018583.

Callus, Anne-Marie. *Becoming Self-Advocates: People with Intellectual Disability Seeking a Voice.* Oxford: Peter Lang, 2013.

Campen, Cretien van, and Jurjen Iedema. "Are Persons with Physical Disabilities Who Participate in Society Healthier and Happier? Structural Equation Modelling of Objective Participation and Subjective Well-Being." *Quality of Life Research* 16, no. 4 (2007): 635–45.

Carson, D. A. *How Long, O Lord? Reflections on Suffering and Evil.* 2nd ed. Grand Rapids: Baker Academic, 2006.

Casás-Selves, Matias, and James DeGregori. "How Cancer Shapes Evolution and How Evolution Shapes Cancer." *Evolution: Education and Outreach* 4, no. 4 (2011): 624–34. doi:10.1007/s12052-011-0373-y.

Chandler, Eliza. "Sidewalk Stories: The Troubling Task of Identification." *Disability Studies Quarterly* 30, nos. 3–4 (2010). http://dsq-sds.org/article/view/1293.

Chapin, Martha H., and Donald Holbert. "Employment at Closure Is Associated with Enhanced Quality of Life and Subjective Well-Being for Persons with Spinal Cord Injuries." *Rehabilitation Counseling Bulletin* 54, no. 1 (2010): 6–14. doi:10.1177/0034355210367685.

Chapin, Martha H., and Donald G. Kewman. "Factors Affecting Employment following Spinal-Cord Injury: A Qualitative Study." *Rehabilitation Psychology* 46, no. 4 (2001): 400–416.

Charlton, James I. *Nothing about Us Without Us: Disability Oppression and Empowerment.* Berkeley: University of California Press, 2000.

Charry, Ellen T. *God and the Art of Happiness.* Grand Rapids: Eerdmans, 2010.

Chen, Roy K., and Nancy M. Crewe. "Life Satisfaction among People with Progressive Disabilities." *Journal of Rehabilitation* 75, no. 2 (2009): 50–58.

Chivers, Sally. *The Silvering Screen: Old Age and Disability in Cinema.* Toronto: University of Toronto Press, 2011.

Clark, Laurence. "Disabling Comedy: 'Only When We Laugh!'" Paper presented at the Finding the Spotlight conference, Liverpool Institute for the Performing Arts, May 30, 2003, http://disability-studies.leeds .ac.uk/files/library/Clark-Laurence-clarke-on-comedy.pdf.

Clifton, Shane. "The Dark Side of Prayer for Healing: Toward a Theology of Well-Being." *Pneuma* 36, no. 2 (2014): 204–25.

————. "Grieving My Broken Body: An Autoethnographic Account of Spinal Cord Injury as an Experience of Grief." *Disability and Rehabilitation* 36, no. 21 (2014): 1823–29.

————. *Husbands Should Not Break: A Memoir about the Pursuit of Happiness after Spinal Cord Injury.* Eugene, Ore.: Resource Publications, 2015.

————. "NDIS, the Disabled Voice and the Church." *St Mark's Review,* no. 232 (2015): 65–80.

————. "Theodicy, Disability, and Fragility: An Attempt to Find Meaning in the Aftermath of Quadriplegia." *Theological Studies* 76, no. 4 (2015): 765–84. doi:10.1177/0040563915605263.

Clifton, Shane, Gwynnyth Llewellyn, and Tom Shakespeare. "Quadriplegia, Virtue Theory, and Flourishing: A Qualitative Study Drawing on Self-Narratives." *Disability and Society,* forthcoming, 2017.

Cohn, Michael A., and Barbara L. Fredrickson. "Positive Emotions." In Lopez and Snyder, *Oxford Handbook of Positive Psychology,* 13–24.

Collins, Susan D., and Robert C. Bartlett. "Interpretive Essay." In Aristotle, *Nicomachean Ethics,* 237–302.

Costanza, Robert, Brendan Fisher, Saleem Ali, Caroline Beer, Lynne Bond, Roelof Boumans, Nicholas L. Danigelis, et al. "Quality of Life: An Approach Integrating Opportunities, Human Needs, and Subjective Well-Being." *Ecological Economics* 61, nos. 2–3 (2007): 267–76. doi:10.1016/j.ecolecon.2006.02.023.

Craig, Ashley. "Resilience in People with Physical Disabilities." In *The Oxford Handbook of Rehabilitation Psychology,* edited by Paul Kennedy, 479–91. Oxford: Oxford University Press, 2012.

Cramp, Jackie D., Frédérique J. Courtois, and David S. Ditor. "Sexuality for Women with Spinal Cord Injury." *Journal of Sex & Marital Therapy* 41, no. 3 (2015): 238–53. doi:10.1080/0092623X.2013.869777.

Creamer, Deborah B. *Disability and Christian Theology: Embodied Limits and Constructive Possibilities.* Oxford: Oxford University Press, 2008.

Crisp, Roger, ed. *How Should One Live? Essays on the Virtues.* Oxford: Oxford University Press, 1996.

Crisp, Roger, and Michael Slote, eds. *Virtue Ethics.* Oxford Readings in Philosophy. Oxford: Oxford University Press, 1997.

Crossan, John Dominic. *The Power of Parable: How Fiction by Jesus Became Fiction about Jesus.* Reprint ed. New York: HarperOne, 2013.

Crysdale, Cynthia S. W., and Neil Ormerod. *Creator God, Evolving World.* Minneapolis: Fortress, 2013.

Cummins, Robert A., and Mark Wooden. "Personal Resilience in Times of Crisis: The Implications of SWB Homeostasis and Set-Points."

Journal of Happiness Studies 15, no. 1 (2013): 223–35. doi:10.1007/s10902-013-9481-4.

Curzer, Howard J. "Aristotle's Much Maligned Megalopsychos." *Australasian Journal of Philosophy* 69, no. 2 (1991): 131–51. doi:10.1080/00048409112344591.

Del Nevo, Matthew, and Robyn Wrigley-Carr. "Spirituality in a Feminine Voice." In *Raising Women Leaders: Perspectives on Liberating Women in Pentecostal and Charismatic Contexts*, edited by Shane Clifton and Jacqueline Grey, 254–73. Sydney: Australasian Pentecostal Studies, 2009.

Dembski, William. *The End of Christianity*. Nashville: B&H Academic, 2009.

Dempster, Stephen G. *Dominion and Dynasty: A Biblical Theology of the Hebrew Bible*. Downers Grove, Ill.: IVP Academic, 2003.

deRoon-Cassini, Terri A., Ed de St. Aubin, Abbey Valvano, James Hastings, and Patricia Horn. "Psychological Well-Being after Spinal Cord Injury: Perception of Loss and Meaning Making." *Rehabilitation Psychology* 54, no. 3 (2009): 306–14. doi:10.1037/a0016545.

Devlieger, Patrick, Beatriz Miranda-Galarza, Steven E. Brown, and Megan Strickfaden, eds. *Rethinking Disability: World Perspectives in Culture and Society*. Antwerp: Garant, 2016.

Diener, Ed, and Carol Diener. "Most People Are Happy." *Psychological Science* 7, no. 3 (1996): 181–85.

Diener, Ed, Richard E. Lucas, and Christie Napa Scollon. "Beyond the Hedonic Treadmill: Revising the Adaptation Theory of Well-Being." *American Psychologist* 61, no. 4 (2006): 305–14.

Diener, Ed, Heidi Smith, and Frank Fujita. "The Personality Structure of Affect." *Journal of Personality and Social Psychology* 69, no. 1 (1995): 130–41. doi:10.1037/0022-3514.69.1.130.

Diener, Ed, Louis Tay, and David G. Myers. "The Religion Paradox: If Religion Makes People Happy, Why Are So Many Dropping Out?" *Journal of Personality and Social Psychology* 101, no. 6 (2011): 1278–90. doi:10.1037/a0024402.

Dobbs-Allsopp, F. W. "The Delight of Beauty and Song of Songs 4:1-7." *Interpretation* 59, no. 3 (2005): 260–77.

Doran, Robert M. *Theology and the Dialectics of History*. Toronto: University of Toronto Press, 1990.

Dorsett, Pat. "The Importance of Hope in Coping with Severe Acquired Disability." *Australian Social Work* 63, no. 1 (2010): 83–102.

Drazin, Daniel, and Maxwell Boakye. "Spontaneous Recovery Patterns and Prognosis after Spinal Cord Injury." In *Essentials of Spinal Cord Injury:*

Basic Research to Clinical Practice, edited by Michael G. Fehlings and Alexander R. Vaccaro, 75–83. New York: Thieme, 2012.

Dunn, Dana S., Gitendra Uswatte, and Timothy R. Elliott. "Happiness, Resilience, and Positive Growth following Physical Disability: Issues for Understanding, Research, and Therapeutic Intervention." In Lopez and Snyder, *Oxford Handbook of Positive Psychology*, 117–32.

Dutton, Jane E., Laura Morgan Roberts, and Jeff Bednar. "Prosocial Practices, Positive Identity, and Flourishing at Work." In *Applied Positive Psychology: Improving Everyday Life, Health, Schools, Work, and Society*, edited by Stewart I. Donaldson, Mihaly Csikszentmihalyi, and Jeanne Nakamura, 155–70. New York: Routledge, 2011.

Echavarría, Agustín. "Thomas Aquinas and the Modern and Contemporary Debate on Evil." *New Blackfriars* 94, no. 1054 (2013): 733–54. doi:10.1111/nbfr.12034.

Eiesland, Nancy L. *The Disabled God: Toward a Liberatory Theology of Disability*. Nashville: Abingdon, 1994.

Emerson, Eric. "The Quality of Life of Disabled Children." In *Enhancing the Quality of Life of People with Intellectual Disabilities*, edited by Ralph Kober, 223–37. Social Indicators Research Series 41. Dordrecht: Springer, 2010. doi:10.1007/978-90-481-9650-0_14.

Emerson, Eric, Maina Kariuki, Anne Honey, and Gwynnyth Llewellyn. "Becoming Disabled: The Association between Disability Onset in Younger Adults and Subsequent Changes in Productive Engagement, Social Support, Financial Hardship and Subjective Wellbeing." *Disability and Health Journal* 7, no. 4 (2014): 448–56. doi:10.1016/j.dhjo.2014.03.004.

Emmons, Robert. "Gratitude, Subjective Well-Being, and the Brain." In *The Science of Subjective Well-Being*, edited by Michael Eid and Randy J. Larsen. New York: Guilford Press, 2008.

Epstein, Marcy. "On Humility." In *Deep: Real Life with Spinal Cord Injury*, edited by Marcy Epstein and Travar Pettway. Ann Arbor: University of Michigan Press, 2006.

Farley, Margaret A. *Just Love: A Framework for Christian Sexual Ethics*. New York: Continuum, 2006.

Felderhof, Marius C. "Evil: Theodicy or Resistance?" *Scottish Journal of Theology* 57, no. 4 (2004): 397–412. doi:10.1017/S0036930604000328.

Ferriss, Abbott L. "Religion and the Quality of Life." *Journal of Happiness Studies* 3, no. 3 (2002): 199–215.

Field, Genevieve. "Should Parents of Children with Severe Disabilities Be Allowed to Stop Their Growth?" *New York Times Magazine*, March 22, 2016, http://

www.nytimes.com/2016/03/27/magazine/should-parents-of-severely
-disabled-children-be-allowed-to-stop-their-growth.html.

Finger, Anne. "Helen and Frida." *Kenyon Review* 16, no. 3 (1994): 1–7.

Finkelstein, Victor. *Attitudes and Disabled People.* New York: World Rehabilitation Fund, 1980.

Foot, Philippa. *Virtues and Vices: And Other Essays in Moral Philosophy.*
Oxford: Oxford University Press, 2003.

Foote, Catherine E., and Arthur W. Frank. "Foucault and Therapy: The
Disciplining of Grief." In *Reading Foucault for Social Work,* edited by
Adrienne S. Chambon, Allan Irving, and Laura Epstein. New York:
Columbia University Press, 1999.

Frederick, Shane, and George Loewenstein. "Hedonic Adaptation." In *Well-
Being: Foundations of Hedonic Psychology,* edited by Daniel Kahneman,
Edward Diener, and Norbert Schwarz, 302–29. New York: Russell
Sage Foundation, 1999.

Gallagher, Deborah J. "On Using Blindness as Metaphor and Difficult Questions: A Response to Ben-Moshe." *Disability Studies Quarterly* 26, no. 2
(2006). http://dsq-sds.org/article/view/690.

Garland, Eric L., and Barbara L. Fredrickson. "Mindfulness Broadens
Awareness and Builds Meaning at the Attention-Emotion Interface."
In Kashdan and Ciarrochi, *Mindfulness, Acceptance, and Positive Psychol-
ogy,* 30–67.

Garland-Thomson, Rosemarie. *Extraordinary Bodies: Figuring Physical
Disability in American Culture and Literature.* New York: Columbia
University Press, 1996.

———. "Misfits: A Feminist Materialist Disability Concept." *Hypatia* 26,
no. 3 (2011): 591–609. doi:10.1111/j.1527-2001.2011.01206.x.

Gaventa, William. "Forgiveness, Gratitude, and Spirituality." In Wehmeyer,
Oxford Handbook of Positive Psychology and Disability, 226–38.

Gervais, Matthew, and David Sloan Wilson. "The Evolution and Functions
of Laughter and Humor: A Synthetic Approach." *Quarterly Review of
Biology* 80, no. 4 (2005): 395–430. doi:10.1086/498281.

Gill, Michael Carl. *Already Doing It: Intellectual Disability and Sexual Agency.*
Minneapolis: University of Minnesota Press, 2015.

Gleeson, Andrew. *A Frightening Love: Recasting the Problem of Evil.* London:
Palgrave Macmillan, 2011.

Gomez, Miriam Taylor. "The 'S' Words: Sexuality, Sensuality, Sexual
Expression and People with Intellectual Disability." *Sexuality and
Disability* 30, no. 2 (2012): 237–45. doi:10.1007/s11195-011-9250-4.

Gosbell, Louise. "Banqueting and Disability: Reconsidering the Parable of the Banquet (Luke 14:15-24)." In *Theology and the Experience of Disability*, edited by Andrew Picard and Myk Habets, 129–44. Burlington, Vt.: Ashgate, 2016.

Green, Joel B. "'We Had to Celebrate and Rejoice!': Happiness in the Topsy-Turvy World of Luke-Acts." In Strawn, *Bible and the Pursuit of Happiness*, 169–86.

Gunn, David M., and Danna Nolan Fewell. *Narrative in the Hebrew Bible*. Oxford Bible Series. Oxford: Oxford University Press, 1993.

Haber, Susan. "A Woman's Touch: Feminist Encounters with the Hemorrhaging Woman in Mark 5.24-34." *Journal for the Study of the New Testament* 26, no. 2 (2003): 171–92.

Hampton, Nan Zhang. "Subjective Well-Being among People with Spinal Cord Injuries: The Role of Self-Efficacy, Perceived Social Support, and Perceived Health." *Rehabilitation Counseling Bulletin* 48, no. 1 (2004): 31–37.

Hartley, John E. *Leviticus*. Word Biblical Commentary 4. Grand Rapids: Zondervan, 1992.

Haslam, Molly C., ed. *A Constructive Theology of Intellectual Disability: Human Being as Mutuality and Response*. New York: Fordham University Press, 2012.

Hassouneh, Dena, Ginger Hanson, Nancy Perrin, and Elizabeth McNeff. "Abuse and Health in Individuals with Spinal Cord Injury and Dysfunction." *Journal of Rehabilitation* 74, no. 3 (2008): 3–9.

Hauerwas, Stanley. *A Community of Character: Toward a Constructive Christian Social Ethic*. Notre Dame: University of Notre Dame Press, 1991.

Hauerwas, Stanley, and Charles R. Pinches. *Christians among the Virtues: Theological Conversations with Ancient and Modern Ethics*. Notre Dame: University of Notre Dame Press, 1997.

Headey, Bruce, Juergen Schupp, Ingrid Tucci, and Gert G. Wagner. "Authentic Happiness Theory Supported by Impact of Religion on Life Satisfaction." *Journal of Positive Psychology* 5, no. 1 (2010): 73–82. doi:10.1080/17439760903435232.

Heiss, Sarah. "Locating the Bodies of Women and Disability in Definitions of Beauty: An Analysis of Dove's Campaign for Real Beauty." *Disability Studies Quarterly* 31, no. 1 (2011). http://dsq-sds.org/article/view/1367.

Hendel, Ronald. *Remembering Abraham: Culture, Memory, and History in the Hebrew Bible*. Oxford: Oxford University Press, 2005.

Hercus, Cheryl. "Identity, Emotion, and Feminist Collective Action." *Gender and Society* 13, no. 1 (1999): 34–55.

Hess, David W., Michelle A. Meade, Martin Forchheimer, and Denise G. Tate. "Psychological Well-Being and Intensity of Employment in Individuals with a Spinal Cord Injury." *Topics in Spinal Cord Injury Rehabilitation* 9, no. 4 (2004): 1–10.

Ho, Anita. "Trusting Experts and Epistemic Humility in Disability." *International Journal of Feminist Approaches to Bioethics* 4, no. 2 (2011): 102–23. doi:10.2979/intjfemappbio.4.2.102.

Hockenberry, John. "Public Transport." In *Voices from the Edge: Narratives about the Americans with Disabilities Act*, ed. Ruth O'Brien, 137–53. Oxford: Oxford University Press, 2004.

Hursthouse, Rosalind. *On Virtue Ethics*. Oxford: Oxford University Press, 1999.

Isherwood, Lisa. *Introducing Feminist Christologies*. New York: Continuum, 2001.

Ivtzan, Itai, and Tim Lomas, eds. *Mindfulness in Positive Psychology: The Science of Meditation and Wellbeing*. Florence, Ky.: Taylor & Francis, 2016.

Jarrett, Carmen Frances, Rachel Mayes, and Gwynnyth Llewellyn. "The Impact of Disablism on the Psycho-Emotional Well-Being of Families with a Child with Impairment." *Scandinavian Journal of Disability Research* 16, no. 3 (2014): 195–210. doi:10.1080/15017419.2013.865671.

Jenkins, Philip. *The Next Christendom: The Coming of Global Christianity*. New York: Oxford University Press, 2011.

Johnson, Elizabeth. *She Who Is: The Mystery of God in Feminist Theological Discourse*. 10th anniversary expanded ed. New York: Crossroad, 2001.

Johnson, Kelley, Jan Walmsley, and Marie Wolfe. *People with Intellectual Disabilities: Towards a Good Life?* Bristol: Policy Press, 2010.

Johnstone, Brick, Bret A. Glass, and Richard E. Oliver. "Religion and Disability: Clinical, Research and Training Considerations for Rehabilitation Professionals." *Disability and Rehabilitation* 29, no. 15 (2007): 1153–63. doi:10.1080/09638280600955693.

Kafer, Alison. "Desire and Disgust: My Ambivalent Adventures in Devoteeism." In McRuer and Mollow, *Sex and Disability*, 331–54.

———. *Feminist, Queer, Crip*. Bloomington: Indiana University Press, 2013.

Kammeyer, Kenneth C. W. *A Hypersexual Society*. Basingstoke: Palgrave Macmillan, 2008.

Kashdan, Todd B., and Joseph V. Ciarrochi, eds. *Mindfulness, Acceptance, and Positive Psychology: The Seven Foundations of Well-Being*. Oakland: New Harbinger, 2013.

Kent, Bonnie. "Augustine's Ethics." In *The Cambridge Companion to Augustine*, edited by Eleonore Stump and Norman Kretzmann, 205–33. Cambridge: Cambridge University Press, 2001.

Khanam, Rasheda, Hong Son Nghiem, and Luke B. Connelly. "Child Health and the Income Gradient: Evidence from Australia." *Journal of Health Economics* 28, no. 4 (2009): 805–17. doi:10.1016/j.jhealeco.2009.05.001.

Kilic, S. A., D. S. Dorstyn, and N. G. Guiver. "Examining Factors That Contribute to the Process of Resilience following Spinal Cord Injury." *Spinal Cord* 51, no. 7 (2013): 553–57. doi:10.1038/sc.2013.25.

Kittay, Eva Feder. *Love's Labor: Essays on Women, Equality and Dependency.* New York: Routledge, 1999.

Kittay, Eva Feder, and Ellen K. Feder, eds. *The Subject of Care: Feminist Perspectives on Dependency.* Lanham, Md.: Rowman & Littlefield, 2003.

Kleege, Georgina. "Blind Rage: An Open Letter to Helen Keller." *Southwest Review* 83, no. 1 (1998): 53–61.

Kortte, Kathleen B., Mac Gilbert, Peter Gorman, and Stephen T. Wegener. "Positive Psychological Variables in the Prediction of Life Satisfaction after Spinal Cord Injury." *Rehabilitation Psychology* 55, no. 1 (2010): 40–47. doi:10.1037/a0018624.

Krause, James S., and K. S. Reed. "Barriers and Facilitators to Employment after Spinal Cord Injury: Underlying Dimensions and Their Relationship to Labor Force Participation." *Spinal Cord* 49, no. 2 (2011): 285–91. doi:10.1038/sc.2010.110.

Krause, James S., Joseph V. Terza, and Clara E. Dismuke. "Factors Associated with Labor Force Participation after Spinal-Cord Injury." *Journal of Vocational Rehabilitation* 33, no. 2 (2010): 89–99. doi:10.3233/JVR-2010-0518.

Lamb, Sharon. "Women, Abuse, and Forgiveness: A Special Case." In *Before Forgiving: Cautionary Views of Forgiveness in Psychotherapy*, edited by Sharon Lamb and Jeffrie G. Murphy, 155–73. Oxford: Oxford University Press, 2002.

Larson-Miller, Lizette. "Healing: Sacrament or Prayer?" *Anglican Theological Review* 88, no. 3 (2006): 361–74.

Laughlin, Peter. *Jesus and the Cross: Necessity, Meaning, and Atonement.* Eugene, Ore.: Pickwick, 2014.

Lawler, Michael G., and Todd A. Salzman. "Virtue Ethics: Natural and Christian." *Theological Studies* 74, no. 2 (2013): 442–73.

Lecavalier, Luc, and Marc J. Tassé. "An Exploratory Study of the 'Personality' of Adolescents and Adults with Down Syndrome." *Journal of*

Intellectual and Developmental Disability 30, no. 2 (2005): 67–74. doi:10.1080/13668250500124976.

Lehrer, Riva. "Golem Girl Gets Lucky." In McRuer and Mollow, *Sex and Disability*, 231–55.

Levy, N. "Deafness, Culture, and Choice." *Journal of Medical Ethics* 28, no. 5 (2002): 284–85. doi:10.1136/jme.28.5.284.

Li, Rongzhi. "The Effect of Community-Based Group Music Therapy on Quality of Life for Individuals with Developmental Disabilities." Master's thesis, East Carolina University, 2010. http://libres.uncg.edu/ir/uncg/listing.aspx?styp=ti&id=6668.

Lindbeck, George. *The Nature of Doctrine: Religion and Theology in a Post-liberal Age*. Louisville, Ky.: Westminster, 1984.

Lindemann, Kurt, and James L. Cherney. "Communicating in and through 'Murderball': Masculinity and Disability in Wheelchair Rugby." *Western Journal of Communication* 72, no. 2 (2008): 107–25. doi:10.1080/10570310802038382.

Llewellyn, Gwynnyth, Rannveig Traustadóttir, David McConnell, and Hanna Björg Sigurjónsdóttir, eds. *Parents with Intellectual Disabilities: Past, Present and Futures*. Chichester: Wiley-Blackwell, 2010.

Lomas, Tim. "Nourishment from the Roots: Engaging with the Buddhist Foundations of Mindfulness." In Ivtzan and Lomas, *Mindfulness in Positive Psychology*, 265–79.

Lonergan, Bernard J. F. *Method in Theology*. London: Darton, Longman & Todd, 1972.

———. "The Redemption." In *Collected Works: 1958–1964*, edited by Robert C. Croken, Frederick E. Crowe, and Robert M. Doran. Toronto: University of Toronto Press, 1996.

Longmore, Paul K. *Why I Burned My Book and Other Essays on Disability*. Philadelphia: Temple University Press, 2003.

Lopez, Shane J., and C. R. Snyder, eds. *The Oxford Handbook of Positive Psychology*. 2nd ed. Oxford: Oxford University Press, 2009.

Lykken, David, and Auke Tellegen. "Happiness Is a Stochastic Phenomenon." *Psychological Science* 7, no. 3 (1996): 186–89. doi:10.1111/j.1467-9280.1996.tb00355.x.

Lyubomirsky, Sonja. "Hedonic Adaption to Positive and Negative Experiences." In *The Oxford Handbook of Stress, Health, and Coping*, edited by Susan Folkman. New York: Oxford University Press, 2010.

MacIntyre, Alasdair. *After Virtue: A Study in Moral Theory*. 3rd ed. Notre Dame: University of Notre Dame Press, 2007.

————. *Dependent Rational Animals: Why Human Beings Need the Virtues.* Chicago: Open Court Publishing, 1999.

————. *A Short History of Ethics.* Notre Dame: University of Notre Dame Press, 1998.

Mairs, Nancy. "On Being a Cripple." In *Plaintext: Deciphering a Woman's Life (Essays, Feminist-Theory, Literary Criticism, Autobiography).* Ph.D. diss., The University of Arizona, 1984. http://disabilitystudies.web.unc .edu/files/2016/01/mairs-on-being-a-cripple.pdf.

Marini, Irmo, and Noreen M. Glover-Graf. "Religiosity and Spirituality among Persons with Spinal Cord Injury: Attitudes, Beliefs, and Practices." *Rehabilitation Counseling Bulletin* 54, no. 2 (2011): 82–92. doi:10.1177/0034355210368868.

Markotić, Nicole, and Robert McRuer. "Leading with Your Head: On the Borders of Disability, Sexuality, and the Nation." In McRuer and Mollow, *Sex and Disability,* 165–82.

Martin, Luther H. "The Hellenisation of Judaeo-Christian Faith or the Christianisation of Hellenic Thought." *Religion and Theology* 12, no. 1 (2005): 1–19.

Matheis, Elizabeth N., David S. Tulsky, and Robert J. Matheis. "The Relation between Spirituality and Quality of Life among Individuals with Spinal Cord Injury." *Rehabilitation Psychology* 51, no. 3 (2006): 265–71. doi:10.1037/0090-5550.51.3.265.

Matsumoto, David, Seung Hee Yoo, and Joanne Chung. "The Expression of Anger across Cultures." In Potegal, Stemmler, and Spielberger, *International Handbook of Anger,* 125–37.

Mattison, William C., III. "Jesus' Prohibition of Anger (MT 5:22): The Person/Sin Distinction from Augustine to Aquinas." *Theological Studies* 68, no. 4 (2007): 839–64.

Mazurek, Micah O. "Loneliness, Friendship, and Well-Being in Adults with Autism Spectrum Disorders." *Autism* 18, no. 3 (2014): 223–32. doi:10.1177/1362361312474121.

McCluskey, Colleen. "Lust and Chastity." In Timpe and Boyd, *Virtues and Their Vices,* 114–35.

McCullough, Michael E., Lindsay M. Root, Benjamin A. Tabak, and Charlotte van Oyen Witvliet. "Forgiveness." In Lopez and Snyder, *Oxford Handbook of Positive Psychology.*

McGrow, Lauren. "Doing It (Feminist Theology and Faith-Based Outreach) with Sex Workers—Beyond Christian Rescue and the Problem-Solving Approach." *Feminist Theology* 25, no. 2 (2017): 150–69. doi:10.1177/0966735016673258.

McLaren, Brian D. *Finding Faith: A Self-Discovery Guide for Your Spiritual Quest*. Grand Rapids: Zondervan, 1999.

McLeod, Carolyn. *Self-Trust and Reproductive Autonomy*. Cambridge, Mass.: MIT Press, 2002.

McNeill, Jay. *Growing Sideways*. Melbourne: self-published on Kindle, 2011.

McRuer, Robert, and Anna Mollow, eds. *Sex and Disability*. Durham, N.C.: Duke University Press, 2012.

McVilly, Keith R., Roger J. Stancliffe, Trevor R. Parmenter, and Rosanne M. Burton-Smith. "'I Get by with a Little Help from My Friends': Adults with Intellectual Disability Discuss Loneliness." *Journal of Applied Research in Intellectual Disabilities* 19, no. 2 (2006): 191–203. doi:10.1111/j.1468-3148.2005.00261.x.

Melcher, Sarah J., Mikeal C. Parsons, and Amos Yong. *The Bible and Disability: A Commentary*. Studies in Religion, Theology, and Disability. Waco, Tex.: Baylor University Press, 2017.

Merriam, Garret. "Rehabilitating Aristotle: A Virtue Ethics Approach to Disability and Human Flourishing." In *Philosophical Reflections on Disability*, edited by D. Christopher Ralston and Justin Hubert Ho, 133–51. Philosophy and Medicine 104. Dordrecht: Springer, 2009. doi:10.1007/978-90-481-2477-0_8.

Michalos, Alex C. "Education, Happiness and Wellbeing." *Social Indicators Research* 87, no. 3 (2008): 347–66. doi:10.1007/sl1205-007-9144-0.

Middleton, J. Richard. *The Liberating Image: The Imago Dei in Genesis 1*. Grand Rapids: Brazos, 2005.

Middleton, James, Yvonne Tran, and Ashley Craig. "Relationship between Quality of Life and Self-Efficacy in Persons with Spinal Cord Injuries." *Archives of Physical Medicine and Rehabilitation* 88, no. 12 (2007): 1643–48. doi:10.1016/j.apmr.2007.09.001.

Miller, Ariel, and Sara Dishon. "Health-Related Quality of Life in Multiple Sclerosis: The Impact of Disability, Gender and Employment Status." *Quality of Life Research* 15, no. 2 (2006): 259–71.

Miller, Mark T. "Imitating Christ's Cross: Lonergan and Girard on How and Why." *Heythrop Journal* 54, no. 5 (2013): 859–79. doi:10.1111/j.1468-2265.2012.00786.x.

Millett-Gallant, Ann. *The Disabled Body in Contemporary Art*. Basingstoke: Palgrave Macmillan, 2012.

Mitchell, David T., and Sharon L. Snyder. "Representation and Its Discontents: The Uneasy Home of Disability in Literature and Film." In Albrecht, Seelman, and Bury, *Handbook of Disability Studies*, 195–218.

Mollow, Anna. "Is Sex Disability?" In McRuer and Mollow, *Sex and Disability*, 285–312.

Mollow, Anna, and Robert McRuer. "Introduction." In McRuer and Mollow, *Sex and Disability*.

Moltmann, Jürgen. *The Crucified God: The Cross of Christ as the Foundation and Criticism of Christian Theology*. London: SCM Press, 1974.

Mona, Linda, Rebecca Cameron, Gali Goldwaser, Aletha Miller, Maggie Syme, and Sarah Fraley. "Prescription for Pleasure: Exploring Sex-Positive Approaches in Women with Spinal Cord Injury." *Topics in Spinal Cord Injury Rehabilitation* 15, no. 1 (2009): 15–28. doi:10.1310/sci1501-15.

Monden, K. R., Z. Trost, D. Catalano, A. N. Garner, J. Symcox, S. Driver, R. G. Hamilton, and A. M. Warren. "Resilience following Spinal Cord Injury: A Phenomenological View." *Spinal Cord* 52, no. 3 (2014): 197–201. doi:10.1038/sc.2013.159.

Morales, Aurora Levins. Foreword to *Exile and Pride: Disability, Queerness, and Liberation*, by Eli Clare. 2015 ed. Durham, N.C.: Duke University Press, 2015.

Morf, Carolyn C., and Walter Mischel. "The Self as a Psycho-Social Dynamic Processing System: Toward a Converging Science of Selfhood." In *Handbook of Self and Identity*, edited by Mark R. Leary and June Price Tangney. New York: Guilford Press, 2012.

Moss, Candida R., and Jeremy Schipper, eds. *Disability Studies and Biblical Literature*. New York: Palgrave Macmillan, 2011.

Murphy, Gregory C., and Amanda E. Young. "Employment Participation following Spinal Cord Injury: Relation to Selected Participant Demographic, Injury and Psychological Characteristics." *Disability & Rehabilitation* 27, no. 21 (2005): 1297–1306.

Neff, Kristen, and Dennis Tirch. "Self-Compassion and ACT." In Kashdan and Ciarrochi, *Mindfulness, Acceptance, and Positive Psychology*, 78–106.

Neimeyer, Robert A., ed. *Meaning Reconstruction and the Experience of Loss*. Washington, D.C.: American Psychological Association, 2001.

Newsom, Carol A. "Positive Psychology and Ancient Israelite Wisdom." In Strawn, *Bible and the Pursuit of Happiness*, 117–36.

Nietzsche, Friedrich. *Beyond Good and Evil: Prelude to a Philosophy of the Future*. Edited by Rolf-Peter Horstmann. Translated by Judith Norman. Cambridge: Cambridge University Press, 2002.

Northway, Ruth. "What Does Independence Mean?" *Journal of Intellectual Disabilities* 19, no. 3 (2015): 203–4. doi:10.1177/1744629515593659.

Nosek, Margaret A., Rosemary B. Hughes, Heather B. Taylor, and Patrick Taylor. "Disability, Psychosocial, and Demographic Characteristics of Abused Women with Physical Disabilities." *Violence against Women* 12, no. 9 (2006): 838–50. doi:10.1177/1077801206292671.

Nussbaum, Martha C. *Aristotle's "De Motu Animalium."* Princeton: Princeton University Press, 1978.

————. "The Capabilities of People with Cognitive Disabilities." In *Cognitive Disability and Its Challenge to Moral Philosophy*, edited by Eva Feder Kittay and Licia Carlson, 75–95. Malden, Mass.: Wiley-Blackwell, 2010.

————. *Cultivating Humanity: A Classical Defense of Reform in Liberal Education*. Cambridge, Mass.: Harvard University Press, 1997.

————. *Frontiers of Justice: Disability, Nationality, Species Membership*. The Tanner Lectures on Human Values. Cambridge, Mass.: Harvard University Press, 2006.

————. "Non-Relative Virtues: An Aristotelian Approach." In Nussbaum and Sen, *Quality of Life*, 242–69.

————. *Sex and Social Justice*. New York: Oxford University Press, 2000.

————. *Upheavals of Thought: The Intelligence of Emotions*. Cambridge: Cambridge University Press, 2001.

————. "'Whether from Reason or Prejudice': Taking Money for Bodily Services." *Journal of Legal Studies* 27, no. S2 (1998): 693–723. doi:10.1086/468040.

Nussbaum, Martha C., and Jonathan Glover, eds. *Women, Culture, and Development: A Study of Human Capabilities*. Oxford: Oxford University Press, 1995.

Nussbaum, Martha, and Amartya Sen, eds. *The Quality of Life*. Oxford: Oxford University Press, 1993.

O'Brien, Mark. "On Seeing a Sex Surrogate." *Sun Magazine*, May 1990, http://thesunmagazine.org/issues/174/on_seeing_a_sex_surrogate?print=all&url=issues/174/on_seeing_a_sex_surrogate&page=1.

————, with Gillian Kendall. *How I Became a Human Being: A Disabled Man's Quest for Independence*. Madison: University of Wisconsin Press, 2012.

Olyan, Saul M. "The Ascription of Physical Disability as a Stigmatizing Strategy in Biblical Iconic Polemics." In Moss and Schipper, *Disability Studies and Biblical Literature*, 89–102.

————. *Disability in the Hebrew Bible: Interpreting Mental and Physical Differences*. Cambridge: Cambridge University Press, 2008.

————. *Rites and Rank: Hierarchy in Biblical Representations of Cult*. Princeton: Princeton University Press, 2000.

Ormerod, Neil. "Chance and Necessity, Providence and God." *Irish Theological Quarterly* 70, no. 3 (2005): 263–78.

————. *Creation, Grace and Redemption.* Maryknoll, N.Y.: Orbis, 2007.

————. *A Public God: Natural Theology Reconsidered.* Minneapolis: Fortress, 2015.

Ormerod, Neil, and Shane Clifton. *Globalization and the Mission of the Church.* London: T&T Clark, 2009.

Ottomanelli, Lisa, and Lisa Lind. "Review of Critical Factors Related to Employment after Spinal Cord Injury: Implications for Research and Vocational Services." *Journal of Spinal Cord Medicine* 32, no. 5 (2009): 503–31.

Overmyer, Sheryl. "Exalting the Meek Virtue of Humility in Aquinas." *Heythrop Journal* 56, no. 4 (2015): 650–62. doi:10.1111/heyj.12009.

Peter, C., R. Müller, A. Cieza, and S. Geyh. "Psychological Resources in Spinal Cord Injury: A Systematic Literature Review." *Spinal Cord* 50, no. 3 (2012): 188–201. doi:10.1038/sc.2011.125.

Peterson, Christopher, Nansook Park, and Martin E. P. Seligman. "Greater Strengths of Character and Recovery from Illness." *Journal of Positive Psychology* 1, no. 1 (2006): 17–26. doi:10.1080/17439760500372739.

Plantinga, Alvin. *God, Freedom, and Evil.* Grand Rapids: Eerdmans, 1973.

Pope, Stephen. "Virtues in Theology." In Timpe and Boyd, *Virtues and Their Vices*, 393–414.

Porter, Jean. "Chastity as a Virtue." *Scottish Journal of Theology* 58, no. 3 (2005): 285–301. doi:10.1017/S0036930605001444.

Potegal, Michael, and Raymond W. Novaco. "A Brief History of Anger." In Potegal, Stemmler, and Spielberger, *International Handbook of Anger*, 9–24.

Potegal, Michael, Gerhard Stemmler, and Charles Spielberger, eds. *International Handbook of Anger.* New York: Springer, 2010. doi:10.1007/978-0-387-89676-2_8.

Quale, Anette Johansen, and Anne-Kristine Schanke. "Resilience in the Face of Coping with a Severe Physical Injury: A Study of Trajectories of Adjustment in a Rehabilitation Setting." *Rehabilitation Psychology* 55, no. 1 (2010): 12–22. doi:10.1037/a0018415.

Rambo, Shelly. *Resurrecting Wounds: Living in the Afterlife of Trauma.* Waco, Tex.: Baylor University Press, 2017.

Ray, Darby Kathleen. *Deceiving the Devil: Atonement, Abuse, and Ransom.* Cleveland, Ohio: Pilgrim, 1998.

Reid, D. Kim, Edy Hammond Stoughton, and Robin M. Smith. "The Humorous Construction of Disability: 'Stand-Up' Comedians in the

United States." *Disability & Society* 21, no. 6 (2006): 629–43. doi:10. 1080/09687590600918354.

Reinders, Hans S. *Disability, Providence, and Ethics: Bridging Gaps, Transforming Lives*. Studies in Religion, Theology, and Disability. Waco, Tex.: Baylor University Press, 2014.

―――. *Receiving the Gift of Friendship: Profound Disability, Theological Anthropology, and Ethics*. Grand Rapids: Eerdmans, 2008.

Reynolds, Thomas E. *Vulnerable Communion: A Theology of Disability and Hospitality*. Grand Rapids: Brazos, 2008.

Richards, Eleanor, Mitchell Tepper, Beverly Whipple, and Barry R. Komisaruk. "Women with Complete Spinal Cord Injury: A Phenomenological Study of Sexuality and Relationship Experiences." *Sexuality and Disability* 15, no. 4 (1997): 271–83. doi:10.1023/A:1024773431670.

Robertson, Rachel. " 'Misfitting' Mothers: Feminism, Disability and Mothering." *Hectate* 40, no. 1 (2014): 7–19.

Rohr, Richard, with Joseph Martos. *From Wild Man to Wise Man: Reflections on Male Spirituality*. 3rd ed. Cincinnati, Ohio: St. Anthony Messenger Press, 2005.

Rose, John, Katie Saunders, Elizabeth Hensel, and Biza Stenfert Kroese. "Factors Affecting the Likelihood That People with Intellectual Disabilities Will Gain Employment." *Journal of Intellectual Disabilities* 9, no. 1 (2005): 9–23. doi:10.1177/1744629505049725.

Rowell, D., and L. B. Connelly. "Personal Assistance, Income and Employment: The Spinal Injuries Survey Instrument (SISI) and Its Application in a Sample of People with Quadriplegia." *Spinal Cord* 46, no. 6 (2008): 417–24. doi:10.1038/sj.sc.3102157.

Rozengarten, Tova, and Heather Brook. "No Pity Fucks Please: A Critique of *Scarlet Road*'s Campaign to Improve Disabled People's Access to Paid Sex Services." *Outskirts* 34 (2016): 1–21.

Ruddick, Sara. *Maternal Thinking: Toward a Politics of Peace*. Boston: Beacon Press, 1995.

Ruether, Rosemary Radford. *Sexism and God-Talk: Toward a Feminist Theology*. Boston: Beacon Press, 1993.

―――. "Talking Dirty, Speaking Truth: Indecenting Theology." In *Dancing Theology in Fetish Boots*, edited by Lisa Isherwood and Mark D. Jordan, 254–67. London: SCM Press, 2010.

Russell, Daniel C., ed. *The Cambridge Companion to Virtue Ethics*. Cambridge: Cambridge University Press, 2013.

Sacks, Daniel W., Betsey Stevenson, and Justin Wolfers. "The New Stylized Facts about Income and Subjective Well-Being." *Emotion* 12, no. 6 (2012): 1181–87. doi:10.1037/a0029873.

Sacks, Jonathan. *The Dignity of Difference: How to Avoid the Clash of Civilizations.* London: Continuum, 2002.

Sanders, Teela. "Sexual Citizenship, Sexual Facilitation and the Right to Pleasure." In Shuttleworth and Sanders, *Sex and Disability*, 139–53.

Schipper, Jeremy. *Disability and Isaiah's Suffering Servant.* Oxford: Oxford University Press, 2011.

―――. *Disability Studies and the Hebrew Bible: Figuring Mephibosheth in the David Story.* New York: T&T Clark, 2009.

―――. "Reconsidering the Imagery of Disability in 2 Samuel 5:8b." *Catholic Biblical Quarterly* 67, no. 3 (2005): 422–34.

Schüssler Fiorenza, Elisabeth. *But She Said: Feminist Practices of Biblical Interpretation.* Boston: Beacon Press, 1992.

―――. *Jesus, Miriam's Child, Sophia's Prophet: Critical Issues in Feminist Christology.* New York: Continuum, 1994.

―――. *Rhetoric and Ethic: The Politics of Biblical Studies.* Minneapolis: Fortress, 1999.

Scott, Catherine. *Scarlet Road.* Documentary, 2011.

Scott, Mark Stephen Murray. "Theodicy at the Margins: New Trajectories for the Problem of Evil." *Theology Today* 68, no. 2 (2011): 149–52. doi:10.1177/0040573611405878.

Seligman, Martin E. P. *Authentic Happiness: Using the New Positive Psychology to Realize Your Potential for Lasting Fulfillment.* New York: Simon & Schuster, 2002.

―――. *Flourish: A Visionary New Understanding of Happiness and Well-Being.* Reprint, New York: Free Press, 2012.

Serlin, David. "Pissing without Pity: Disability, Gender, and the Public Toilet." In *Toilet: Public Restrooms and the Politics of Sharing*, edited by Harvey Molotch and Laura Noren, 167–85. New York: New York University Press, 2010.

Shakespeare, Tom. "Coming Out and Coming Home." *International Journal of Sexuality and Gender Studies* 4, no. 1 (1999): 39–51. doi:10.1023/A:1023202424014.

―――. *Disability Rights and Wrongs.* New York: Taylor & Francis, 2006.

―――. *Disability Rights and Wrongs Revisited.* 2nd ed. New York: Routledge, 2014.

Shakespeare, Tom, Kath Gillespie-Sells, and Dominic Davies. *The Sexual Politics of Disability: Untold Desires.* London: Cassell, 1996.

Shapiro, Joseph P. *No Pity: People with Disabilities Forging a New Civil Rights Movement*. New York: Broadway Books, 1994.

Sheldon, Kennon M., and Richard E. Lucas, eds. *Stability of Happiness: Theories and Evidence on Whether Happiness Can Change*. London: Academic Press, 2014.

Shepherd, Carrington C. J., Jianghong Li, and Stephen R. Zubrick. "Social Gradients in the Health of Indigenous Australians." *American Journal of Public Health* 102, no. 1 (2012): 107–17. doi:10.2105/AJPH.2011.300354.

Shildrick, Margrit. *Dangerous Discourses of Disability, Subjectivity and Sexuality*. London: Palgrave Macmillan, 2012.

Shuttleworth, Russell P. "The Search for Sexual Intimacy for Men with Cerebral Palsy." *Sexuality and Disability* 18, no. 4 (2000): 263–82. doi:10.1023/A:1005646327321.

Shuttleworth, Russell, and Teela Sanders, eds. *Sex and Disability: Politics, Identity and Access*. Leeds: Disability Press, 2010.

Siebers, Tobin. "Disability Aesthetics and the Body Beautiful: Signposts in the History of Art." *Alter-European Journal of Disability Research* 2, no. 4 (2008): 329–36.

Singer, Peter. "Why We Must Ration Health Care." *New York Times Magazine*, July 30, 2009, http://www.nytimes.com/2009/08/02/magazine/02Letters-t-001-001.html.

Sirgy, M. Joseph. *The Psychology of Quality of Life: Hedonic Well-Being, Life Satisfaction, and Eudaimonia*. 2nd ed. Dordrecht: Springer, 2012.

Smith, Dylan M., Kenneth M. Langa, Mohammed U. Kabeto, and Peter A. Ubel. "Health, Wealth, and Happiness: Financial Resources Buffer Subjective Well-Being after the Onset of a Disability." *Psychological Science* 16, no. 9 (2005): 663–66.

Snow, Nancy E., ed. *Cultivating Virtue: Perspectives from Philosophy, Theology, and Psychology*. Oxford: Oxford University Press, 2014.

————. "Virtue and Flourishing." *Journal of Social Philosophy* 39, no. 2 (2008): 225–45. doi:10.1111/j.1467-9833.2008.00425.x.

Sparrow, Robert. "Implants and Ethnocide: Learning from the Cochlear Implant Controversy." *Disability & Society* 25, no. 4 (2010): 455–66. doi:10.1080/09687591003755849.

Spinka, Marek, Ruth C. Newberry, and Marc Bekoff. "Mammalian Play: Training for the Unexpected." *Quarterly Review of Biology* 76, no. 2 (2001): 141–68.

St Leon, Sharna, Desiree Kozlowski, and Stephen Provost. "Resilience and the Role of Savouring Pleasure." *Frontiers in Psychology* 6 (2015). doi:10.3389/conf.fpsyg.2015.66.00010.

Stark, Christine, and Rebecca Whisnant, eds. *Not for Sale: Feminists Resisting Prostitution and Pornography.* Melbourne: Spinifex Press, 2005.

Stenberg, Joseph. "Aquinas on Happiness." Ph.D. diss., University of Colorado at Boulder, 2016.

Stoeber, Michael. *Reclaiming Theodicy: Reflections on Suffering, Compassion and Spiritual Transformation.* New York: Palgrave Macmillan, 2006.

Strawn, Brent A., ed. *The Bible and the Pursuit of Happiness: What the Old and New Testaments Teach Us about the Good Life.* Oxford: Oxford University Press, 2012.

Stubblefield, Anna. "Living a Good Life . . . in Adult-Sized Diapers." In *Disability and the Good Human Life,* edited by Jerome E. Bichenbach, Franziska Felder, and Barbara Schmitz. Cambridge Disability Law and Policy Series. New York: Cambridge University Press, 2013.

Stump, Eleonore. *Aquinas.* London: Routledge, 2003.

————. *Wandering in Darkness: Narrative and the Problem of Suffering.* Oxford: Oxford University Press, 2012.

Swinburne, Richard. *Providence and the Problem of Evil.* Oxford: Oxford University Press, 1998.

Swinton, John. *Raging with Compassion: Pastoral Responses to the Problem of Evil.* Grand Rapids: Eerdmans, 2007.

Tada, Joni Eareckson. *A Place of Healing: Wrestling with the Mysteries of Suffering, Pain, and God's Sovereignty.* Colorado Springs, Colo.: David C. Cook, 2015.

Taylor, Judith, Josée Johnston, and Krista Whitehead. "A Corporation in Feminist Clothing? Young Women Discuss the Dove 'Real Beauty' Campaign." *Critical Sociology* 42, no. 1 (2016): 123–44. doi:10.1177/0896920513501355.

Tessman, Lisa. *Burdened Virtues: Virtue Ethics for Liberatory Struggles.* Oxford: Oxford University Press, 2005.

Thill, Cate. "Listening for Policy Change: How the Voices of Disabled People Shaped Australia's National Disability Insurance Scheme." *Disability & Society* 30, no. 1 (2015): 15–28. doi:10.1080/09687599.2014.987220.

Timpe, Kevin, and Craig A. Boyd, eds. *Virtues and Their Vices.* Oxford: Oxford University Press, 2014.

Torrance, Thomas F. *Trinitarian Faith: The Evangelical Theology of the Ancient Catholic Faith.* 2nd ed. London: T&T Clark, 1997.

Tucker, M., and Orna Johnson. "Competence Promoting vs. Competence Inhibiting Social Support for Mentally Retarded Mothers." *Human Organization* 48, no. 2 (1989): 95–107. doi:10.17730/humo.48.2.d64q452755008t54.

Tugade, Michele M., and Barbara L. Fredrickson. "Resilient Individuals Use Positive Emotions to Bounce Back from Negative Emotional Experiences." *Journal of Personality and Social Psychology* 86, no. 2 (2004): 320–33.

Tzonichaki, Ioanna, and George Kleftaras. "Paraplegia from Spinal Cord Injury: Self-Esteem, Loneliness, and Life Satisfaction." *OTJR* 22, no. 3 (2002): 96–103.

Uppal, Sharanjit. "Impact of the Timing, Type and Severity of Disability on the Subjective Well-Being of Individuals with Disabilities." *Social Science & Medicine* 63, no. 2 (2006): 525–39. doi:10.1016/j.socscimed.2006.01.016.

van Inwagen, Peter. *The Problem of Evil.* Oxford: Oxford University Press, 2008.

Vanier, Jean. *Becoming Human.* 2nd ed. Mahwah, N.J.: Paulist, 2008.

Volf, Miroslav. *Exclusion and Embrace: A Theological Exploration of Identity, Otherness, and Reconciliation.* Nashville: Abingdon, 1996.

Vorhaus, John. "Disability, Dependency and Indebtedness?" *Journal of Philosophy of Education* 41, no. 1 (2007): 29–44. doi:10.1111/j.1467-9752.2007.00537.x.

Watson, Nick. "Researching Disablement." In *Routledge Handbook of Disability Studies*, edited by Nick Watson, Alan Roulstone, and Carol Thomas, 93–106. New York: Taylor & Francis, 2012.

Wawrykow, Joseph P. "The Theological Virtues." In *The Oxford Handbook of Aquinas*, edited by Brian Davies and Eleonore Stump. Oxford: Oxford University Press, 2012.

Weaver, J. Denny. *The Nonviolent Atonement.* 2nd ed. Grand Rapids: Eerdmans, 2011.

Wehmeyer, Michael L., ed. *The Oxford Handbook of Positive Psychology and Disability.* Oxford: Oxford University Press, 2013.

Wehmeyer, Michael L., and Todd D. Little. "Self-Determination." In Wehmeyer, *Oxford Handbook of Positive Psychology and Disability*, 116–36.

Weitzner, Eleanor, Susan Surca, Sarah Wiese, Andrea Dion, Zoe Roussos, Rebecca Renwick, and Karen Yoshida. "Getting On with Life: Positive Experiences of Living with a Spinal Cord Injury." *Qualitative Health Research* 21, no. 11 (2011): 1455–68. doi:10.1177/1049732311417726.

White, Brian, Simon Driver, and Ann Marie Warren. "Resilience and Indicators of Adjustment during Rehabilitation from a Spinal Cord Injury." *Rehabilitation Psychology* 55, no. 1 (2010): 23–32.

Whiting, Beatrice Blyth, and Carolyn Pope Edwards. *Children of Different Worlds: The Formation of Social Behavior.* Cambridge, Mass.: Harvard University Press, 1992.

Williams, Simon J. "Is Anybody There? Critical Realism, Chronic Illness and the Disability Debate." *Sociology of Health & Illness* 21, no. 6 (1999): 797–819. doi:10.1111/1467-9566.00184.

Wishart, J. G., and F. H. Johnston. "The Effects of Experience on Attribution of a Stereotyped Personality to Children with Down's Syndrome." *Journal of Intellectual Disability Research* 34, no. 5 (1990): 409–20. doi:10.1111/j.1365-2788.1990.tb01551.x.

Worthington, Everett L., Charlotte Van Oyen Witvliet, Pietro Pietrini, and Andrea J. Miller. "Forgiveness, Health, and Well-Being: A Review of Evidence for Emotional Versus Decisional Forgiveness, Dispositional Forgivingness, and Reduced Unforgiveness." *Journal of Behavioral Medicine* 30, no. 4 (2007): 291–302. doi:10.1007/s10865-007-9105-8.

Wotton, Rachel, and Saul Isbister. "A Sex Worker Perspective on Working with Clients with Disability and the Developments of Touching Base Inc." In Shuttleworth and Sanders, *Sex and Disability*, 155–77.

Wright, N. T. *Jesus and the Victory of God.* Christian Origins and the Question of God 2. Minneapolis: Fortress, 1996.

Yazicioglu, Kamil, Ferdi Yavuz, Ahmet Salim Goktepe, and Arif Kenan Tan. "Influence of Adapted Sports on Quality of Life and Life Satisfaction in Sport Participants and Non-Sport Participants with Physical Disabilities." *Disability and Health Journal* 5, no. 4 (2012): 249–53. doi:10.1016/j.dhjo.2012.05.003.

Yong, Amos. *The Bible, Disability, and the Church: A New Vision of the People of God.* Grand Rapids: Eerdmans, 2011.

————. *Theology and Down Syndrome: Reimagining Disability in Late Modernity.* Studies in Religion, Theology, and Disability. Waco, Tex.: Baylor University Press, 2007.

Young, Stella. "To My Eighty-Year-Old Self." In *Between Us: Women of Letters*, edited by Marieke Hardy and Michaela McGuire. Melbourne: Penguin, 2014.

Scripture Index

Subject Index

CPSIA information can be obtained
at www.ICGtesting.com
Printed in the USA
LVHW112140231119
638280LV00006B/627/P